Bicycling
beyond the
Divide

Outdoor Lives

Daryl Farmer

# Bicycling beyond the Divide

Two Journeys into the West

University of Nebraska Press | Lincoln & London

Library of Congress
Cataloging-in-Publication Data
Farmer, Daryl, 1965–
Bicycling beyond the divide:
two journeys into the west /
Daryl Farmer.
p.   cm.
ISBN-13: 978-0-8032-2034-8 (cl.: alk. paper)
ISBN-10: 0-8032-2034-0 (cl.: alk. paper)
1. West (U.S.)—Description and travel.
2. Bicycle touring.   I. Title.
PS3606.A716B53   2008
814'.6—dc22
2007025087

Set in Sabon by Bob Reitz.

For my parents,

DORIS J.,
who through her music
taught me the value of art,
and through her faith
the power of prayer,

and

DONALD L.,
for whom success and integrity
are one and the same.

And for JOAN,
who knows that dreams
are meant to be lived.

To travel best is to be of the sportsmen of the road. To take a chance, and win; to feel the glow of muscles too long unused; to sleep on the ground at night and find it soft; to eat, not because it is time to eat, but because one's body is clamoring for food; to drink where every stream and river is pure and cold; to get close to the earth and see the stars—this is to travel.

—MARY ROBERTS RINEHART, from *Through Glacier Park in 1915*

When man invented the bicycle he reached the peak of his attainments. Here was a machine of precision and balance for the convenience of man. And (unlike subsequent inventions for man's convenience) the more he used it, the fitter his body became. Here, for once, was a product of man's brain that was entirely beneficial to those who used it, and of no harm or irritation to others.

—ELIZABETH WEST, from *Hovel in the Hills*

# Contents

Acknowledgments | ix
Prologue | xi

COLORADO
Departure | 2
On How Not to Begin | 4
Florissant to Fairplay | 7
Hoosier Summit | 13
Below Freezing | 19
A Colorado Cow Patch South of Baggs | 25

WYOMING
Outlaws, Antelope, Prairie Dogs, and Sage | 34
Night at the Antelope Saloon | 49
To Jackson | 52
Elkfest | 59
Signal Mountain Lodge | 61
How to Bicycle through a Buffalo Herd | 68
Richard I | 75

MONTANA
Another Log on the Fire | 84
Paradise Valley to Ennis | 88
Virginia City to Opportunity | 99
Anaconda to Missoula | 105
Face-planting on Highway 2 | 114
Glacier National Park | 122
Kalispell Again | 127
Libby to Troy | 135

IDAHO
Karaoke Night in Bonners Ferry | 142

WASHINGTON
Fire Trucks and Rodeo Queens | 152
Okanagan to Friday Harbor | 158
The San Juan Islands | 168
Anacortes to Port Angeles | 179
A Side Trip to Victoria | 185
Port Angeles to Shoalwater Bay | 190
Winnefred | 200

OREGON
Astoria to Newport | 208
On a Sunday Morning | 213
A Coming to Peace | 220
At the North Bend Airport | 235

INTERMISSION: *San Francisco*
Like a Haggard Ghost | 238
City of Hills | 246

RETURN TO OREGON
North Bend to Gold Beach | 254

CALIFORNIA
To Eureka | 262
From Modesto to Yosemite and Mammoth Lakes | 267
From Mammoth Lakes to Mono Lake | 280

NEVADA
Tonopah | 284
The Extraterrestrial Highway | 293

UTAH AND ARIZONA
Modena to Kanab | 306
At Jacob Lake | 311

# Acknowledgments

Grateful acknowledgment is extended to the editors of the following journals, in which sections from this book first appeared:

Portions of "Prologue," "Outlaws, Antelope, Prairie Dogs, and Sage," and "To Jackson" appeared in a somewhat different form as "Bicycling the Cowboy State" in the Winter 2007 issue of the *Laurel Review* 41, no. 1.

"Like a Haggard Ghost" appeared as "Like a Haggard Ghost: A San Francisco Journal" in the 2007 issue of *Paddlefish*.

This book came to be only through the generosity and encouragement of many. I would especially like to thank Tony and Michelle Koester for their bicycle expertise and neighborly ways; Diane Boney for her friendship and kindness; Cathy and Mary Ebers for the writing cabin; Deb Snyder for typing the transcripts; and Elizabeth Gratch for her fine editing skills; and all the good people at the University of Nebraska Press.

Thanks also to Jim Reese, Kelly Carlisle, Kati Cramer, and Luan Pitsch for their feedback on early drafts; Erin Flanagan and Ty Jaeger for their help and friendship along the way; Ladette Randolph, whose generosity feeds the spirit of writers everywhere; Ted Kooser, Gerry Shapiro, Judy Slater, and Andrew Graybill for their mentorship and encouragement; and for her unlimited supply of generosity and for being an advisor, mentor, and friend, a very special thanks to Jonis Agee.

This journey was enhanced by more people than I can thank, but I am especially grateful to Father Schray and the good people at Divine Redeemer in Coos Bay, Oregon; Winnefred Revenaugh; Vince and Carol Price; and Randy and Carolyn Randall for sharing not only their home but their spirit and faith. Finally, thanks to the other six D's—Donald, Doris, David, Denise, Dede, and Debbie—as well as Mike, Reed, Lisa, Bill, Kathy, and all the Essers and Trettins. Thanks to Tyler and Abby for their notes of well wishes along the way.

And special gratitude to Joan for her patience and love.

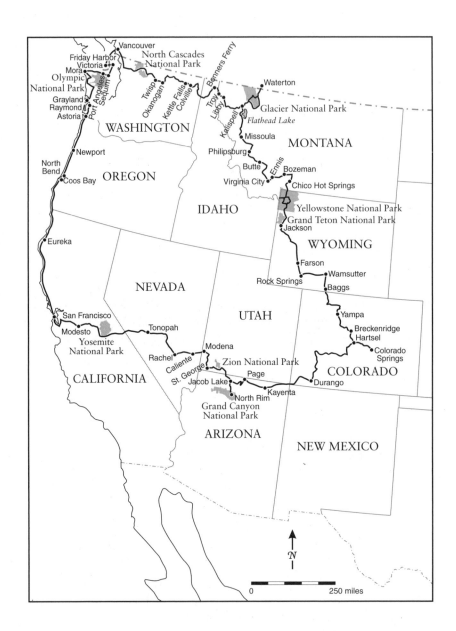

Vancouver
Friday Harbor
North Cascades
National Park
Victoria
Mora
Olympic
National Park
Benners Ferry
Waterton
Grayland
Raymond
Astoria
Twisp
Okanogan
Kettle Falls
Colville
Troy
Libby
Kalispell
Glacier National Park
*Flathead Lake*
Port Angeles
Sequim
WASHINGTON
Missoula
MONTANA
Newport
Philipsburg
North
Bend
Coos Bay
OREGON
Butte
Ennis
Bozeman
Virginia City
Chico Hot Springs
IDAHO
Yellowstone National Park
Grand Teton National Park
Jackson
Eureka
WYOMING
Farson
NEVADA
Wamsutter
Rock Springs
Baggs
San Francisco
UTAH
Yampa
Modesto
Tonopah
Breckenridge
Hartsel
Yosemite
National Park
Rachel
Modena
Caliente
Zion National Park
Page
Colorado
Springs
CALIFORNIA
St. George
Jacob Lake
North Rim
Kayenta
Durango
COLORADO
Grand Canyon
National Park
ARIZONA
NEW MEXICO

N

0          250 miles

1985 Route

# Prologue

*The pronghorn was running beside me.*

*I glanced over at him, saw the thin brown mane of his neck, the black patch on his cheek. In the large brown eyes I expected to see panic, but what I saw was determination instead, and muscles churning beneath the tan and white skin. We raced beneath an overcast sky, on a road that ran through rust-colored hills covered with yucca and sage. Side by side we moved, and I could hear the hum of my tires rolling over the pavement shoulder, the rush of the antelope's hooves on the sandy soil at the edge of the road, my CatEye cyclometer showing a speed of nearly thirty-five miles per hour as we moved together, miles of highway stretching out ahead and not a car in sight.*

*I had first seen the antelope moments before, standing by the side of the road. It's hard to imagine what he must have thought when he looked up and saw me, just yards away, pedaling silently on my bicycle, but he lifted his head, stiffened and watched, just long enough to determine that what-ever was the vehicle, there was a human attached. And then he jumped into forward position and was off. There was a barbed wire fence to the right of the road, and at first he had moved toward it, but in the frantic stride of his sprint, didn't jump and moved back toward the shoulder. He was galloping now as I rode beside him, and I could hear him, clods of the Wyoming dirt rising around his feet.*

*I'd been riding three hours since leaving Rock Springs early that morning, without encountering another living being, save for the occasional pickup or RV, and I pedaled furiously, determined to keep up, and it seems now, as I remember it, that we rode and ran together throughout the morning, but in reality it must have been just seconds. Finally, unable to maintain the sprint, I slowed to a stop, and breathing heavily where I stood straddling the bike, I watched as the antelope veered right, slipped beneath the fence, and disap-peared over a distant rise. Then, reemerging on a farther hill, he stopped, and I saw him standing, watching.*

. . . . . .

It was the summer of 1985. Ronald Reagan was in his second term. The Los Angeles Lakers, led by Magic and Kareem, were on their way to their third championship in six years. A music festival called Live-Aid played to audiences around the world in order to raise money for the world's starving children. It was a time of optimism.

I was twenty.

It is winter now, and nearly twenty years have passed since I rode beside that antelope. I sit in my small writing studio in Walton, Nebraska, and look at an old photo, at the lean legs that straddle the Trek touring bicycle, the still unused tent and sleeping bag strapped to the rear rack, fully packed panniers draped over each tire. The picture was taken by my mother, and I remember the moment after she snapped it, how we had each stood, not knowing what else to say, and then she hugged me good-bye. I lifted the bike, and in small stuttered steps turned and pointed it toward the street. With the tires wobbling under the weight of my gear, I pedaled off the curb and rode south to the end of Crown Ridge Drive, before finally turning right and heading west on a journey that would take me through the Rocky Mountains of Colorado, Wyoming, Montana, Alberta, and Idaho, across Washington, into Vancouver, before returning down the coast, through Oregon and half of California, east across Nevada, Utah, Arizona, one tire carefully set into New Mexico at the four corners (I wanted to tell people that I hadn't been to New Mexico but my bicycle had), and finally, a five-day push back to Colorado Springs, where a small group of friends, family, and neighbors had gathered on the front lawn to welcome me home.

The journals from that trip are old now, the pages worn and yellowed. I take the first and gingerly turn over the cover, which has long been torn from its binding. It contains daily entries, scribblings of mileage, average speed, distance, and day-to-day life bicycling solo over back western roads. Stuck within the pages are various business cards and brochures, information on campgrounds and motels, and an old note, left on the seat of my bicycle by my older brother, David, the morning I left: *Keep your eyes on the road and your nose off the pavement.* It was a mandate I had managed mostly to adhere to.

What endures also are fragments of memory, pieces that no longer flow together as a whole but remain scattered, like a puzzle once put together, now strewn about: a rattlesnake on a desert highway, a drenching hailstorm, a small town Montana bar in the rain, a Navajo man named Verl, a night of fireworks on an Oregon beach, an elderly couple in Raymond, Washington, who took me in and fed me. I remember turtling across highway 95, Nevada's most desolate highway. The winds, rebelling in true Nevada fashion, had reversed their usual westerly flow. For three days I'd averaged a measly six miles per hour, while bomber planes from a nearby military range flew overhead.

In Yellowstone I woke among a herd of elk; in Waterton, Alberta, to a pair of mountain goats licking the salt from my sweat-stained bicycling gloves. In Sequim, Washington, I woke to a bag of donuts left by a teenage girl whose mother had invited me to sleep in her family's yard.

Consider him, that twenty-year-old boy. (Knowing who I was then, I can't think of myself back then as anything but a boy.) Naive, sheltered, painfully shy. In the year that preceded the summer, I'd quit my second college and moved back in with my parents. I was working at a downtown soda fountain called Michelle's. Two nights a week I cleaned an office building. I opened the junior high school gym for the Park and Recreation Department. Three part-time dead-end jobs. My father wanted me to go back to school. I drank beer instead. I had a girlfriend. Cynthia. We spent evenings drinking coffee, taking walks around Broadmoor Lake, parking in the Garden of the Gods. She told me her life goals, none of which seemed to include me. I felt an anxiety I didn't understand, a longing for something I couldn't define. So I did what countless other lost young men have done in this country. I headed west.

Think of the changes the last twenty years have wrought. In 1985 there were no cell phones or even phone cards. A call home required a pocketful of quarters or a voice on the other end willing to accept a collect call. There were no ATM machines. Money had to be wired or taken as an advance on a credit card during normal banking hours.

Computer use required an understanding of foreign languages today more outdated than Latin: FORTRAN, BASIC, and COBALT.

Much has changed in the West. Major urban areas are sprawling. Recent years have seen drought conditions and a rise in fires. There are increasing tensions between states and communities over water rights and legal battles between state and federal government agencies over where to store nuclear waste. Immigration across the southern U.S. border has emerged as one of the most hotly contested political issues. In the West, where capital is still tied to land, ideological battles rage on between conservationists and economic developers.

Worldwide, tensions are mounting, and the United States is embroiled in a war that feels like it will never end. Ronald Reagan has passed away and Magic Johnson has become the face (albeit still smiling and vibrant) of a devastating disease. World hunger and poverty have not diminished.

As for me, I'm no longer skinny, not so naive. My blood pressure's high, and I recently broke my hand after slipping and falling on ice. I spend most of my time working and studying in an academic building called Andrews Hall, in an office with no windows. Beer is more a condiment than a meal. Exercise is a walk from my office to the library. Cynthia is a pleasant nostalgic memory.

I schedule an appointment, walk across campus to the University Health Center. I'm breathing heavily by the time I get there.

"The first thing," says the nurse, jotting a number down on her chart as I'm standing on a scale, "we have to do something about the weight problem." Weight problem. The number one piece of evidence I'm no longer the kid I was then. That first trip was not only twenty years but also seventy pounds ago.

"Of course, I'm wearing shoes," I say.

"Whatever makes you feel better," she says.

I sigh. I once ran the Pikes Peak Marathon. Now I have to stop to rest after climbing a flight of stairs. I have fallen increasingly into a life that moves me away not only from good health but also from a relationship with that land of the West, the day-to-day connection of a life lived outside, in physical exertion, among the elements. What I fear is that all I learned on that journey is lost. I'm a different person now, thank God, but I want to feel the road beneath my tires again. I want to apply what I've learned in the last twenty years to the journey, and I want to apply the journey to the next phase of my life. In February I will turn forty. My longing for the West has never diminished. To think of that summer on the bicycle is to dream myself home, and home is an endless space, a roof of big sky, a bed of dry earth.

I've decided to retrace that route, to ride it again.

I work at convincing myself that in some ways it'll be easier now. I know more, can better take care of myself. I'm banking on wisdom to make up for the lard.

"Do you think I can do this?" I ask the nurse.

"I think you better do something," she says.

I walk down the creaky steps into the dank and dusty cellar, the smell of cold dirt, the soft hiss of the furnace. The old bicycle leans at an angle against the concrete wall. The tires are flat, the leather of the seat rippled and torn, the handlebar tape unraveled. How long has it been since I've ridden the bike? I can't remember. Fifteen years, maybe.

I carry the bike into the yard, lean it against a tree. I fill a bucket with soapy water and an old rag and start to clean, embarrassed at my neglect.

I purchased this bike in 1984. It's a Trek 520. It has old-school caliper brakes. The gearshift levers are on the down tube of the frame, and shifting is made by feel rather than by clicking into place. The bike was made specifically for touring, which means its longer wheel base covers more ground per pedal rotation than a mountain or racing bike. Riding this bicycle after riding a mountain bike is something like the difference between driving a Cadillac and a jeep. Right now it's like a Caddy on blocks, but I didn't even consider buying a new one. A good bicycle, even when neglected, will last a lifetime. But the bike needs work. Quality work. And probably parts that are no longer made.

I call my neighbor Tony.

Tony Koester is one of those I-know-a-guy kind of guys. You need something, anything, in Nebraska, if Tony can't get it, he knows a guy who can. If there are twenty-year-old bicycle parts anywhere in Nebraska, I know he'll find them.

Sure enough, just weeks later, Tony delivers the bike to my door. The tires and seat are a polish of black, the new chain sharp silver. The handlebar tape has been replaced. I ride the bike down the driveway and to the end of the gravel road. Rides smooth. The gears shift easily. I replace the old rusty rearview mirror and add a new cyclometer. A week before I'm ready to leave, I lean the bike against our elm tree and step back to admire it.

The bicycle sparkles in the sun. Good as new.

Bicycling
beyond the
Divide

# Colorado

# Departure

TO GET TO THE JOURNEY was a journey in itself. Purple redwood tree blossoms lined Lincoln residential streets as I made my way to campus to finish and turn in final grades, the end of a hectic semester. I had a lunch meeting with two of my University of Nebraska colleagues then the handing in of my final comprehensive exam portfolio, a culminating semester-long project that accompanied a forty-eight-book reading list. The day was characteristic of the semester—scheduled to be finished by noon, I left my office at four.

It was warm and sunny, that time of quiet afternoons, before public schools officially ended and summer settled in. I walked out the sliding glass door off our living room and onto the redwood deck. It needed staining, something I'd planned on doing before I left. Now there wouldn't be time. Oscar, the neighbor's cat, sauntered over and rolled onto his back. I reached down to pet him. Soon Joan would arrive. I took a deep breath and walked inside, started to pack for our eight-hour drive.

We drove west on I-80, neither of us talking much, just looking out the window at the night sky, stopping only once for gas at Big Springs and then spending a night in Sterling, Colorado. In the morning we headed south on Highway 71, through the eastern Colorado ranchlands, the mountains far on the western horizon, cirrus clouds against a light-blue sky. At Limon we turned west on Highway 24, through Calhan, and into the mad traffic of Colorado Springs, the city of my birth, which grows ever more unrecognizable with each visit, past the cloned home developments, the endless traffic lights, past the Citadel Mall, what once was the eastern edge of the city but is now in the center, zigging our way to Uintah Street, 19th, King Street, and finally, onto Crown Ridge Drive, the home of my parents, and my youth, the exact spot where I'd begun my trip twenty years before and in two days would begin it again.

One day, weeks earlier, I had been sitting at an English department social in Dudley Bailey Library with the fiction writers Gerry Shapiro and Judy Slater and the poet Grace Bauer. The talk turned to my impending journey.

"So you must be doing a lot of training, then?" said Grace.

"No, I really haven't," I said.

Grace started to laugh but then realized I wasn't joking. She blinked a couple of times. Judy looked down, took a sip of her tea.

I had doubts of my own to contend with, but I knew that an advantage to a solo bicycle tour was that you could ride at your own leisure. It would be slow going, but on a bicycle, slow was the point. The goal was neither adventure nor fitness, though if those became by-products, fine. What I wanted was not only to see the West but to experience it—to feel its changing day-to-day moods, to see its geography in terms not of pockets of beauty but of a continuous and changing landscape. And more than that, I wanted to be a part of it, to lend my own respiration to the air.

The disadvantage, obviously, to a solo bike trip is loneliness, which brings me to what I knew would be the most difficult part of the trip.

Consider all the men throughout history who have left their families behind: soldiers off to war, men who took jobs on expeditions of discovery, sometimes gone for years, before phones or even telegrams and letters. What must that yearning for their lives back home have felt like for explorers such as those on the Grinell expeditions in the 1850s, men for whom, as Chauncey Loomis and Constance Martin write in their introduction to Grinell's *Arctic Explorations*, "must have felt deeply the great distances between themselves and their homes and suffered a sense of hopelessness, especially when they brooded on a second winter in the arctic." What I will be doing pales in comparison, obviously.

I will try not to belabor this point, other than to say that in the twelve years we'd been married, Joan and I had lived in ten states, many for a short period of time. This meant that she was not only the most important person I knew in town but often the only person I knew. In Alaska, due to our jobs, we had lived apart for several months, seeing each other only on occasional weekends. When people talk about difficult times in their marriages, they tend to mean times when they weren't getting along. For us difficult means being apart, and because we know what that feels like, we don't waste much time not getting along.

It wouldn't be storms or wind, mountain passes or sore muscles that would cause me the most hardship on this journey.

As antidote, we had splurged on two flights for Joan. We would meet first at the end of June, in Friday Harbor, on San Juan Island in Washington, and then again in San Francisco in July. Optimism assumed I'd make it that far.

That night I stayed up late, packing my bags and then repacking them, whittling my gear down to the most basic of needs. I didn't get to bed until one. I was nervous, and not without reason.

## On How Not to Begin

SATURDAY, MAY 7. I said good-bye to Joan and my parents, wobbled down the driveway, pedaled to the end of the street, King to 30th, and onto Pikes Peak, to the four-way stop on 36th. The mountain air was cool, the sun behind me, the shadows long. I crossed Colorado Avenue and merged onto Highway 24 and Ute Pass. I rode for about a mile, but the seat wasn't set right, so I stopped to adjust it. After placing my tools back into the front pocket of my rear pannier, I neglected to cinch it. As I pedaled, the strap caught in my spokes and ripped. Then I realized that my cyclometer wasn't working. Not used to the altitude, or the climb, I was already panting. I hadn't ridden for nearly three weeks, was in probably the worst shape of my life, and it was clear I'd packed too much gear. I stopped to catch my breath and tried to decide what to do about the cyclometer. I didn't want to ride without it, and I wouldn't be near a bike shop until Breckenridge, maybe three days away. Best to get it fixed now, I thought.

I struggled to the Cliff Dwellings entrance, where I called Joan.

"How's it going?" she asked.

"Never felt better," I said.

"How far have you gone?"

"'Bout a mile and a half. And I've only stopped to rest twice," I said.

"Might as well pace yourself," she said.

"Can you come get me?" I said. "I'm having trouble with my speedometer."

Because it was early and the bike shops weren't open, we drove into Manitou, where we sat at an outdoor café sipping coffee in the sun. At the table next to us, a group of friends were laughing. A young couple with a dog showed up and joined them. Being in the morning mountain air watching the dog wag its tail reminded me of all the things I missed about western mountain towns. My discouragement faded a little.

We finished our coffee, and Joan drove me to Old Town Bike Shop, where I bought a new cord and mount for the Sigma. Then she drove me back to the highway. She said she'd leave for the cabin at noon, and she'd pick me up wherever she found me. She wished me luck, and then she drove away. I took a deep breath and started to pedal again.

Ute Pass was named after the Ute Indians, who used the route to follow bison herds back and forth from the mountain meadows today known as South Park. The Utes were nomadic, and by the time the Europeans arrived, their culture had spread throughout what is now western Colorado. Later the route served as a wagon road and then, during the height of the mining operations in the towns of Victor and Cripple Creek, the Colorado Midland Railway. As I rode, I could still see train tunnels carved into the cliffs on the southern side of what is now four-lane Highway 24. Once I was in the narrows, Pikes Peak disappeared from view. I pedaled slowly. Twenty years earlier the day had been warm, sunny. Now the day started clear, and I expected a midday heat. Instead, it grew colder, and clouds rolled in over the mountain, darkening the sky. Furious gusts of wind blew fine specks of sand into my eyes. The temperature dropped quickly. There was a brief flurry of snow. I stopped to rest often. When Joan found me three hours and just ten miles later, I was sitting on a guardrail, eating dried apricots.

5

"You're doing well," she said. Said it like she meant it, which I appreciated.

"This road's steeper now than it was twenty years ago," I said.

We drove together to the cabin, where we were met by my parents, my brothers and sisters, their spouses and kids. Everyone brought food and gave me a send-off celebration. I was embarrassed to tell them I hadn't actually made it to the cabin on the bicycle. In fact, I hadn't even made it to Woodland Park.

That night, unable to sleep, I stepped out onto the wooden deck and stood beneath the black sky. I listened to the stillness, let it calm me. I knew that in the morning Joan and I would take a short hike through the forest, find an outcropping of rock where we could sit and sip coffee. The whole morning would be spent avoiding our inevitable good-bye.

I'd been planning this trip for years, but now I considered all that might happen—lightning, snowstorms, hypothermia, accidents, injury. When I'd left on that first trip, I faced similar fears, had put off leaving for a week, had almost decided not to go.

I thought of the mountains I'd soon ride over. Colorado would be the most difficult part of the trip. If I could make it to Wyoming without pulling a muscle or blowing out a knee, I'd know I could do it. I walked inside, lay down next to her. The last few weeks had been filled with the frenetic pace of graduate school and of preparation for this trip, and I lamented my self-absorption, the writing and graduate school life that left her with her own dreams unfulfilled and a debt that she didn't deserve. Real men hold steady jobs and provide, I thought. They don't pedal off trying to be twenty again.

"You okay?" she asked.

"I'm not going, I decided," I said.

"You'll be fine," she said. She cuddled close, and we fell asleep.

Early Sunday afternoon I watched her drive away. I was on my own.

# Florissant to Fairplay

MONDAY, MAY 9. I pedaled the fully loaded bicycle up the gravel road and followed it to the intersection of Twin Rocks Road, heading west. The mountain air was cool as I rode through Trout Haven pine and aspen, the wildflowers not yet in bloom. The sky was clear. The roads were rough and steep. On Teller County Road 1 I passed Fossil Beds National Monument. Around thirty-four million years ago, a volcanic eruption had created a mudflow here that covered lake shale, protecting it from erosion. The result was a natural preservation of fossils, including over one thousand different types of insects, and petrified redwood trees that stood as evidence that the Colorado climate was once similar to that of the current northern California coast.

To the south lay evidence of a more recent history, the Hornbeck Homestead. An old weathered home and barn sat empty in a field at the edge of the pine forest. The site was homesteaded by Adeline Hornbeck in 1878, just three years after the mysterious disappearance of her husband. Hornbeck became a prominent citizen in nearby Florissant, where she worked at the Florissant Mercantile and served on the school board. In less than ten years she had managed to increase the value of her property more than five times its original cost. Now an old wagon was parked in the yard, its tongue dragging with age, the horses that once pulled it long since deceased.

The county road ended at Florissant and Highway 24. The town rested quietly in the cool morning sun. Both cafés were closed, even though they each had signs advertising breakfast. One of the closed restaurants was the Fossil Inn, a place partially made from an old railroad car. I wondered if it had changed at all, if the old slab of pine wood, stained and shaped into the state of Oklahoma and displaying several samplings of rusty barbed wire, still hung on the wall. I remembered the restaurant as a comfortable place, with chicken fried steak and warm rolls. Somewhere still, I had an old matchbook from the restaurant, which included a whole list of daily events in the town, including an 8:30 P.M. "Coyote Quartet" and the 9:00 A.M. opening of the post office. At 2:00 one could "drive down Main Street," a journey that ended, according to the schedule, at 2:01.

I rode to a small convenience store at the edge of town.

The woman stood about four-foot-ten, and at first I thought she was a child. She stood facing a newspaper vending machine. It unnerved me when she turned, and I saw her wrinkled skin, the gray hair sticking out from beneath a green army camouflage cap.

"There's a girl in there, got struck by lightning." She gestured toward the machine, as if the girl in question lived inside.

I looked at the headline. Sure enough, lightning had struck a girl in Denver.

"Bet they don't treat her like they did that Terry Schiavo," said the woman, referring to the recent Florida case that pitted a husband against his in-laws. The woman ambled off, not waiting for agreement or argument.

Inside, I bought coffee and a poppy seed muffin, and I ate the breakfast while sitting on a concrete wall in the cool sunshine. Florissant had grown, but the tour through town, even by bicycle, still took only the minute prescribed on that old book of matches.

After a short steep hill, the road flattened into an easy ride through Lake George, before the long gradual incline to the 9,500-foot summit of Wilkerson Pass. To the west, hills covered with grass the dry color of wheat led into a valley, with forests of pine and aspen beyond. Cumulus clouds covered most of the sky, and a blue range of mountains spread across the horizon. The mountains were the result of the Laramide Orogeny, a mountain-building episode that occurred roughly sixty-five million years ago. Colorado's Rocky Mountains spread along what was once a soft zone where tectonic stresses caused the area to lift, fold, and in some cases erupt. During the Ice Age much of this region became glaciated, resulting in the mountains that characterize the state today. The earth had its own definition of slow.

For a guy on a bicycle Wilkerson Pass was unique among Colorado passes. The east side was a slow gradual twenty-mile climb, but the west was a steep three-mile no-holds-barred descent. My ride was smooth and quick, tempered only by a stiff westerly wind. I was expecting an easy ride into Hartsel, but the wind was relentless, and though I could see the town in the distance, in the distance it remained. I stopped often, to rest and take swallows of water in a failing attempt to thwart the dryness in my throat. Sparse, straw-colored grasses danced in the fields. I stopped at a guardrail and looked back at the road I'd come down, which disappeared around a curve. My knees ached, but I'd made it over my first mountain pass without incident.

Hartsel, Colorado, was a small outpost at the intersection of highways 24 and 9, with a handful of huddled wind-battered buildings. In a window I saw a sign advertising Buffalo Burgers. I walked inside expecting a café but found a bar instead. There was no music. The barstools were full of customers, but the tables were empty. The chairs were shaped from old beer kegs, and when I sat in one, it wobbled on uneven legs, and I flailed my arms, thinking I was falling. The wind still rang in my ears, and my throat was so parched I could barely speak. When the waitress asked for my order, my words came out in squeaks that I had to repeat. I sat at the table, drank four Sprites, and listened to the conversation at the bar. Teenage tattoos and body piercings were the topic of the day and kids whose parents had no better sense than to forbid such portending of apocalypse.

"My kids know," said a large man in suspenders, "they come home looking like that, I'll take the laser to 'em myself." He said it loud, and I wondered if that was for my benefit. A stranger comes to town, might as well let him know where things stand. My bicycle attire had "city boy" written all over it.

I finished my Sprite, stood slowly on stiff muscles, and walked out onto the boarded walk. There was a single bench outside. Twenty years earlier I'd met a six-year-old Hispanic girl named Mary here. I'd been sitting on that bench when a school bus pulled up and unloaded a small group of children. The children stood staring at me, until one of the older boys, probably seven or eight, walked over. Mary stood behind the others. The boy asked me what I was doing, and when I told him, he shook his head, and then all but Mary walked into the Hartsel store. As soon as the others had gone, she sat on the bench beside me.

"That's your bike?" she asked, pointing, and I told her it was. It was leaning against a wooden rail at the edge of the parking lot. We stared at it for a long time. Still relatively new, it sparkled in the sun. The bike bags, two in front and two in back, held nearly forty-five pounds of gear. Had she stood beside it, the top of Mary's head wouldn't have reached my seat post.

"What's that?" she asked, pointing to two full stuff sacks bungee-corded to the rear rack.

"That's my tent and a sleeping bag," I said.

She looked at the small bundles, furrowed her eyebrows.

"You don't have a house?" she asked. I'd been on the road for all of six hours, had yet to spend a night alone in that tent. For the next three months "home" would be wherever I stopped at night.

"Just the tent," I said. The other kids walked out of the store and started walking on the side of the road toward Fairplay. She watched them.

"Do you have a bicycle?" I asked her.

"My father has a truck," she said. And then, without saying good-bye, she jogged toward the others but stopped before she had caught up with them, careful to walk a short distance behind.

Now I walked into the store, which I remembered as a friendly place. An elderly woman stood behind the counter. She greeted me but didn't smile. The inside seemed to be wilting, like an oak tree in a drought. Old merchandise hung from the ceiling, from the shelves. In the cooler were packaged sandwiches. I took one, checked the date, then put it back. The café that was once in back was mostly gone. I grabbed a cold drink from the cooler, carried it to the counter.

"Is there any camping between here and Fairplay?" I asked the woman.

"No," she said. "It's all private land that way."

Outside, the expanse of land stretched out in all directions. Miles and miles of it, none of it groomed for crops, and yet there seemed to be nowhere a man could pitch a tent. I still hadn't eaten. I walked into a small building that advertised fresh tamales. Through a narrow hallway into a kitchen I could see a woman working at a stainless steel sink. I stood waiting. The woman looked up but didn't acknowledge me, just continued with her work. Off to the side was a small seating area, but it was blocked off with yellow CAUTION tape.

Already it was five o'clock. I had maybe three hours of daylight left, my muscles were sore, I was wind-beaten, and I wasn't sure where I was going to sleep. There was a small bell on the counter and I hit it twice. Finally, the woman came, and I ordered an enchilada platter, took it outside to eat at a picnic table in a yard beside the restaurant. A man at another table was eating alone, and when I sat down, he greeted me, asked me where I was headed. He had a Middle Eastern accent, said he was a trucker. His truck sat idling in front of the building, and I could smell the exhaust.

"Where'd you start from?" I asked, nodding toward the truck.

"I live in New York," he said. "I'm working for this moving company, and I'm headed to a place called Houston, Washington. Have you heard of it?"

"I've heard of Houston, Texas," I said.

He looked at me with a hint of disgust and shook his head.

"No," he said. "Not Texas." He finished his meal and got up to leave, wished me luck with a tone that seemed to suggest I'd need it.

I walked back inside. The woman looked up, and when she saw me, her face dropped. I wondered who she was expecting.

"Is there any place to pitch a tent between here and Fairplay?" I asked her.

She shook her head. "It's pretty much all private land," she said.

"You think you could fill my water bottles?" I asked.

"This water is non-potable," she said.

So I rode to the convenience store–gas station at the edge of town. A middle-aged couple worked behind the counter. The man wore overalls over a flannel shirt. I asked him if he could fill my water bottles.

"I can sure fill them for you," he said, "but I should tell you, I don't drink Hartsel water myself."

"Why's that?" I asked.

He reached behind him and grabbed a plastic gallon milk jug, which was about a quarter full of liquid. The liquid was the color of rust.

"This is what it looks like coming out of the faucet. We use it just to water the plants. It's probably fine to drink, but it tastes like sulfur."

Behind the glass door of the walk-in cooler, shelves were lined with bottled water. "Aqua Fina," I said.

"Probably a good idea," he said. "You're bike touring?"

"Yes," I said.

"God, I used to do stuff like that. I first moved here in the '70s—my dad and I toured all over. Back then you could ride right down the middle of the highway, there was so little traffic." I looked out the window. Seemed to me not much had changed.

"We should do something like that," he said, looking at the woman.

She nodded. "I could use a getaway," she said.

"Is there a place to camp between here and Fairplay?" I asked as I paid for the water.

The man scratched his neck, looked at the woman. "Boy, there's not much."

"It's pretty much all private land," said the woman.

Just past the turn onto Highway 9, a single bison grazing behind a barbed wire fence watched as I passed. Behind him lay Pike National Forest. The Buffalo Peaks rose in the distance. Soon the sun would be behind them. But I was heading north now and no longer fighting the wind.

I stumbled wearily into Fairplay at dusk. The temperature was dropping quickly, and my hands were numb and stiff. I stopped at a motel that doubled as an RV park. Inside I asked if there was a place to pitch a tent. The man behind the counter said he wasn't sure. They had just bought the motel, he and his wife, he said, and had taken over that very day.

"I'm not really sure how everything works yet," he said. "I don't think we're ready for tent camping."

I asked him how much for a room. When he told me, I said, "Look, all I need is a plot of land big enough to lie down on."

"The thing is, I'm just not sure what . . . our liability is. How it all works. We just kind of started." He sighed. "I guess, just go out at the edge of the lot, past the RV sites, see what you can find, and then come in, and we'll settle up."

In the darkness I found a small plot beneath a tree. There was a streetlight not far away, and the intersection where the highway met Main Street was just yards past the lot. Not exactly wilderness camping. Or quiet. I was tired and wanted a good night's sleep.

"I'll tell you what," said the man as soon as I walked back inside. "I can give you a room for forty. I'm just not sure we're set up to do tent camping yet."

I was already tired, and the temperature was getting colder. I'd have to set up the tent in the dark with numb hands. I thought the light and traffic might keep me awake.

"I'll take it," I said. There'd be plenty of time for roughing it later.

The room was clean, with a king-size bed. I lay down, forced myself to not fall asleep. I'd ridden fifty-nine miles.

That long ago spring of 1985 I'd ridden all the way to Alma on my first day out and stayed in a friend's cabin. The cabin had no electricity. By match light I found a table and chair, and I slumped down and rested my head on the table. It was cold in the cabin, and I knew I needed to change into warmer clothes. I hadn't eaten, and I was shivering. I'd ridden nearly eighty-seven miles, the last several in the dark without a light, and I had pushed myself to illness. I unrolled my sleeping bag on the floor and lay shivering until I had finally fallen asleep.

Now at least, in the comfort and warmth of my motel room, I wasn't sick. Sun-and windburned. Tired and sore. Out of shape and not at all acclimated to the altitude. But I'd made it through the first day without making myself ill. Maybe this was some of that wisdom-that-comes-with-age people were always talking about.

## Hoosier Summit

ALMA, COLORADO, sits at an elevation of 10,578 feet, and the timber line was clearly visible on the mountains to the west. The sky was clear, but the sunshine was cold. *Crisp* is the word Coloradans use to describe such mornings. I took deep breaths, trying to inhale large volumes of the thin air.

Two fully loaded bicycles leaned against the front of a small store. The riders, two men in their young twenties, introduced themselves as Brian and Dave. They were from Albuquerque, they said, and had already been on the road for over a week. They were young and lean. Their bikes were new. Brian was tall, had blond hair. He looked at my bike.

"Old school," he said.

"Only bike I've ever needed," I said.

"You ready for this pass?" asked Dave. He wore a thin and tight hood, which outlined the oval of his face. His tone disguised it politely, but I noted the skepticism in his voice. I wasn't sure what concerned him most, the age of my bike or the size of my gut.

"Sure," I said. "I'm ready." The pass he meant was Hoosier, and the truth was, I was dreading it. I'd been lingering all morning trying to avoid it.

"You guys had a pretty smooth trip so far?" I asked, changing the subject.

"We had a problem in New Mexico," said Brian. "It was late, dark, and we were a long way from the next town. We just pulled over right off the road, set up our tent. We could hear the traffic."

"The highway patrol stopped, woke us up, asked a bunch of questions," said Dave. "But they let us stay, just told us to leave early in the morning. They were really nice about the whole thing, actually."

"You ever get caught like that?" asked Brian.

I laughed. "Well, I only left yesterday. But when I've toured in the past, I've had to sleep in all kinds of places," I said.

"It's weird. You know you're not supposed to, but you don't know what you are supposed to do," said Brian.

"Just not get yourself in the situation, I guess," said Dave.

Part of the joy of bicycle touring was not having to plan ahead, to just sleep where the daylight ended. I hadn't thought about how it might be different now than twenty years before, when I had generally been indulged. I'd slept in parks, baseball dugouts, playground forts, the yards of abandoned houses. I'd even camped on a golf course once. Once schools were out for the summer, I figured I could rely again on high school football field bleachers. Would it be the same at age forty? Along with private land comes a low tolerance for trespassers, and in the last twenty years both the encroachment and the land ownership had increased. I wasn't sure what I'd do if I was caught between towns after dark. Sleeping by the side of the road seemed ripe with potential trouble. Trouble, though, can find you anywhere, even, as I would later learn, in the quiet darkness of a small town football field.

"Have you had a lot of trouble finding campgrounds?" I asked.

"A lot of them aren't open this early, especially since we got here to Colorado," said Dave. "We didn't expect that."

He put on his helmet. "We'll see you on the pass, maybe?" said Brian.

I laughed. "Odds are I won't catch up to you."

Hoosier Pass summits at 11,500 feet. You would think, given the elevation of Alma itself, the summit wouldn't be much of a climb. From the bottom of the pass to the top was only four miles. It was not the distance, though, but the grade. The ascent didn't rely on a series of switchbacks but for the most part was one straight and steep incline. For a slightly overweight, middle-aged man who'd been living four years in the relatively low and flat state of Nebraska, the pass loomed daunting ahead.

I decided to ride in quarter-mile increments, dividing the climb into sixteen stages. I tried to focus on the scenery, but I couldn't keep myself from watching the slow change of the numbers on my cyclometer, and I had to push myself to make each quarter-mile before stopping to gasp for the thin air, the cold stinging my lungs. I felt each turn of my tire, watched the road beneath me, could see every stick and pebble, and the white smears of paint where the road crew had long ago strayed from the straight line. I moved forward slowly, embarrassed at my plodding speed. When cars approached from behind, I tried to pedal faster, to do my best impersonation of a real bicyclist. By the time I reached the snow line, I was coughing like a pack-a-day smoker. But then I heard the ethereal rustling of pine trees, which didn't have the tambourine effect of deciduous trees but something more haunting, like a Gregorian chant, a building wave of harmonious unity. I had grown up in these mountains, and through my struggle up the pass I felt an unexpected joy, as if the mountain itself were singing me to the top. Occasionally, a gust of wind caught me from behind like a hand of God, gently pushing me onward.

When finally I arrived at the summit, I wanted to raise my arms in celebration. But I was too tired. I leaned the bike against the stone wall of the summit sign that marked the Continental Divide, between Park and Summit counties and the Atlantic and Pacific watersheds. It would be the highest point, elevation-wise, of my journey. The wind continued to blow cold, and I felt mildly light-headed.

To the mountains humans have always come, seeking wisdom, solace, peace. In *The Satanic Verses*, Salmon Rushdie's novel about the forces of good and evil, the character Alleluia Cone says that mountains are "where the truth went . . . just upped and ran away from these cities where even the stuff under our feet is all made up, a lie, and it hid up there in the thin air where the liars don't dare come after it in case their brains explode." Peter Mathiessen, in *The Snow Leopard*, writes that the "mountains draw near, and in such splendor, tears come quietly to my eyes and cool on my sunburned cheeks." It is not only the physical beauty of the mountains that move him but the power they evoke. "Still, all this *feeling*," Mathiessen writes, "is astonishing: not so long ago I could say truthfully that I had not shed a tear in twenty years."

Hoosier Pass, admittedly, was not the Himalayas. Still, I sensed the mountains' power, even as I struggled to catch my breath. I looked out across the snow-covered peaks. It was hard to imagine violence there. It was hard to stand there and imagine violence anywhere. And yet the top of Hoosier Pass brought a memory of a violent act.

It was a Monday night in April 1999. I'd driven seventeen straight hours, all the way from Lakeview, Oregon, and was in that odd intersection between exhaustion and joy that long drives always seem to inspire; I had parked my car at this summit and stood outside, happy to be back in the Colorado mountains. It was nearly two in the morning. The snow was still piled high at the edge of the parking lot, and the moonless sky was clear, multitudes of shimmering stars. I remember that night for that surreal feeling of calm that humankind must once have known so intimately. But mostly I remember that night for the tragedy of the following morning, when two boys dressed in trench coats and carrying guns and explosives walked into their high school and opened fire.

I had driven slowly down the mountain pass, my windows down, the hair on my arms standing up, not from the cold so much as from the charged elation of being back in my Colorado mountains, my home. It was a night of staggering beauty, and I could not have felt more removed from a violent instinct. I could not have imagined that just miles away those two boys must have been awake, a perverse adrenaline coursing through their veins as they imagined the plan they would soon carry out.

It was a hard world to wrap your mind around. Always there's been violence. Still, something of the contemporary rage felt new somehow. Twenty years earlier there were no high school shootings, were there? No planes crashing into buildings?

It was a world that made you want to disappear at times, to hide forever in the thin air along with Alleluia's truth.

Now low clouds moved swiftly across the sky, and I felt the temperature drop. It would be a cold descent, and I waited for my sweat to dry. The ride down was eleven winding miles, my eyes watering in the wind.

Twenty years earlier I had watched a beaver move through the water of a dark-blue pond. Truth or false memory, wherever that pond had been, it was gone now. In its place were cabins, homes, private driveways, condominiums. I was on the outskirts of one of Colorado's most famous winter recreation towns.

Contrary to what it seems today, Breckenridge wasn't founded on skiing—it was founded on gold. In the mid-nineteenth-century miners discovered placers, and in 1859 it became the first mining boomtown on the western slope. The town was named after a politician from Kentucky, John C. Breckinridge. Locals liked to say the different spelling was an intended improvement on the man's name.

A bicycle trail led clear to Frisco. Suddenly I was surrounded by cyclists, all built like models from *Outside* magazine, lean and fit, their bicycles as finely tuned as the muscles that churned them. Cycling had long been popular in Colorado. In the early 1900s Denver had the most bicycles per capita of any American city. Now cyclists passed me easily as I plodded forward, a rhinoceros in a herd of gazelles.

The late-afternoon sun created long shadows and light through the trees caused a strobe-like effect as I made my way along the trail. My map showed campgrounds near Frisco, but when I found them, they were closed, in part due to spring runoff, which had caused flooding. And once again (at the age of forty, you would think I wouldn't continually be caught off guard by this), darkness was falling.

A Day Use Area near a section of cross-country trails had a small lodge that was closed for mud season. Behind the lodge lay a large grassy field. A guy could probably, I thought, wait until just before dark and then pitch his tent.

A man pulled up in an official state truck. He told me he was a caretaker nearby. I asked him about camping. Told him my plan.

"You do that," he said, "you'll be arrested for vagrancy for sure. They patrol the hell out of this area. I'm sorry." Sleeping, I thought, was a most peculiar crime. The man started to drive off, but then he backed up. "I'll tell you, if you head up this road, 'bout half-mile, then turn right on the gravel road—you'll see it—and go back a ways, then go back into the forest up there, you probably won't get caught. Understand, I'm not saying it's okay or that I think you should do that—I'm just saying you probably won't get caught."

"Sounds good," I said.

"Now, I'm not giving you permission. Someone asks me, I'll say I never talked to you."

I nodded. "Thank you," I said, because I was grateful. I vowed to protect the man's good name. I'd tell no one he'd committed an act of generosity.

# Below Freezing

A FROST-COATED MORNING, the instant coffee already lukewarm by my second sip. I walked in circles to keep warm. After packing the bike, I rode into Frisco, waiting in vain for a warming sun. What came instead were flurries of snow, which by early afternoon had turned into full-fledged flakes. The forecast called for night temperatures of less than ten degrees, which could have been a good test for the lower limits of my warmest clothes and sleeping bag. Instead, I sat in a Laundromat and wrote postcards and read from John Steinbeck's *Travels with Charley*: "Having a companion fixes you in time, and that the present, but when the quality of aloneness settles down, past present and future all flow together." And I felt it, knew exactly what Steinbeck meant, this merging of time. It was a winter day in spring, and I was in pursuit of a past and future summer. I could feel schedules as defined by a clock or calendar slowly fading. It was not for me to wish the snow to stop. Better to let the weather fall as it may, to embrace rather than fight it. I checked into the cheapest motel I could find.

By night the snow had stopped. The air was still, and what clouds remained moved swiftly across the sky, last stragglers of a migrating herd. It was mud season, that time between skiing and summer, and I was the lone tourist on the downtown street. The orange glow from the few open restaurant windows gave the off-season solitude a ghostly charm. Following a sign and the sound of muffled music, I walked up a flight of stairs and into a bar, looking for conversation, if only to eavesdrop. But beneath the warm lights there was only the bartender. He brought me a Fat Tire beer.

"What brings you to town?" he asked.

When I told him, he asked if it wasn't too cold for long-distance bicycling, and I agreed that it probably was. In all, only a couple of inches of snow had covered Frisco, but I was worried about the trail over Vail Pass, and I asked the bartender about it.

"There might be places where you'll have to carry your bike over drifts," he said. "And toward the top it might be iced over and slick. It'll be cold, and there's supposed to be a storm moving in. But you should be able to make it to the top of the pass okay."

And the ride down the other side?

"Now that," he said, "I couldn't say."

When the song on the jukebox ended, he brought me a second beer, and we watched a muted basketball game on the TV.

Back outside the streets were empty, and the night was filled with percussive dripping, the sound of melting snow falling from eaves. The whole town smelled of pine. I pulled my cap over my ears and walked alone beneath the streetlights. The clouds were gone now, revealing a sky full of stars and a sliver of moon.

My concern about Vail Pass was an informed one. On my trip in 1985 the backside of the trail had been covered with old snow drifts. By the time I reached the summit, storm clouds formed, and I'd pedaled through flurries of snow. I was shivering when I finally started my descent, anxious to get to the warmth of a Vail lunch. But as I rode, the drifts became deeper and more frequent. Plowing forward, I could barely keep my balance. When I came to a sign that said X-COUNTRY SKIERS STAY RIGHT, I knew it was time to give up.

I had lifted my bike and started walking up to Interstate 70. From the trail to the road was a steep hike on a slippery hill, and carrying the bike, I slipped twice, falling in the snow, careful to hold onto the frame and not let the bike roll down to the bottom of the hill. Finally, I reached the interstate and rode down the pass slowly, wary of occasional patches of ice. The snow and clouds cleared, and by the time I had arrived in Vail it was sunny and warm.

Now the skies were so clear it was hard to imagine clouds moving in. I left early the next morning, dressed in my warmest clothes. They were barely enough.

The temperature in Copper Mountain had risen to seventeen degrees by the time I entered the small resort town. A woman bundled in an old brown jacket was walking in front of the ski lodge, and I asked her where I might get some food. She smiled, shrugged, and explained that she didn't speak English.

"Vives aqui?" I asked.

She shook her head, no. She didn't live in Copper Mountain.

"Trabajo," she said, or at least, that was the one word I understood. Like most of the upscale ski resort villages in Colorado, the people who worked them couldn't afford to live in them.

"Comida aqui?" I asked, pointing toward the hotel.

"No aqui," she said, and she pointed me to the only open café in Copper, and I rode over the cobbled streets until I found it.

Inside I begrudgingly ordered a three-dollar cup of coffee and an eleven-dollar turkey sandwich with a thin slice of cheese. At the table beside me four women discussed the impending marriage of one of their friends. Of the groom, it was clear, they did not approve.

"Everything revolves around him," said an immaculately dressed woman with expensive jewelry. "We can't even go out to coffee anymore. I think he just doesn't like me."

"It's not just you," said one of the other women. "He totally controls her."

"Do you know she's not even having a bachelorette party?" said the first woman, and they all shook their heads and started grumbling at once. "We should just skip the wedding altogether and have a party of our own." It was a sentiment that held, for them, unanimous appeal.

The trail continued uphill and wound through pine forests and willow marsh. The ground was covered deep in snow, but the trail was clear, even the short wood bridge that crossed a creek. Near the top of the pass it merged with the highway, and a turn lane led into a parking lot, where a carload of people were feeding a red fox from their rolled-down windows.

The streaming wind howled in my ears as I descended along streams and ponds and piles and drifts of leftover snow. The sky had grown cloudy, a reminder how fast weather could change in these mountains. I sped down the pass, hoping to evade the inevitable storm.

The snowfall waited until I was nearly down, and then, three miles from Vail, it fell, large sleet pellets at first and then wet, feather-like flakes. Shoots of yellow grass stood in the patches of white that covered the hillsides. Flakes fell like the inside of a newly shaken snow globe, and I, in my yellow and black rain gear, wove around the curves, moving easily through the snow, skirting a golf course that, try as I might, I didn't recognize. It was lined with what seemed to me an unnecessary abundance of NO TRESPASSING signs. The message was clear: there would be no camping here this time around.

In '85 it had been sunny and warm when I'd arrived in Vail. The trail had run right through the golf course. I had stopped to drink from my water bottle when two men came walking up the trail. They said they were firemen. It was their day off, and they'd just come from having lunch. The taller of the two had blond hair and a mustache. The other man was shorter but had broad shoulders and curly brown hair. They seemed to be in a very good mood, and it occurred to me that, in the early afternoon of a sunny day in Vail, "lunch" may very well have been a euphemism for "beer."

"It's a good time to be in Vail," said the tall one. "It's quiet, no tourists, everyone's happy."

"In two months we'll all be grumpy," said the other.

"Tourists," said the first, and he shook his head.

Technically, I thought, I was a tourist. But I kept it to myself.

"The stupid questions," continued the tall fireman. "I could write a book."

"What kind of questions?" I asked.

"'At what elevation do deer become elk?' 'Why do they chop down all the trees on the mountain tops?'"

"One guy last summer wanted to know if I could tell him where some fortune in gold was buried. I mean, if I knew, I already took it, right?"

Tourist bashing, despite the fact that tourism was an industry that drove the economy, was an honored Colorado tradition. In an essay from a 1954 issue of *Harper's Magazine*, for example, Thomas Hornsby Ferril, who was a member of Denver Chamber of Commerce wrote: "I loathe tourists. I hate myself when I get crowded into being one; my dearest friend, in the role of tourist, becomes leprous in my sight."

A Steller's jay landed on the bush to our left, looked us all three in the eye, and then flew away. At the risk of adding to the list, I ventured a question of my own. Where might a guy set up a tent around here?

"You could set it right there," said the first man, pointing to a flat patch of high grass behind some bushes at the edge of the golf course.

I must have looked skeptical because the other man said, "Seriously. No one'll bother you. There's really no one around this time of year anyway."

Because they were firefighters, I figured their consent was as good as any. I thanked them, and they wished me luck.

That night I set up my tent behind a bush on that golf course, not far from the trail. I fell asleep to the soft sound of rain. In the morning, when I emerged from the tent—still rubbing sleep from my eyes, my hair in a rat's nest—an elderly woman was walking two white poodles on the trail. She took one astonished look at me and started to walk faster, muttering under her breath to her dogs. I watched her and imagined the story she'd later tell: *Stupid tourists. All these mountains, and they set up camp on a golf course.*

I looked up at the mountains now as I rode through the falling snow. The aspen trees that once covered the hillsides were gone. In their place stood condominiums packed together so tight, it was hard to tell if there were many buildings or just one, fortress-like and stretching for what seemed miles.

Was it the world that had changed, or was it me? Now, during a time of heightened security, it was difficult to imagine that I would get away with camping on a resort town golf course. Terrorism and war. Civilian Minutemen with guns "protecting" our southern border. It was a time when a government-issued color code was used to gauge our risk, and freedom itself was being reconfigured to fit the changes. A dosage of fear was fed to us daily. Vitamin or sugar pill, who could say? The news seemed gloomy, and yet in 1985 the news had been of starving children, environmental degradation, crisis in the Middle East.

At twenty I had feared nothing. One day in late July, on a busy California highway, I'd left my helmet by the side of the road. By the time I realized my mistake and went back to retrieve it, the helmet

23

was gone. I shrugged it off, didn't buy a new one. For the remainder of the trip I rode without it, unconcerned with the tenuous security of my human skull. Now it was all I could do to not wear a helmet every moment of my day-to-day life. At forty I considered all the ways a man on a bicycle in the western United States might die: lightning, flood, tornado, earthquake, volcano, collision with car, falling rocks, bike crash, gun fire, grizzly bear attack, human attack, heart attack, heat stroke. Was it naïveté then, or was I now a product of a culture of fear? Where exactly was the line between faith and common sense?

What was clear enough, given the vast number of NO TRESPASSING signs, was that there would be no one camping on the Vail golf course anytime soon.

Just past Vail I waited out a pounding rain inside a covered bus stop. But when the sun returned, it came with a sheriff's swagger, and the clouds scattered, petty crooks running scared. As if to merge with the changing mood, I rode out of the development and into open space, reaching Wolcott just before sundown. The lone store was closed. Beside it a quaint-looking green, two-story house glimmered in the fading light. A sign outside said ROOMS. There was a parking lot in front. Faded Visa and MasterCard stickers hung on the door, which was unlocked. I walked inside. A large brown dog, lying on a throw rug, raised its head to look at me and then put its head back down. I waited, looked around. There wasn't really a front desk or even a bell to ring for service. I leaned down to pet the dog.

"Hello?" I called.

A woman appeared at the top of a stairway. She was not happy to see me.

"How," she asked, "did you get in my house?"

"Your . . . I thought this was . . . Don't you have rooms?" I asked.

"This is my *house*. That door is supposed to be locked," she scolded.

I stammered an apology and commented on the friendly disposition of her dog.

She sighed. "There's a campground just down the road, less than a mile."

The campground was an abandoned mess, the garbage bins overflowing, trash lying all over the grounds nearby. Large crows were rifling through the debris, scattering it further. I walked through the campsites, looking for a quiet spot as far away from the stench as possible. One of the campsites had been abandoned, the past occupants having left dirty diapers and opened cans of dog food on the picnic table. I wondered how long it had been that way. I wondered, too, what animals it might attract. I found the campsite farthest from the bins. The site was near a river, and I fell asleep to the sound of distant trucks and honking Canada geese.

## A Colorado Cow Patch South of Baggs

THREE MILES PER HOUR into an unrelenting wind, and the last three towns on my map were ghost towns, entirely devoid of human life or stores or cafés. My water bottles were quickly dwindling, and my chain was making a clunking noise that all the White Lightning in the world wouldn't make go away.

I grew weary from hunger and soreness and elevation. My throat was dry. I cursed myself for not buying more food in Vail. I came around every bend in the road, anticipating a summit, but each time the road continued to rise. Fatigued, I stopped and lay down on a grassy hill, protected from the wind, and I watched the clouds until I fell asleep to the mild warmth of sun on my face.

I woke rested but hungry. It was just past six. Finally, I came over the crest of the final climb. Even downhill, I had to pedal hard, such was the wind. When the road leveled out, the resistance of the wind was so strong, I had to strain against my pedals in a low gear, the chain crunching with each spin.

Twenty years earlier I would have been too proud to do what I did next. With age, though, comes humility. First truck I saw, I stuck out my thumb, and when I arrived in the high valley town of Topanas, it was on the bed of a flatbed truck, my bike and I both hunkering low—as if in shame—to avoid the wind.

At the Topanas Store a woman behind the counter rang up my

25

food. When I asked if there was a place to sit, she pointed to a stack of folded aluminum-frame lawn chairs, told me to help myself. I settled back, enjoying my meal and the cold drink against my throat. The woman asked about my trip, and I told her how I'd come through the same way once before.

"Didn't there used to be an antique store and a bookshop here?" I asked.

"Yeah," she said. "All that's been closed a long time now."

She called her husband, told him about me. When she hung up, she said, "When my husband gets here, we'll give you a ride into Yampa. There's a couple motels there. One's run by some friends of ours, the Royal. It's cheap—you can get a good night's sleep there."

"Think they have rooms available?" I asked.

She thought. "I don't know." She picked up the phone and dialed.

"It's me," she said into the phone. "You got rooms available?" She held the phone away from her ear. "They got plenty," she said to me.

On the drive into Yampa the evening sun cast a golden glow over the high valley, where the grass performed a synchronized sway.

The Royal Hotel had upstairs rooms above a bar and restaurant. The room was just big enough for a queen bed and a nightstand. The hotel was dorm style, with shared baths down the hall. A sign said: PLEASE DO NOT STEAL LINENS, AS IT WILL BE A DETRIMENT TO THE OTHER GUESTS. Another warned: ATTENTION: THE HOT AND COLD ARE REVERSED IN THE SHOWERS.

It was Friday night. Downstairs a jukebox was playing country songs. I walked down, sat at the bar, and asked to see a menu.

"Kitchen's closed, Hon," said the bartender, a rugged-looking woman. Attractive. Looked like she could be sweet and mean all at the same time. "You still want to see a menu?"

"Sure," I said. I was so hungry, I thought maybe just the descriptions themselves might help.

Unlike mud season in a ski resort town, Friday night in a cowboy town bar, and no matter the size of the crowd, it's going to be lively.

A young woman sat between two men at the other side of the bar. "What time we brandin' Sunday?" she asked one of the men.

"I don't know," he said. "Early."

"Well, what time?" she asked.

"Why you gotta know right now?" he said.

"I need to know to what extent to pace myself," she said, nodding toward her beer. Cowboy logic.

A woman came out from the kitchen, wiping her hands on an apron. She saw me looking at the menu.

"You going to eat?" she asked.

"Not if the kitchen's closed," I said.

"I ain't closed if you're hungry," she said.

"I don't want to keep you here—you probably just cleaned the kitchen," I said.

"I got no where I gotta be. What do you want?"

"What's easy to make?"

"Whatever you want. I should tell you, I been told here recently I can't cook," she said, looking sideways at a man sitting on the other side of the bar. The man chuckled.

"It's your funeral," he said to me.

"Least he won't die starvin'," said the cook. "What would you like?"

"I like rellenos," I said.

"Coming right up."

I looked around. The bar was a big square room with tables on two sides and strings of light hung from the tops of the walls. A large-screen TV was showing country music videos.

"You want another drink?" the bartender asked the man sitting to my left.

"Yeah, hell. Might as well drink. I ain't gettin' laid," he said.

"Not with an attitude like that, you ain't," she said. Said it as if attitude alone was the secret to it all.

Shortly, my meal came. A heaping plate of rellenos, deep fried with beans and rice. I was feeling the happy sort of tired that comes from a good day of making sore muscles, and the meal tasted as good as any I'd had in a long time.

"How is it?" asked the cook.

"It's as good a meal as I've had in a long time," I said.

"Really? Earl!" she said looking around the bar. "Did you hear what this man just said? Hey, where'd he go?"

"He left," said the bartender.

"Well, heck. The one time someone says somethin' good about my cookin'. The one time I'd a been happy to look over and see the man sitting there, and he's gone," she said, shaking her head. "That just figures."

In the morning I coffeed over a copy of the *Steamboat Today*, where I saw this advertisement: MARMOTS IN YOUR ROCK WORK? SKUNKS UNDER THE DECK? PORCUPINE GNAWING ON YOUR HOT TUB? CALL VARMINTS UNLIMITED WILDLIFE DAMAGE CONTROL.

Always good to know, I thought, what needs can be met by the spirit of human enterprise. Exactly how common *was* a porcupine-gnawed spa?

I had my own problem to deal with: squeaks in my chain. There was no ad for that. At the Yampa Post Office I was loaned a bucket and sponge. I cleaned the chain, link by link, wiping clear the mud and grease. Then I patched punctured tubes, and I washed the entire bike until it glimmered in the morning sun. The sky was clear. Twenty years earlier it hadn't been, and I'd been caught in a storm between here and Phippsburg.

I had been pedaling along the Yampa, teals and mallards in the river, occasional robins on fence posts. The road was flat, there was a tailwind, and I was so into the ride and the green of the scenery that I barely noticed the darkening sky.

Ahead, unbeknownst to me, within the cumulonimbus clouds forming in the sky, supercooled water droplets were attaching to pellets of ice. Wind updrafts were causing the pellets to move through the clouds in a roller coaster cycle. The pellets were growing with concentric layers of ice. Their timing with gravity, assuming I was the target, was perfect.

One more reason to wear a helmet: hail.

At first I felt a smattering of rain, and I thought I could ride it out. But then it started to pour. The world suddenly became a shelling attack of pinball-sized ice, accompanied by a downpour of merciless rain, thunder, and lightning. There was nowhere to hide, so I kept pedaling. I felt the sting against my shoulders and back, bouncing loudly against my helmet, clinking against my spokes. By the time I pulled into Phippsburg, I was drenched.

I sheepishly stopped at a store at the edge of the town. I was dripping wet, and I stood in the doorway, looking in through a screen.

"Well," said a woman behind a single register, "come in."

"I don't want to track in," I said. "I was just wondering if you might fill my water bottles."

She laughed. I guess because a soaking-wet man asking for water struck her as funny. "It's fine," she said. "Come in—a little water won't hurt nothin'."

I opened the screen and stepped into the store. The woman looked at me, shook her head. She was probably in her mid-sixties. "You get in here and dry off," she said. "You're lucky you didn't get caught in that hail they got just south 'o here."

"Yes," I said. "Lucky me."

She walked into a back room and returned with a stack of towels. "Now," she said, "go get dried up." She pointed toward a steep stairway. My shoes squeaked on the wood floor, and my heels squished with every step. I climbed up a flight of stairs and walked into a small bathroom, where I dried off the best I could. When I returned, there was a man talking to the woman. He wore a cowboy hat and boots. They both turned to stare at me when I walked back down the stairs.

"Feel better," she said. It sounded more like a command than a question, but I nodded anyway.

"Quite a storm you got caught in," said the cowboy. "Woulda' been a nice free car wash, 'cept for the new dents in my pickup. Didn't do you any brain damage did it?" he asked.

"Hard to tell," I said.

"Well, how many fingers am I holdin' up?" he asked, holding up three, which is what I answered.

He nodded. "Helps to have a hard head," he said, and the woman laughed.

How fleeting, that youth. I had ridden into that storm, had laughed out loud, the bombardment of hail a perverse joy. Now, the day before, I had caved at the mere hands of a little wind and just miles from town.

I pedaled north, taking a back route, past Stagecoach State Park, over rolling hills and a blue lake with motorboats in the distance, crows overhead, a red-winged blackbird on a fence post, grazing cattle on the hillsides, the buzzing of a dragonfly.

Steamboat Springs was a friendly town, with families playing Frisbee in a park and the laughter of friends over drinks on a sidewalk café. I walked my bike through the downtown and at a corner, while I waited for a light, a teenage boy on a red single-speed asked me where I was headed. When I told him, his eyes lit up.

"That's cool," he said, and I realized I would soon be in Wyoming, that I had made it over the highest of the mountains I would have to climb.

I rode in the shadow of a cliff with high walls and then past ranches and rivers and horses standing proud on green hills. Just before Hayden, the sun low in the sky, a small herd of antelope ran across a field, and a group of mule deer lifted their heads to watch me pass.

I camped in woods overlooking the river, and as night fell a half-moon rose over the horizon, its reflection of flowing light undulating in the river.

Craig, Colorado. Sunday at noon, seventy degrees. A small western town at a BBQ café, the sun warming a wood deck patio, a good book, and a sweating glass of ice-cold water. My last day in Colorado. It was healthy, this travel by bicycle. The unsequestered movement away from the confines of walls and television and career. And the goose bumps on arms, this electricity that humans must once have felt more regularly, reawakened. How carefully we have numbed ourselves from the rhythms of nature. On the bicycle the whole notion of outside and in was flipped. In offices and homes we lived in and occasionally went out. On the bike I was living out and occasionally going in. Comfort was a matter of slowly adapting to change, rather than relying on an artificial and confining building environment. When I pedaled, I sensed every change in the light, in the land, in the air, in the temperature.

What I felt was something I had not expected or had forgotten: that sense not of accomplishment but of relief. For twenty years I had been traveling these American highways, long dusty roads through the desert, the plains, the mountains and coasts. And for twenty years I have felt a sadness, a longing for this slow movement: to move through the world not as observer behind windshield glass but as participant, to feel the wind and the cold and the sun on my skin. To be back on the bicycle after twenty years was to reconnect with all that I'd been seeking since that original trip. The why of the matter had nothing to do with fitness or health or recapturing my youth but, rather, with the reacquaintance with this West I'd left behind but had never let go of. The West—like all environments—was a region that was only felt fully when we joined its center. Thoreau talked about living "simply," but to me that marginalized it somehow. It was not simplicity that brought us to nature but a desire for transcendence, for awakening. More than the need for preservation of the "pristine" (the very use of the word implies a division, a sense of categorizing and ranking) was a reclaiming of this relationship with the environment, a means of reconnecting with an inherent worldview, an understanding that "we" and "environment" were not separate but one and the same. From the bicycle I was able not just to observe the natural world but to enter it.

I left town and rode along the river. To my right, swaying from its perch on the top of a cattail, a red-winged blackbird sang out to me, and I returned its call. Then the bird led me, flying from stalk to stalk, staying just ahead, turning to watch me before it flew, as if encouraging me on.

Early evening through smooth rolling hills of sage, the grass a fertile valley green past ranch houses, horses, cattle. I pulled off on a county road and camped in a cow patch behind willow brush, where a lone pronghorn supervised the pitching of my tent from roughly a hundred yards away. Twenty years earlier it was very near here that I had seen a different antelope, about fifty yards from the road, his head caught in a barbed wire fence. With grand delusions of setting it free, I took just two steps toward it before, frantically, it shook loose, and

I could hear the creaking of the rusty fence, even after the antelope had sprinted away.

Now, my tent secured, I turned around. This antelope, too, was gone.

To view the setting sun, I walked to the top of a nearby hill, where a small group of pronghorn ran across a field of plowed black dirt. Further from the mountains now, night fell slower. I lay back against my panniers and waited patiently for stars. Ambition willing, breakfast would be in Wyoming.

# Wyoming

# Outlaws, Antelope, Prairie Dogs, and Sage

BAGGS, WYOMING, sits at an elevation of just over 6,000 feet in the state's Little Snake Valley. The town was named after George Baggs, a rancher who settled in the area in the early 1880s, along with his wife, Maggie, whom he'd met in a Chicago dance hall. By most accounts Maggie had a notorious mean streak: she'd once had a man horse-whipped simply for making an off-color comment at her expense. She was also a habitual philanderess, with a weakness for ranch hands, including one Mike Sweet. Maggie and Sweet made little effort to hide the affair, and when George found out, he divorced her. With her half of the ranch money, she fled to California, taking Sweet with her. George ultimately moved farther west, near the Utah border, where he continued to ranch.

The town was in the midst of a small oil boom, and I tried to mesh what I saw with my memory of it. The setup seemed backward, my memory like a film negative or like looking at a mirror reflection, all the elements of the town reversed. I parked my bike near the Butch Cassidy cabin, which was closed, and walked across Main Street to a Catholic Church with a freshly painted red door. In a vent beneath the cross on the roof, mother birds had built two nests side by side. A sign indicated the church doubled as a Visitor Center. I tried the door. Locked. A Monday in May, and I was the only visitor.

Twenty years earlier it had been a Sunday evening when I'd ridden into Baggs. The town had smelled of rain-dampened sage as I passed an old faded HOTEL sign with an arrow pointing toward a side street, but when I followed it, it led only to a group of numbered trailers. Some of the windows were broken or boarded over, and there was no office in sight.

So I'd returned to Main Street and pulled up to a church, hoping maybe there'd been an evening service, someone still milling about. But the church stood quiet. Across the road and up a block a sign said: LIQUOR.

In the West, aside from the prohibition experiment, booze and religion had a long-standing and cordial, if not outright friendly, relationship. An 1880s Rawlins newspaper, for example, once reported that "the temperance organization at Carbon is thriving nicely, and the saloons are doing well as ever, so all parties are satisfied." Sunday, and the church was closed, you found the next best thing. I walked across the street.

"You in need of a prayer?" asked the woman behind the register. She was pushing fifty, slightly plump, with brown hair. I hadn't talked to or seen anyone else for hours, and even though I'd seen her behind the register when I walked in, her voice startled me.

"What?" I asked.

"I saw you over at the church. No one'd be over there this late."

"Actually, I was just wondering if there was a place I could pitch a tent," I said.

"I got a hotel, just up a block. It's not much, just a few trailers. You can stay there if you like. I'm Elaine, by the way." She meant the hotel I'd already seen. I was curious what she'd charge for a place so clearly out of commission.

"How much?" I asked.

"I couldn't rightly charge you, since there's no water," she said. "There's no bedding. I trust you have a sleeping bag?"

She took a purse from beneath the counter, removed a single key, and handed it to me.

"They're not in great shape, but at least you'll stay dry if it rains," she said. "Keep your food wrapped tight—there might be mice. Watch your step—there might be glass. If you're hungry, you could try Virginia's. Mexican place. I think they're stayin' open tonight."

I thanked her, embarrassed that I'd been afraid she'd charge too much.

At the trailer hotel I had checked all the rooms before deciding on the last one, the farthest from the road. The room was a single bed, a bare light bulb above a dresser against the wall. The carpet was worn and gray, and the room smelled of mildew and dust. The screen door didn't latch. A six-inch gap separated the end of the top step and the trailer door. I carried my bike into the room, leaned it against the bed.

The whole place had a holed-up feel, like it would be a good place to hide. The room darkened as the sun slid low in the sky. I had imagined myself a wanted man, running from the law.

I ordered a plate of huevos rancheros at a restaurant called El Rio's, and I peered out the window as I sipped a hot cup of coffee. Across the highway I could see Cassidy's cabin, resting empty in the sun. Cassidy's gang had been popular in Baggs, for in addition to their rowdy nights of drinking and gunfire, they always brought with them plenty of money. Cassidy sightings were reported in Carbon County into the 1930s, despite the conventional wisdom that he had been killed in Bolivia in 1909. Was it possible that he faked his own death, just as a way to keep the law off his back?

I pondered the question over my eggs.

If he did fake his death, who could blame him? Who among men had not considered the same? Disappearing. Whatever impulse would inspire one to fake his death, it was an impulse I understood.

At night in that trailer room twenty years earlier I had looked at myself in the distorted reflection in the mirror above the dresser. What was I doing in Baggs on a bicycle? Trying to disappear? Back then I often thought I could be happy if I were invisible. I didn't want the life that it was assumed every American wanted. It wasn't just the "American Dream" of the big house, expensive cars, prestigious job. I didn't want to make a name for myself. What I wanted was to move like a ghost through the world, to go from one town to the next, never sleeping in the same place twice. There was freedom in walking into a bar on a stormy night in a strange town, and though all heads would turn and look, size me up, within minutes I would be happily ignored. For the first time I saw my shyness not as an illness but as a gift. "Speak up," I'd been told all my life, as if listening were not also a conversation skill, as if the ultimate goal were a discourse in which every person's voice was not heard but expressed. That whole trip, the very act of riding away from the only home I'd ever known, had allowed me to move away from the life in which I'd always felt like a stranger. I'd always been out of the mainstream anyway, but before that bicycle tour it had been because of my shyness—the feeling that I was unable to fit in. What the bike trip had taught me was that life offered more than the mainstream allowed—fitting in could be a crutch. I hadn't ridden away from my comfort zone. I had ridden into it.

Because to live only in the mainstream was to risk trudging up the side of the highest mountain simply by moving forward in a single-file line. What the bike trip had taught me was that I could move out of that line. I could fly to the top or go around to the other side. I really didn't have to climb the mountain at all. I could climb other mountains. Or climb down canyons. Or fly to the moon. Or sit down and watch the clouds. There were many other choices. In all of our talk about the value of freedom how rare is it we ever fully explore all of its possibilities? I thought back to my education up to that point, how all the best teachers had always been the ones who asked me to consider possibilities, to think in new ways, to travel, to consider the lives of others. At its best my education opposed what the psychoanalyst Eric Fromm termed "necrophily." In his book *The Heart of Man*, Fromm writes, "The necrophilous person is driven by the desire to transform the organic into the inorganic, to approach life mechanically, as if all living persons were things. . . . Memory, rather than experience; having, rather than being, is what counts. The necrophilous person can relate to an object—a flower or a person—only if he possesses it; hence a threat to his possession is a threat to himself; if he loses possession he loses contact with the world. . . . He loves control, and in the act of controlling he kills life."

What the first bike trip had taught me was that experience lifted life beyond the static and inhibitive world. The assumption had been that I would finish that trip and then return to a "normal" life, get a degree and a salaried job, a 401K, a life insurance policy. The trip was just a diversion, a young man's whim, like hitchhiking through Europe. I couldn't have known then, as I stood in that trailer in Baggs, that in the end that trip would change the way I prioritized oftentimes over the last twenty years in ways that had made life more of a struggle than it would have been otherwise. That life would have been easier had I not learned to challenge the assumptions I'd been raised on, had

37

I not considered other possibilities, had I not learned that a home can be made with a tent and a sleeping bag.

But easy has never been the point.

A tailwind on a slight downhill, and I rode into the West of old range songs—sage, antelope, distant bluffs. Black volcanic soil, green thick grass, creek-carved draws. A handful of ranch houses stood far at the end of gravel roads, their pastures full of horses, cattle in the fields. Traffic was sparse, and the few truckers and cars that did pass gave me plenty of room, even though the shoulder was wide. Easy was the ride, and by the time I arrived in Creston Junction, I'd ridden fifty-two miles in just over three hours.

Wind, though, is the devil's tool and not to be trusted.

I stopped at a small pull-out area with two trailers, one a fireworks stand. I tried the door, but it was locked. A teenager, maybe sixteen, walked out from the other trailer, asked if he could help me.

"Do you sell cold drinks?" I asked.

"Nope," he said.

"Is there anywhere around here a guy could set up a tent?"

"Not really," he said. We both looked around. Nothing but space as far as the eyes could see. I sighed.

"How far's Wamsutter?" I asked.

"Thirteen miles," he said.

I looked to the west, where the sun had moved behind low-horizon clouds.

"How much daylight you think I got left?"

He shrugged. "Half-hour—maybe an hour," he said. I waited for him to deduce my dilemma—sun going down, next town miles away, man on bicycle. But if it all ever registered, he didn't show it. He turned and walked back inside.

I merged onto I-80 and headed into a rushing westerly wind. Had I been heading east, the interstate followed a direct line all the way back to Lincoln and Joan. Not a bad idea, and the wind seemed hell-bent on driving me that way. Tempting. Instead, I plowed forward, and it raged on, a mocking laughter in my ears. Eighteen-wheelers passed, seventy, eighty miles per hour. No matter how hard I strained against the wind, my cyclometer registered no speed higher than eight. Ahead I could see a steep climb.

I did not want to ride Interstate 80 in the dark.

After a couple of very slow miles, the sun growing ever lower in the sky, I saw gravel to my left, a retreating line that ran parallel to the interstate. A frontage road. I took the next exit and rode onto the gravel. Taking that exit was the first act in a night full of a comedy of errors.

At first the road was smooth, so long as I stayed in the tire grooves. But the farther I went, the rougher the road became. The sun broke through the clouds, casting long rays of orange light over the high desert. Then I heard a hissing rush of air, and I felt a very unwelcome wobble coming from my rear tire.

The temperature was dropping. I stopped to fix the flat, and my hands grew numb as I worked. There were no signs, and I could only hope the road continued into Wamsutter. But darkness was falling quickly, and I looked around for possible places to camp. I fixed the tire. The gravel road turned into hard-packed clay, first red and then white. Then the road narrowed into two tracks through the grass. Finally, it became hard-packed mud sediment. It was hard to know if there was really a road there at all.

And then, a fence with a locked gate. Dead end.

I had ridden six rough miles since leaving the interstate. All I could do was turn and head back. The sun was already partly behind the horizon.

Roughly two miles back, I had passed a small, square red-brick building surrounded by a barbed wire fence. I biked back to it and pitched my tent nearby, out of the view of I-80 and hopefully out of the wind. There were no clouds directly overhead, and the stars and moon were already bright in the sky. Lightning flashed in the eastern sky, but it seemed far off. Without my tarp, I thought, I could star gaze through the night. A couple hundred yards from where I lay in my sleeping bag, a steady run of trains rumbled through at roughly half-hour intervals. Eventually, I managed to fall into a restless sleep.

I woke to the plunk of a raindrop landing on my face. I got up, pulled out the tarp, and crawled out of my tent. But in the darkness, and with the hard blowing wind threatening to take the tarp for a long ride into the sage, I gave up. I looked at the sky, which was only partially covered with clouds. There was distant thunder. With the wind direction I thought perhaps the storm would blow over. I went back to sleep.

When I woke again, I woke wet. The rain was pounding me and my tent. Wind blew hard. The trains and thunder played percussive chaos. I was starting to shiver. I took the tarp and tucked it around the bottom of my sleeping bag, and I pulled it up over my head, an attempt to keep the sleeping bag dry.

Six in the morning was a cold drizzle. Small puddles of water stood in the corners inside my tent, and the foot of my sleeping bag was wet. Mostly, though, I had managed to stay dry. I rose, pulled rain gear from my pannier, and quickly loaded my bike. Standing water lay in the bottom of one of my front panniers, which I'd left partially open.

To get back to the interstate I had two options: go all the way back to the exit I'd taken or lift everything over the barbed wire fence, cross the eastbound lane of I-80, then the median, which I knew would be muddy and soft, and then head west again, once on the other side. The latter seemed the better option. I carried the bicycle to the fence, lifted it over, and threw all my bags alongside it. Then I hopped over and walked my bike to the shoulder. There were trucks screaming past, and I waited for a break, and then ran my bike across the lanes. The median was wider than I expected but the ground more solid, and I managed to roll the bike across, and just like that, I was riding again. Wet. Cold. Cursing the wind. But at least I was headed west. Jumping that fence had saved me about eight miles of riding. Smart decisions weren't coming routinely, but that was one of them. Storm clouds were moving fast, and, optimistically, I believed the sun would soon break through.

Minutes later I rode into face-stinging pellets of freezing rain. Then it began to snow, large flakes that fell not down but sideways, directly into my eyes. My glasses fogged. Without them my vision was poor. With them, though, I couldn't see at all. I took them off. I battled the wind soaking wet. Remarkable, really, how quickly water and wind could conspire to chill. I kept pedaling, refusing to hitch but hoping someone would stop, offer me a ride. No one did. Probably looked like I was having too much fun. I wouldn't know. I couldn't see.

At long last I arrived at an exit.

Wamsutter was a weather-beaten town at the edge of Wyoming's Red Desert. A scrawny man wearing a greasy ball cap was walking toward the truck stop door when suddenly arose a large gust of wind, and the man whirled a pirouette, just quick enough to snatch his now airborne cap from the air.

"Son bitchin' Wyoming. Does it ever get warm here?" he asked me, as he pulled the cap down tightly on his head. I shrugged.

Inside my numb hands wrapped around a coffee cup; an elderly woman with crooked teeth looked across the aisle at me.

"Hell," she said. "What this is. God made hell, and he called it Wyoming."

I wasn't convinced of her theology. I didn't think Wyoming was hell—I just thought the devil kept his wind in cold storage there.

Truckers were grumbling. "Can't even keep my rig between the lines," said one. Not a happy thought for a guy on a bicycle.

I spent the morning sitting at that truck stop drinking coffee until I finally felt warm again. A radio announced the wind speed: thirty-five. On flat ground, with no wind, my best speed was probably just over twenty. I'm sure a physics professor could show me the error in my thinking, but my arithmetic had me moving backward. Rock Springs seemed a long ways away. I begged for rides from the truckers, all of whom looked at me as if I'd asked for their firstborn. A FedEx driver explained that it was against company policy. I asked, what if I wrapped myself and paid the shipping cost? She laughed, thinking I was kidding. At the pump the drivers looked at me as if I might rob them. My appeals to their sympathy were unanimously shut down, even when I offered to fill their tanks. The day never warmed, and the forecast called for more of the same. Everyone seemed lethargic. It was the wind. It's a lot of extra stress when gravity's working on you sideways. I checked for bus service. There was nothing. Rock Springs, which was only seventy miles away, might as well have been on an island in the ocean.

At the Wamsutter Motel I rented a tiny room, with timeworn carpet and a double bed with a sagging mattress. I hung my tent, sleeping bag, and all my clothes to dry, laid out my gear on the dresser.

I knew for fact that it did get hot in Wyoming, even in May, had experienced it myself on this very stretch of road.

Back in '85 I'd made it peacefully into town on a calm and sunny evening. At a gas station I asked about a place to pitch a tent, and the teenage boy who ran the register suggested I ask at the town hall. It had been late, nearly seven, and I questioned if maybe the town hall might be closed.

"There'll be people there," said the boy. "There's a town hall meeting."

"I hate to interrupt a meeting," I told him.

"Don't worry," he said, "they ain't talkin' 'bout nothin', trust me."

At the Town Hall building a hallway had led into a large carpeted room, and people sitting in chairs were gathered in a circle. I stood, hoping someone would notice me. Finally, a woman turned, saw me, and walked over.

"Can I help you?" she said.

I asked for permission to sleep in the park.

"Wait here," she said.

I could hear her. "There's a kid (*kid?*) out here, wants to know if he can pitch a tent in the park?" she said.

"We got a motel," said a male voice.

"He's got a tent," repeated the woman.

Then I heard a second male voice, calm, a voice of authority. "Tell him its fine. If he camps south of the restrooms, they'll block him from the wind."

It had been my first full day ever out of Colorado on my own, and the drinking age in Wyoming was nineteen. After dark I walked into town and purchased a four-pack of California Coolers. I sat on a picnic table, looked at the stars, and drank like the adult Wyoming considered me to be. Wyoming. As a young boy, I'd traveled here with a children's church choir—the Sunshine Singers. We'd performed in a number of churches, but what I remembered most was riding the bus, looking out my window, and watching the dark band of blue on the horizon fading into night, and the stars, a thin sliver of moon, the occasional lights from passing cars reflected in the glass. While others slept, played games, or read, impatient for home, I wanted the ride to last. It had ignited a wanderlust in me, the thrill of moving through new places filled with unfamiliar people and long stretches of landscape.

I remembered, too, the high school baseball tournament where teammates and I had placed our sleeping bags in the outfield grass, and when we were done laughing and listening to Eddie Foley's dirty jokes, and I'd recovered from getting sick off my first experience with Skoal, and the others had all gone to sleep, I looked up at the night sky, and, not remembering the names of the constellations, I'd connected the stars in my own way, creating my own mythological gods.

That summer of the first bike trip, I finished that last cooler and reluctantly entered my tent. I fell asleep listening to the distant humming of the interstate traffic and longing for the road ahead, for the West I had yet to see. The night had been warm, the wind calm.

Now the night was frigid, and the wind howled. I napped through the afternoon, and when I woke, the wet clothes and gear hung like old ghosts from a dream. I walked outside. A local café was filled with large tattooed men in old black T-shirts and ranchers in cowboy hats and boots. A woman in blue jeans watched the CMT Music Award from the edge of her seat with an intensity of one who had money down on the nominees. She cursed out loud when the stars she wanted to win didn't.

In the morning, with sheet metal roofs shaking and the cold penetrating all layers of clothing, I returned shivering to the same café for breakfast. I checked the paper for a weather report, which confirmed my fears. Wind speeds between thirty and thirty-five. It was going to be a hard day—no way I'd get to Rock Springs in less than two days. In the adjoining store, in a last-gasp effort, I asked the woman behind the counter if she knew of anyone with a pickup going to Rock Springs.

"That guy that was just in here, he might be going there," she said.

"He just left?" I asked.

"He's coming back. He just went home to get us some tamales his wife makes. I don't know if he'll give you a ride. I'm not asking him for you," she said.

I waited for the man to return.

His name was Todd, and he was small and wiry and wore a cowboy hat with boots to match. The lines on his weathered face revealed a life lived mostly in wind and sun. They say you can tell a real cowboy by the size of his wrists, and Todd's were substantial. He smiled often, even later, when he talked about liberals and environmentalists.

"Sure," he said, "I'll give you a ride, if you help me carry these tamales." There were boxes of them, freshly made. I'd devoured two of them in the café the night before. They were as good as any tamales I'd ever had. I asked him how long his wife had been selling to the café.

"We used to own this place," he said. "Sold it about a year ago. Now I'm mostly retired, but I still help them out."

I loaded my bike in the back of his white pickup, and just like that, I was headed toward Rock Springs at seventy miles per hour.

"I got a son about your age, used to do some biking. Led tours for awhile," Todd said as we drove. "He lives in Durango now. Was a mountain climber too. Now he leads climbing tours all over the world."

"You ever go on one of his tours?" I asked.

"Naw," he said. "I never did much athletic stuff. I used to rodeo, though. My knees are so shot now I can barely walk. Not a lot of rodeo people walk real nice."

He pointed to some horses standing in the distance, their manes blowing in the wind.

"Wild horses," he said.

I asked him if there was a large population of them here.

"Too many, maybe," he said. "Environmentalists want to save them, but people back east, they don't understand how fast the horses breed. The desert can't sustain them. When they breed so fast, it weakens them. Environmentalists raise all kinds of hell. They take

44

pictures of the antelope, say the oil digging's killing them off. They don't take pictures of the antelope resting in the shade created by the oil tanks." He chuckled. "The controls aren't all bad, though. Like in Russia, they had no controls, and the oil seeped into the water. Some control's important."

We continued to drive. I could hear the wind through the glass, could feel it pushing against us. The shoulder was wide, but I had only a small tinge of remorse for not biking it. George Nellis, during his 1887 bicycle ride across the country, described the Wyoming landscape as "bare and bleak." About the route between Rawlins and Rock Springs, he wrote, "If there are one hundred and twenty miles of railroad on this earth so utterly devoid of humanity, civilized humanity, as the expanse of waste between Rawlins and Rock Springs, then let some knowing cyclist point it out." Nellis rode from New York to San Francisco, and despite not having the luxuries of paved roads (he occasionally rode on railroad ties) or even a multi-geared bike, he managed to complete the trip in just seventy-two days, setting a new transcontinental record. Nellis's trip is chronicled in a book called *An American Cycling Odyssey* (1887) written by Kevin Hayes.

I didn't think of this desert as a wasteland at all but as an increasingly rare expanse of open space, with red sand and sage, wild horses and, of course, antelope. To Nellis's credit, though, he hadn't hitched a ride.

We passed an old gas station, which slumped in ruins. I once knew the guy who had run the place.

"You ever know a guy named Marvin, who ran that station?" I asked Todd.

"Oh yeah," he said. "I know him."

When I'd ridden through before, I'd met Marvin, an unabashed right-winger who believed America's downfall began with the rise of feminism. "What d'you do? Kill rabbits and eat 'em along the way?" he had asked me.

"Mostly," I said, "I stop at cafés." When I told him I didn't hunt, he shook his head in disgust, told me the first thing I needed to do when I got to Rock Springs was buy myself a gun, even told me what kind to get. I had pretended to write it all down.

I'd seen Marvin a handful of times since. A woman once told me she thought he had died.

"He died, didn't he?" I asked Todd.

"Naw, he's still alive as he ever was."

"Really?" I said. "He must be about ninety now?"

"Naw, hell. He's my age. He's always looked like that," said Todd. "He has a different station now, just farther up the road. He won't sell you a partial tank of gas. Either you fill it up, or don't waste his time." Todd smiled. "I get along with him fine, but not everyone does.

"That university you teach at," he asked, "is it pretty liberal?"

"Well," I said, "it's not Boulder."

"Oh, God, no, I hope not," he said.

I laughed. Throughout much of the rural Rocky Mountain West, Boulder had long been regarded as bleeding heart central.

"It's probably like your university here in Laramie," I said.

"Our university's liberal. I had a girl call me; they were fund-raising, trying to get money for the university. This was before the election. I said 'Who're you going to vote for?' She said 'Kerry.' I said, 'Let me give you some advice. If you're going to be calling people here in this state asking for money, don't tell them who you're voting for. If they ask, just say you haven't decided yet.'" He chuckled. "She said she'd consider that."

Politics aside, I was grateful not only for the ride but also the company. Todd's smile was infectious. That morning Rock Springs had seemed a world away. Todd had me there before eleven.

About Rock Springs Jack London wrote in his journal in 1894, "It seems to be a mining town. I went to a saloon, got a glass of beer, and had a fine wash in warm water . . . it seems to be the wild and wooly west with a vengeance."

If you'd lived in this region during the fall of 1872 and had a little money to invest, you might have been swept up in the excitement that was created by the prospect of southern Wyoming becoming the diamond capital of the world. That summer a Kentuckian named Philip Arnold, with the help of a cousin, showed up at a California bank with handfuls of diamonds. Word spread. Some of the richest men of the time, including Horace Greeley and Charles Tiffany, invested in the "mines." By the time a government geologist named Charles King exposed what would become known as the Great Diamond Hoax, Arnold had made over a half-million dollars. This, on an original investment of just over thirty thousand, most of which was spent on diamonds purchased in Europe and used to salt an area south of Rock Springs.

For his part Arnold came out of the scandal unscathed, save for various lawsuits, which still left him with nearly three hundred thousand dollars. Back in Elizabethtown, Kentucky, he was considered a hero and his scam the act of an astute business mind. He built several of the town's most prominent buildings and started his own bank.

His was not a happy ending, however.

Angered by Arnold's business tactics, he was challenged to a duel by a rival. In the Elizabethtown street the two bankers fought it out. Arnold was shot. He died of pneumonia while recovering from the gunshot wound. Like Butch Cassidy, who was seen by many as a Robin Hood character who "only stole from the railroads," Arnold was lauded for taking the wealthy investors' money. And like Cassidy, assuming the truth of his Bolivian demise, they each died a violent death.

Prairie dogs disappeared into their holes and then reemerged, standing for a better look, their curiosity ultimately stronger than their fear. I talked to some of the closer ones, inquired about the weather and how they liked it, this prairie. I realized that what for me was open space full of solitude, for the prairie dog was a highly populated community, with no shortage of social opportunities.

The sky was clear save for the few cumulous clouds that floated lazily above the horizon. I was headed north now on Highway 191. Traffic was light, and I reveled in the solitude, the slow pace, noticed the subtle changes in the landscape, drank in the surreality of being alone in the wide-open space. From distant hills members of the Sublette antelope herd stood alertly, watching me.

I stopped to watch them back. The oldest surviving animal species in North America, the American pronghorn is a singular animal, worthy of admiration. To see them sprinting across the prairie or desert was akin to watching any migrating herd on an African safari.

The pronghorn is in the family of neither deer nor goat, though it shares characteristics with both. Despite the common use of the term, they're not technically antelope. They have branched horns, not antlers, and all bucks grow and shed them annually, the only species to do so. Less than half of all does grow horns, though sans prong. Able to run up to sixty miles per hour, they are the fastest species in North America and the second fastest in the world. They don't jump fences but squirt underneath, maintaining their speed with a seamless grace. A quirky mix of curious and shy, they are by reputation skittish and yet have been known to race along side cars, horses, trains. Even bicycles.

While there has been a push by conversation groups to seek protection for the pronghorn habitat, especially in the Red Desert, Wyoming is the only state in the union exempt from the Antiquities Act, which allows for the creation of national monuments by the federal government.

I hadn't said so to Todd, but the truth was that by interfering with migration routes, oil drilling *had* adversely affected the pronghorn habitat. Since 1985 the antelope population had decreased by roughly 40 percent. While gas fields weren't the only factor in this decline, they did contribute to it. Still, the pronghorns were plentiful, and no one was yet arguing that they were an endangered species. One wonders, though, is depletion the only argument for preservation?

Twenty years earlier, late in the morning, after I had raced beside that antelope, I was sitting on a picnic table eating an apple. Two golden eagles struggled into the wind but then turned and glided skillfully as they rode the currents, rising high over mesas of sedimentary rock and rippling cliffs.

A car pulled up, and a man and a woman got out. They didn't speak at first, and I sensed that they might have been arguing, were doing their best to leave me out of it.

The woman looked at me, sized me up. I nodded, said hello. She looked at my bike, shook her head.

"How can you ride out here in this ugly place?" she asked. "God, aren't you lonely?"

I looked out across the highway, to the mesas and cliffs far off on the horizon. I smiled shyly, mumbled something about the solitude, how it grows on you.

"There's nothing out here," she said.

"Well," I said, "there's antelope."

"Antelope, sure," said the man, while taking a cigarette from his front pocket and lighting it. "But I mean, they're not even deer. And they're always so far away."

Now I wondered where those people were, if they were still together, if they still believed in the fallacy of this desert as empty, when in truth it was so full.

## Night at the Antelope Saloon

AN ABANDONED HOUSE—its windows boarded and the wood stripped and sun-faded—sat among the high desert wheatgrass. Two oak trees stood skeletal against gray clouds, and an old army-green pickup rested peacefully in the backyard. The house was two stories, with large white beams stabilizing a roof over a large porch. I love that word: *stories*. What better to describe the different levels of the house?

Whoever had built the house built it solid. The roof didn't sag, the porch didn't lean. Once, I imagined, it had been a dream home. I could envision children playing in the yard, a tail-wagging golden retriever standing by the gate, the still-young mother standing on the porch, one hand on her hip, the other shading her eyes. And a man, with callused hands and dirt beneath his nails, greeting her, kissing her.

In the upstairs window, which had no glass or screen and hadn't been boarded, I searched for ghosts. But all was silent, save for the rustling of the grass in the breeze.

I rode through Eden and then into Farson, a small highway town, with a gas station, a small café, and a bar aptly named the Antelope Saloon. I stopped for chicken fried steak, which was delivered by a tall waitress wearing a tight yellow T-shirt with the image of a blue teddy bear on the front, and the words YOUR BOYFRIEND SNORES.

It was already evening, and I needed a place to sleep.

"Is it legal to camp in the park here?" I asked her.

"I don't know if it's legal," she said, "but I've seen people do it."

"Is there a sheriff in town, or someone I could ask?"

The woman laughed. "There's no sheriff anywhere near here," she said.

I waited until just before dark, and I pitched my tent beneath a tree in the park. The Antelope was just on the other side of the park, and I could hear the thumping bass of its music.

Just past the fall of night, I walked to the bar, which was filled with loud music, cigarette smoke, voices, laughter, the smacking of pool balls. The crowd was mostly truckers and the road crew that was working on the highway project. A large muscular man greeted me at the door. He was about six-foot-six, with a full brown beard and a back so tattooed that he barely needed the orange tank top he was wearing. Clearly an outcast, I walked over and sat at the bar. It wasn't just that I had no tattoos or piercings. What concerned me most was that the bicycle jersey I was wearing had a hoody. It occurred to me that a man with a hoody in a place like this might expect to become fodder for bully practice. I sat at the end of the bar and tried to remain inconspicuous. Two seats down sat a man with long stringy hair. He wore an orange vest and what I thought were bicycling gloves.

"Are you biking?" I asked.

He looked confused. "No. I'm here working on the road crew. All these guys are," he said gesturing.

"Going well?" I asked.

"It sucks," he said. "We're on our third foreman, we're behind schedule, nobody knows when the next shipment of supplies is going to get here. The third guy's threatening to leave, and you know who's next in line?"

"Who?" I asked.

"Me," said the man. "And as bad as things are now, it'll be a living disaster with me in charge, trust me." Then the man bought a twelve-pack from the bartender. "I'm going to my room," he said.

"Tomorrow's just going to suck." And on that note of optimism, he turned and walked out the door.

The bartender brought me a beer. I looked at her. She was about six feet tall, with long hair and several ear, eyebrow, and nose piercings. There was something athletic and attractive about her, in a very she-could-hurt-you kind of way. I thought I had seen her before, but I couldn't imagine where.

She shrugged. "I was the third-ranked junior middleweight boxer in the world for awhile," she said. "Some people recognize me from that."

And then I realized who she was. I had read about her in *Sports Illustrated* and seen her on ESPN. There was a small controversy a few years earlier, because Muhammad Ali's daughter Laila had been anointed Champ of the World, even though she hadn't actually fought any ranked opponents. Debbie Foster was one of the women she refused to fight.

"What are you doing here?" I asked her.

"I'm retired now," she said. "We live out on a ranch. I like it here. It's quiet."

"Do you miss boxing?" I asked.

"No," she said. "I have a lot of great memories, but my focus is on working with the high school kids here, teaching them about health issues. I'm setting up a boxing program. I really like working with the kids."

About her own boxing past, she spoke graciously, but I knew the questions I asked she had answered hundreds of times before. But when she spoke of the Farson youth, she spoke with passion. It was this she had most to offer the world now.

"Do you get much resistance about teaching boxing to girls here?" I asked.

"Some," she said. "Not a lot. I have to do everything after school and have to try not to interfere with other extracurricular stuff. People think boxing is brutal. But it teaches a kind of discipline and confidence that you can't get any other way. But mostly," she emphasized, "everything's been positive. I just really like working with the kids."

Suddenly, there was a ruckus behind me, raised voices. I turned to see two men argue. They'd been playing pool. The tension rose quickly in the bar. One of the men raised his pool cue, ready to swing.

"Excuse me," said Foster. She calmly walked from behind the bar and stood between the two men. "Knock it off," she said, without raising her voice. Duly admonished, the two men lowered their pool cues and moved to opposite sides of the room. Foster picked up two empty bottles from a table and carried them back to the bar, dropping them in the trash on the way.

"You want another?" she asked when she returned, and I said yes because I didn't want to leave. Hoody or no, I suddenly felt safe.

Later, the man in the orange tank came and sat at the bar. He was Foster's husband and had been her promoter during her boxing days. He himself had been an Ultimate Fighting competitor. We sat and ate peanuts and told stories well into the night. I told them about my bicycle trip, and we talked about cycling, fighting, sports, and about quiet nights spent beneath western skies. When I looked around later, I realized the bar was nearly empty. It was closing time.

We'd become friends, I guess, in that temporary way that people whose lives cross briefly forge bonds. Before I said good night and rose to leave, he nodded at me and said, "You must be tough to ride this far." Foster nodded. I imagined what I must look like next to them—me in my frilly bicycling shorts and jersey—and I had to laugh. Yeah, I thought, I'm the tough one here.

# To Jackson

THE HIGH COLD DESERT between Farson and Boulder, as seen from a bicycle, was not a bland colorless place. At seventy miles per hour it might have been. Slowed down, I observed: the green of the sparse clumps of grass, the brown and red of the sandy soil, the olive sage, the occasional dots of yellow dandelion, the bright red of the spring willow, the blue of the mountain base, the white of the fair-weather clouds hovering over the snow-capped Wind River peaks, and the turquoise of the midmorning sky.

And lying happily discarded by the side of the road, a dust-covered pair of Levi's blue jeans.

Twenty years earlier the ride out of Eden had started smoothly, and I'd pedaled with enthusiasm, anxious to get to Jackson and back into the mountains. But then a raging wind developed, blowing from the north, and I plowed ahead. The never-changing landscape surrounding me made me feel like I was riding stationary, and I rode on, playing songs in my head, thinking of my girlfriend back home, missing her, longing for two things at once, to return home and yet to keep moving forward. I tried to keep my mind calm, to think of her, the night we'd spent walking around Broadmoor Lake, holding hands, kissing beneath the lamplight; long drives through the Garden of the Gods or afternoons spent in downtown Colorado Springs, watching people, making up stories about them, or laughing and drinking coffee in all-night cafés. I moved slowly, north on 191, a steady eye on the map placed in the map holder on top of my handlebar bag, trying to match it with the scenery around me, looking for any sign that I was making progress. I kept moving forward. And why? For what reason to keep pedaling, to feel the weight pushing against me with each turn of the wheels? I felt that if I turned around, the wind would sail me all the way back home to her. Who would fault me? Damn the wind. It inspired an anger I couldn't get control of, and I swore myself northward, trusting that the loneliness and frustration would die when the wind did. Few cars passed, but when they did, I could feel their passengers looking at me, and I pedaled forward, refusing to look back. I wanted to stop, to scream, to throw rocks. But I pedaled forward, letting my rage propel me on. I raged forward until I came to a sign that showed a campground, and I turned onto a gravel road, thinking the change in direction would lessen the headwind, but it didn't, and instead the wind blew at an angle such that it was coming at me from both the front and the side. I made my way down the gravel road until I came to the camp site which was entirely vacant, not even an RV in sight.

In the reservoir I watched the turbulent water lapping noisily onto the shore. I lay my bike on the ground, knowing that if I leaned it against a tree, it would be blown over. I fought my tent from the stuff sack, the first stake coming free from the rocky ground, my hand stabbing out just in time to grab a handful of the nylon, enough to keep it from blowing away. If it had, it would have flown into the lake, and I imagined myself struggling in the choppy water, trying to rescue it.

Several yards from the campground was a small area, dug out and squared off, as if for a foundation. There was a tractor there and mounds of dirt and gravel. I carried the tent over and pitched it beneath the rise, where it was shielded from the wind. I ate a peanut butter sandwich dinner and the last of my granola bars. It was early; the sun wouldn't be down for a couple of hours. Sitting at the picnic table where I ate, I tried to write in my journal, but the pages kept flapping shut, so I took it and sat in the portable outhouse that had been placed there for the construction crew, and I listened to the wind slam against the sides, felt the wobble of the small space as I wrote. When I was done, it was still light, but I walked out, put my head down as I walked against the wind, and made my way to my tent and crawled inside. I spent a restless night listening to the flapping tarp of my tent and the wind and the water from the lake. When I slept, I dreamed tension-filled dreams of anger, and I was shouting, shouting at a faceless stranger, shouting against a grating noise.

In the morning I woke feeling completely rested. Outside it was calm, and I rose, squinting into the sunlight.

Now I rode through Boulder and into Pinedale, where I walked through gusts of wind, squinting against the grainy air. I bought a new tent stake, some granola bars, visited with a woman and her dog at the Chamber of Commerce. I ate a salad at a bar and grill, where, according to a sign on the wall, beer had been "helping white men dance since 1833." Pinedale was a friendly town, growing but still unjaded by the tourist trade.

I arrived at Warren Bridge Campground just after sunset, with plenty of light to spare. I had ridden over eighty miles since leaving Farson, and I knew I would wake sore in the morning. I carried Advil now, and SportsCreme, two items I hadn't needed twenty years earlier.

Yet the trip seemed easier somehow. My world was smaller. I knew what to expect and was better able to deal with complications as they came up. Instead of the manic graph of highs and lows, I was more patient now and less susceptible to bouts of boredom, and instead of exploring what was for me new territory, I was revisiting a memory, and the new exploration was not only in place but also in memory and time. It was not physical youth I was trying to recreate but that youthful sense of wonder, of joy in the world. Imagine a young boy out in the rain, drenching wet, walking along train tracks. The adults who pass shake their heads, maybe offer a ride, feel sympathy. But the boy is laughing, joyful, not worried about the potential for cold, not miserable at all but engaged in the moment.

Maybe what I craved now was a reattachment to discomfort, risk, a break from a focus on security and stability. It had grown easy to fall into mediocrity, blandness, routine, and then to seek fulfillment in material goods or in synthetic and packaged experience such that authentic human and nature interaction had become increasingly rare.

Maybe all I'm doing here is justifying the journey. A forty-year-old on a three-month bicycle trip seems out of the normal order of things, like a drenched man laughing and walking in the rain along the railroad tracks. It was easy to believe I should have been home, working.

But it felt right to me, that journey, felt like the perfect way to begin the last half of my life. I would return to my work, my day-to-day life, soon enough. When I did, I hoped to hold the memory of wind and sun and rain; of the fecund scent of marsh; of wildflowers dancing in a breeze. The knowledge of a child.

Past the willow a meandering stream moved through the valley. It was warm. Twenty years earlier it hadn't been, and I had packed the bike in a cold rain. I had only a single pack of oatmeal left, but I couldn't start my stove to boil the water. So I began the morning hungry, which didn't help the cold. On the highway, which set higher, less protected than the campground, a furious wind blew. Once moving, I didn't want to stop, and by the time I changed into warmer clothes, I was shivering. The ride was all uphill, and after about eight miles I felt weak and dizzy and wet and cold. I wanted to pull over, to find a spot beneath a tree to curl up and rest, but I knew the best way to stay warm was to keep pedaling. Bondurant was another twenty miles or more, and I didn't know if there was anything before it. I didn't think I could make it that far without food, and I started looking for a shelter of trees that might provide me enough dry ground to start my stove. But I'd ruined my last book of matches that morning trying to start the stove in the rain.

So I was relieved when, near the top of the steep hill, I saw a log building with a parking lot. I rode closer and saw the sign I was looking for: OPEN.

The Rim Store doubled as a café. Even after I removed my rain gear, I was soaking wet and my shoes were covered in mud. When I entered, I smelled the fresh scent of burning pine. I apologized for tracking in. A woman behind the counter looked at me.

"Oh, Honey," she said. "You come on in, sit yourself by the fireplace." The store was a large building, could have doubled as a dance hall. The fireplace was made of stone. There was a sofa in front of it. "You go on," she said. "I'll bring you some hot tea to drink."

I nodded my thanks and did as I was told.

In front of that fire my feet slowly warmed, my clothes began to dry. The woman brought the tea, and I drank it slowly, the fire warming me and lulling me into a blissful comfort. For nearly an hour I watched the flames, before ordering a western omelet, and she brought it to me, let me eat it on the couch as if I were a guest in her home.

By ten o'clock I was toasty and rested. Outside the rain had slowed to a soft drizzle. I wanted to get to Jackson. The woman refused to take money for the tea when I went to pay ("You didn't order it—I gave it to you," she said), and I thanked her with words that had seemed entirely inadequate.

Now I looked out across the willow and the deer and the meandering stream moving through the valley. I wished I could remember that woman's name, wished I could describe her. But all that remained in my memory was the warmth of that fire and her act of generosity.

I pedaled out the campground and began the ascent, surprised at how gradual it was, how easy to climb. Not at all the struggle I remembered. I was anxious to see that Rim Store again, but when I arrived there, a chain barrier blocked a narrow driveway, and a sign stated: PRIVATE RESIDENCE KEEP OUT. I stopped, took a long sip of water from my bottle. Go with God, I thought, as I looked at the old building. It had been a business when I needed it, and now I was happy to leave it with the peace of the privacy it craved.

The shoulder was wide, but it had ruts, and I tried to stay within the narrow space—roughly five inches—between the ruts and the white line, and I kept my mind occupied by taking an inventory of the items seen by the side of the road: broken glass, a diaper, a condom wrapper, one large plastic antifreeze jug, Kleenex, a Marlboro cigarette box. Plastic soda pop bottles, a white fence post, an old tire, a new tire, a not-quite-empty tube of Neosporin. Mostly the roadsides of Wyoming were lined with beer bottles—Budweiser, Coors, the cardboard remains of a Michelob Light twelve-pack.

At the bottom of the pass a dead moose was slowly decomposing to the delight of a flurry of gnats. Just left of the moose, lying in the weeds, a discarded sign said, JESUS SAVES.

Nothing creates hunger like a closed sign in a café window just minutes past noon. Orange construction cones created an obstacle course as I wove through Bondurant, which, though technically not a ghost town, appeared as one. I rode until I came up to a woman in an orange vest with a STOP sign in her hand.

"It'll be maybe five, ten, minutes," she said. "Gotta wait for the pilot car."

"Not much open," I said.

"Well, it's not tourist season yet," she said. "There'll be a café and store up ahead, 'bout two miles or so, just past this construction."

Gradually, a handful of cars lined up behind me. When the pilot car showed, I let them all pass and then pedaled furiously, visions of oncoming traffic inspiring me to keep up. It seemed to me that I had seen fewer RV's than twenty years before. On the first trip it seemed that most of the traffic was Winnebago's, but now it was mostly truckers, construction crews. Wyoming was growing, so they said, but traffic still was light.

At the café outside Bondurant a black dog, its leash tied to a post, wagged its tail when I pulled into the parking lot. The dog had been left that morning. Abandoned. This I was told by the waitress who said she had given the dog water and food, would continue to take care of it, as whoever left it there must have known she would.

In the café restroom I looked in the mirror. My second chin was missing. Good riddance, I thought, and vowed to try not to recover it.

A river flowed next to the highway, and a raft full of people waved as they went rushing by. Twenty years earlier I had stopped in Hoback Junction, at an ice cream and antiques store, was sitting at the counter working on a root beer float when three men in cowboy hats, chaps, boots, and spurs came in. They had been covered in mud, unshaven, muttering beneath their mustaches into their coffee. Now the ice cream store was gone, and in its place was a convenience store and a fully stocked grocery.

I remembered this ride from that long-ago summer, when, late in the afternoon, the sun had finally come out, and a rainbow had formed over a pasture full of horses. Like the twenty-year-old who'd come before, I felt the rush that accompanied the realization of how far I'd come. Soon I would be in a comfortable room in a favorite western haunt.

A bicycle trail led me past a newly built strip mall and real estate offices, hotels, and restaurants on the clearly expanding outskirts of town. I followed the trail, which meandered along a creek, through trees, park benches, past the backsides of new condominiums, and then I was in Jackson, a town that, like many people who didn't actually live there, I considered my own.

I made the last push into the town square. Jackson was an important stop, the end of my first leg, and I was in the mood to celebrate. I needed to find a motel and a Laundromat. I needed to mail some postcards, clean the bike, purchase some spare tubes and $CO_2$'s, which are cartridges the size of a screwdriver handle used to inflate a tire quickly. But first things first.

Twenty years earlier I had leaned my bike against a bench near the elk antler arch and walked across the street to the Million Dollar

Cowboy Bar, where a man could sit in a saddle, order a cold beer, drink it from a bar inlayed with silver dollars, all while listening to country and western music. And that's exactly what I had done.

Then I had made it to Jackson in eleven days. This time it had taken me twelve, though that included at least a day's worth of hitchhike rides. Still, I thought, adding only a day to my time in twenty years wasn't bad. A comparison of numbers from the two rides from Warren Bridge was eerily similar:

|  | 1985 | 2005 |
|---|---|---|
| Distance (miles) | 58.66 | 58.58 |
| Time (hrs., mins., sec.) | 4:31:25 | 4:29:46 |
| Average speed | 12.9 | 13.2 |
| Maximum speed | 34.7 | 32.2 |

I wished I could meet that kid now, buy him a drink, teach him a thing or two. Instead, I ordered a beer in his honor and drank it to the past. Then, just to make things square, I ordered another and drank to the present.

## Elkfest

ON THE CROWDED PLAZA vendors sold antlers and skulls. Buffalo skulls, antelope skulls, deer skulls, wolverine skulls. There were mounds of antlers—moose and elk and deer—all for sale. Hanging from a NO RV PARKING sign hung a complete set—elk skull with five-point antlers, each nearly five feet in length. There was a pink tag clipped to the antlers—$1,595. Cub Scouts were holding an auction. Two of the boys struggled to hold a single elk antler to display to the crowd, as the auctioneer on a makeshift stage behind them rambled off the rising price until, "Sold!" and a man came to help the boys carry the antlers away. Men on horses wearing cowboy hats and sheriff stars patrolled the square. A taxidermy exhibition displayed lion and gazelle heads and a rhinoceros tusk. The sun shone in a clear blue sky. The mood was festive, a cheery blend of commerce and death. This was the annual Jackson Elk Fest.

I joined the crowd and made my slow way through the street, along the boarded sidewalk. A large man in a raccoon hat and a deer hide vest was shaking hands, like a politician campaigning.

On a side street a mounted mule deer buck head and an old miner with one hand shading his eyes and the other holding a dynamite pack lay side by side in the back of a pickup truck. I did a double take. The man was carved in wood, his clothes and facial features literally painted on.

I found a table in a crowded café just off the plaza, where I read from Robert Pirsig's *Zen and the Art of Motorcycle Maintenance*, and a passage about the value of solitude. Pirsig uses the example of someone on a fishing trip. "Often," he writes, "they're a little defensive about having put so much time to 'no account' because there's no intellectual justification for what they've been doing. But the returned fisherman usually has a peculiar abundance of gumption, usually for the same things he was sick to death of a few weeks before. He hasn't been wasting time. It's only our limited cultural viewpoint that makes it seem so."

Pirsig's *gumption* was a word related to *enthusiasm*, which at its root meant to be "filled with God." A person becomes filled with gumption, according to Pirsig, "when one is quiet long enough to see and hear and feel the universe."

Whether this idea of being "filled with God" was taken in the literal theological sense, or in a more metaphorical way, I thought I knew what he meant. Bicycling in the mountains through the various forms of spring weather wasn't easy, but the effort was invigorating. Somehow the combination of bicycling and being outdoors provided for me a felt universe.

It filled me.

Dawn was mountain cool, the sun out, no clouds in the sky. I felt good, rested, and clean, could feel my body slowly changing toward fitness. I'd been losing weight and was now over the steepest of the mountains. I was feeling confident, alive. I rode to the plaza, pulled up to the curb. But when I lifted my leg over the crossbar to dismount, my heel caught, and in trying to regain my balance, I overcompensated, and the bike leaned and fell, taking me onto the ground with it. Remarkably, I had wrecked.

While I was *stopped.*

This struck me as funny, and I sat up on the curb laughing. The middle-aged couple walking on the boardwalk who had seen me tip over approached warily. It was Sunday morning. The woman's mouth was open. They seemed unsure about what course of action to take. It occurred to me that a guy falling down laughing might appear to be drunk. This thought made me laugh even more. Finally, I stood up and picked up the bike.

"I'm glad you folks were here to see that," I said. "I'd hate to be embarrassed all by myself."

"No need to be embarrassed," said the woman, which was kind of her. But all three of us knew the need was great.

## Signal Mountain Lodge

THE CAMPGROUND AT JENNY LAKE was for tents only—no campers or RV's—and because it was early in the season, I had my choice of spots. I set up camp and walked along the lakeshore. Teton Peak loomed just on the other side of the water.

The Grand Tetons. In less than a month tourists would arrive in droves. The campground would be full, boats would cruise the water, the trails would be crowded. I was grateful for the solitude. Gazing up at the mountains filled me with a familiar sense of melancholy, though, and I wondered if landscape could hold its own mood. If so, did it rise from the land itself or from the human stories it held? No doubt there were tragic histories here. But such histories were everywhere, and my mood wasn't a sense of mourning so much as a sort of wistful longing. What was it about these mountains that inspired it? I walked until nearly dark, and then I sat at the edge of the lake and watched stars slowly appear over the water.

In the morning I returned to the lake. The scenery was beautiful, the carved striations of the mountain peaks visible in the sun, smooth ripples on the dark-blue water. But the wistful feeling remained.

Whatever caused it was a mystery. Experience, though, had taught me the cure for such bouts with Teton melancholy. I packed my bike and headed to Signal Mountain Lodge.

It was almost noon, and a busload of elderly tourists was standing in line at the café. I browsed in the small store, and then I ate lunch in the bar, where a bartender named Stan and I talked about a local novelist, Tim Sandlin. Sandlin once worked as a dishwasher at Signal Mountain, and in fact, the lodge makes an appearance in his novel *Sex and Sunsets*.

"He shows up here once in a while," said Stan. "He's very generous." He pulled a copy of the novel from a shelf above the bar. "I've read this several times," he said. I had also. The book opens with a soon-to-be bride in her wedding dress punting a football across a church lawn. The story is filled with quirky characters and a perfect mix of humor, raunch, tequila, human folly, and heart.

And it happened again, just as it always had at Signal Mountain. Conversation in the small lounge, and like that, my mood changed.

I set up camp on a bluff overlooking Jackson Lake, its rocky shore, Mount Moran in the distance. Then I rode down to the junction, where three moose stood grazing in the nearby willows.

Once, while hiking near here, I had walked around a bend in the trail and was startled to find myself nose to substantial nose with a cow moose. She had stood, facing me. Then we both backed away slowly.

Now several cars were parked on the shoulder, and people stood on the road with cameras. Moose paparazzi. I once watched a photographer with a large zoom lens walk directly to within just feet of a bull moose. Miraculously, the moose never charged. Another time, a horde of tourists walked beside a bull moose as he made his way along the edge of the Snake River at Oxbow Bend. When the moose started to trot, the people ran with it, a most peculiar Teton version of the running of the bulls. Finally, clearly agitated, the moose had sprinted across the road and up over a hill.

Now, though, the people kept a respectful distance. The moose gave sidelong glances as they grazed on the willows but didn't seem at all irritated.

At Oxbow Bend a woman sat before an easel and canvas. She was painting the bend of the Snake River, with Mount Moran beyond. The mountain breeze was cool, and the aspen trees along the banks were starting to bud. I sat on the hill and listened to the flow of air, of water.

Two blackbirds flew low, skirting the surface of the river, giving a throaty chirp as they passed. I stood and walked my bike back along the edge of the parking area, passing the woman, who was still painting.

"A beautiful spot," I said.

"I keep coming back," she said. "It's never the same place twice."

I knew what she meant. You could paint a lifetime here.

I rode to Jackson Lake Lodge, where rooms ranged from $145 to $525 a night. I was paying $5 to camp at Signal Mountain. The grandiose lobby was filled with an interesting and diverse mix of people milling about: grungy backpackers just returned from an expedition, RV and family campers, naturalists, photographers, artists, and conference attendees in business suits. The rooms overlooked willow marshes and the Teton range beyond. The view made the value, I'm sure. But it was the backpackers who were looked upon with envy. The roof full of stars was the real luxury here.

I sat at one of the long counters inside the café. A college student with a name tag—Ryan from Idaho—brought me tea. It was his second season working in the area.

"Last year I worked at Bay Bridge," he said. "In Yellowstone."

"How was that?" I asked.

"Not good. At first I was just happy to be in the park. I imagined a summer hiking, camping, enjoying being in the world's most famous wilderness." He laughed. "But we were way understaffed, to the point I was working triple shifts. When I did have a day off, I slept from exhaustion."

"There must have been a lot to see there, though?" I asked.

"No," he said, "not really. I mean, there's not much in Bridge Bay. No animals, no geysers, none of the things I'd come to Yellowstone for. I was kind of bitter a lot."

"So you came here this year," I said. "Is it better?"

"We'll see," he said. "I just started yesterday. But it feels better. I'm hoping for a good summer."

In the past time off enough to experience the backcountry of the parks had been part of the deal for the employees. It was not merely an issue of recreation. By staffing the parks with young people from across the country and allowing them the chance to experience these places, the park service ensured a future of people who understood the importance of the wilderness beyond tourist services. Forcing employees to work triple shifts felt incongruous with the opportunity. Ryan's bitterness was understandable.

"I hope you get some days off this time," I told him when I left.

"I'm keeping my fingers crossed," he said.

Back at Signal Mountain the warm sun balanced a cool breeze, and water lapped gently against the shore. A man threw rocks into the lake, and a golden retriever ran joyfully into the water, splashing, swimming, diving for the rocks and returning them, tail wagging. Nearby, a woman and her toddler son watched. I could hear the boy's joyous laughter each time the dog sprinted into the water.

Inside, the dining area had large, plate glass windows that overlooked the lake, the mountains, the setting sun. The sun was low in the sky, causing me to squint.

"Would you like me to close the blinds?" asked the waitress. Her name tag said Jill.

"No," I said. "I don't mind." She smiled, nodded.

I finished my dinner and walked back to the lounge. For the last several days I'd been avoiding people, retreating into my own solitude. Now, though, I realized how much I craved company, friendship. I saw Stan, a customer now, and I invited him to join me. We talked books, travel, politics, sports. As the night progressed, we were joined by others. Jill came in, along with Andy, her boyfriend, who guided raft trips on the Snake River. Andy and Jill had spent a year living in Amsterdam before moving back to the States. He was scheduled to begin graduate school at the University of Washington in the fall, where he would be teaching and studying literature.

"Are a lot of these people here from college?" I asked Stan. Twenty years earlier almost all of the employees at Signal Mountain were college students, and they'd come from all over America to spend their summers there.

"Not many. Most of the people are locals from Jackson who work winter jobs and then take summer jobs here. It's hard to live in Jackson," he said. "Most people I know work two, sometimes three, jobs."

The bar grew crowded. It was early in the season; the workers were all just getting to know each other. Someone bought me a beer. Stan introduced me, told people about my bike trips.

"Has this lodge changed much in twenty years?" asked Jill.

I thought back. "Not much," I said. "Actually, when I was here the first time, I had a night pretty much like this one."

And it did feel the same—had begun with the same melancholy then this lodge, this bar, the group at my table. Back then the staff had come from North Carolina, Michigan, Iowa. I'd met a raft guide, Tim, who invited me to stay in his room. Tim was from Maine, skinny with red hair and a New England accent. He had been kind, enthusiastic. We became fast friends.

Because I was the same age as most of the employees then and because it was so early in the season, I'd fit in, had stayed for several days, hiking all day and then spending evenings in the bar.

When I had first arrived at the lodge, I'd met a waitress named Susan, a diehard North Carolina Tarheel. That night we sat in the bar and spoke our lives over Moosehead beer. Later she had invited me to join a small group of Signal Mountain employees on an evening trip to a place called Huckleberry Hot Springs. It was nearly dark when we arrived at the small gravel parking area, and we'd walked through the forest, crossed a wide stream on a makeshift bridge. The springs were natural and we'd soaked in the hot water. A sliver of moon sat in the sky, and occasionally falling stars streaked across the night. Just at the edge of dusk, before the last remnants of blue on the horizon had faded to black, a bull moose stood in silhouette. I was twenty years old, in love with the people, the wine, the West, the stars. We drank in the night, singing songs, spilling our lives and souls in the dark.

Now, though older, I was among friends again, and with each new round of beer, time merged, and for one blurry evening I felt twenty again.

In the morning I slept late and woke warm and feverish with the sun piercing my tent.

I dragged myself out of my sleeping bag. The sun was over the mountains, and the diamonds of light flickering on Jackson Lake stung my eyes. I walked down to the lodge. Jill was working the breakfast shift. She took one look at me, and before I even had a chance to order, she delivered a breakfast of yogurt, toast, and coffee.

I spent the day reading, soaking up sun by the lake, cleaning my bike. It was nearly two before I left, destination Yellowstone. But the nearest open campground was in Madison, nearly eighty miles away. Deep down, even as I turned at the junction, I knew the ride would require energy I didn't have. I rode ahead anyway.

I made it all of ten miles, just past Colter Bay and Lizard Creek, but it was windy and cold, and I knew I'd sabotaged it from the start. I turned around. That evening I watched a young bull moose standing up to his knees in marsh. He dipped his head beneath the water in order to procure his aquatic plant dinner. Water dripped from his chin as he chewed. The low sun cast a golden light that stretched across the valley, and in the stream behind the willows two trumpeter swans drifted lazily in the water. It was a moment of singular beauty in a well-known tourist hot spot, and I had it all to myself.

Later, in the lounge, all eyes gazed upon the dark-gray storm thundering outside the plate glass windows. Clouds curled like a sea tempest, and raging wind rattled the glass. Lightning flashes illuminated the lake.

It was May 24. On the first trip I'd made it all the way to Missoula, Montana, by the 1st of June. Now Missoula was at least two weeks away.

I was falling behind schedule.

I limited my nostalgia to remembering rather than reliving and ordered only Sprite, of which I had several. The bar was less lively, but Andy was there, along with two of his assistant guides.

The four of us sat at a table. His guides deferred to Andy when I asked questions, and I noticed how they gauged his reactions out of the corners of their eyes, secretly seeking his approval as they told stories about the river. It was easy to see what they admired about him. He was articulate, and when he spoke of his river experiences, he did so in a way that revealed his skill and knowledge and yet not his ego. He struck a perfect balance between rugged and intelligent, and he listened intently to each of us, never seeking to dominate the conversation himself. He spoke passionately, both about literature and wilderness.

"You used to work here?" asked one of the guides.

"No," I said. "I wish I had." Andy told them about my bike trip, and I told them about that night at Huckleberry Hot Springs and how on the way back I had fallen asleep in the back of a pickup. When I woke the next morning, I hadn't been alone.

"Her name was Lori," I said. Andy and the guides looked at me, wondering if they'd missed something. They hadn't.

"Anyway," I said, "Tim from Maine had this roommate named Earl. Earl was stocky, strong. Muscular. A little on the edgy side. Scary, actually. Lori just happened to be the girl Earl had been looking to hook up with. I didn't know about any of this. It all had nothing to do with me, really. So anyway, Lori woke up.

"G'morning," I said. She looked at me, as if trying to place me from a bad dream. Then she sat straight up like a shot, cursing.

"Why didn't someone wake me?" she mumbled.

"Then she opened the topper, poked her head out, looked both directions, and jumped out of the truck. I could hear socked feet running over the rocks, followed by a door opening and closing. I thought nothing about it. It was all very innocent. But rumors did what rumors do. By the time I went back to Tim and Earl's room, Earl was there. He had piled all my gear by the door.

"You find a place to camp yet?" he asked me.

"What?" I said.

"Camp. Find a place to camp. There's plenty of places. Find one," he said.

I took a sip from my Sprite. Outside the storm had calmed, but rain still fell against the windowpane. "So I left," I said.

One of the assistant guides, a Brad Pitt look-alike, was staring at me. "You're saying nothing happened?" he said.

"Trust me. I didn't even know she was there until that morning. Tim never knew why I left, I don't think." I laughed. Signal Mountain Lodge, 1985. The moose in the moonlight, Huckleberry Hot Springs, a quirky New Englander, a misunderstanding, and a jealous hunk named Earl. The situation with Earl gave it just enough drama to make the story. But it was the romance of the night sky among new friends that I remembered most. After I left Earl that morning, I saw Susan walking back from breakfast. We sat at a picnic table in the sun and promised to write.

And we did write, stayed in touch for several years. We used to talk about bicycling around the world together. I hadn't heard from her in at least fifteen years. But now, in the very bar where we'd first met, her memory haunted me. I could hear her laughter, her Carolina accent. She once told me the summer she spent at Signal Mountain was the best summer of her life. I wondered if she ever returned, and if so, if she felt her own past still lingering there.

Now I looked around the bar. Almost everyone there I now knew by name.

"To Signal Mountain," I said, "a special place." Andy, his guides, and I all touched glasses. Twenty years later, and I was still among friends.

# How to Bicycle through a Buffalo Herd

THE COYOTE ON THE ROAD AHEAD turned to look over his shoulder and then pranced into the picnic area just past the Yellowstone entrance. I followed, not because I meant to but because the coyote was going right where I was headed. He looked well-fed. When he turned and saw that I was gaining ground, he sprinted into the woods. As I ate a lunch of noodles and gorp, I sensed him there, waiting for any food I might leave behind.

And then I was pedaling again, uphill through lodgepole pines, occasionally skirting the Lewis River. The shoulder was narrow, but traffic was light, and the forest floor next to the road was covered with residual snow, which stood deeper as I gained altitude. At Lewis Lake I stopped and walked along the shore, following a haunting music until I discovered its source: ice at the edge of the water had broken into glass-like fragments so when waves tumbled against them, they played the sounds of chimes along the water's edge.

I continued to climb until the road flattened through an area of sparse trees. The elevation was nearly eight thousand feet. Clouds formed quickly, and a sudden flurry of snow had me scrambling for my jacket. It was forty degrees. From one of the thawed ponds I heard the croaking call of boreal chorus frogs.

In West Thumb the store and gift shop were closed. A strong scent of sulfur emanated from the rising steam. Standing as close to the barrier as possible, I held my hands to the steam to warm them.

Once again, the road climbed, curved, and dipped. By the time I reached the Craig Pass summit I was chilled from the cool damp air. But it felt good, the cold, and made climbing in the mountains comfortable and pleasant. I looked out over Shoshone Lake and beyond to where the Pitchstone and Madison plateaus met. On the west end of the lake lay the Shoshone Geyser Basin. It was a good time to be in Yellowstone, before the summer crowds, when one could sense the magnitude of what early explorers must have felt, looking out over such vistas.

I crossed the Continental Divide for the third time that afternoon, and then it was a chilly and exhilarating descent. By the time I finally pulled into Old Faithful, I was cold, tired, and thirsty. Twenty years earlier I'd rented a small room in the snow lodge, which had a shared bath down the hall. I had dined on sautéed mushrooms, with crepes, potatoes, and rolls and a chocolate sundae for dessert. I'd sat at the candlelit table, my stomach full, ecstatic at the ride, had felt a joy of being young and knowing that I had made it all the way to Yellowstone. I now hoped to have a similar experience. More than anything, I wanted a shower.

The lodge was a two-mile ride off the main road. The parking lot wasn't full, and there were no people milling about. So I was surprised when the clerk at the registration desk informed me that all of the rooms were booked.

"Most of the lodge isn't open for the season yet," she explained. "Just the snow lodge."

I had paid twenty-nine dollars for the room back in 1985, and I was curious how much the rooms were now.

"Ninety dollars ten cents," said the woman. "But we're entirely booked, I'm afraid."

"How far is the next campground?"

"Madison is about twenty miles," she said, "but they might be full also. Let me call."

A moment later she said, "Sites are still available in the hiker-biker area. They'll hold the site for you until nine o'clock." It was nearly seven. I asked her about the road.

"It's flat mostly. Nothing like the road you just came over. But listen, be careful. There are a lot of bison, and the moms have their babies right now."

I stopped at the lodge lounge to get my water bottles filled. The woman behind the bar was young, slender in her uniform lodge clothes, the white shirt, and name tag. In the adjacent dining area the tables were full, the people all richly dressed and newly cleaned. I noticed them looking up from their meals with interest. I hadn't showered since Jackson. I must have looked like a remnant of the wilderness they'd come to see.

"Is there a place to shower here?" I asked.

"The public showers aren't open yet," she said.

"What about the campground?"

"There are no showers in the campgrounds, I'm afraid." She seemed genuinely sympathetic to my plight. "You might ask the rangers there, though. They might let you shower at the station, I'm not sure."

"'Bout two more days, and they'll be asking me, instead of me asking them," I said.

She laughed. "I think what you're doing is great," she said. I was tired, having believed when I'd arrived at Old Faithful that my day was through. But her words were all the encouragement I needed to get me pedaling again.

The road was flat, and the sun shone low enough in the sky to cast a golden light over the green valley but not so low that I felt I was racing against nightfall. I could smell sulfur, and puffs of rising geothermal steam dotted the view.

In the mid-nineteenth century, initial reports of Yellowstone's fire and brimstone geothermal features—bubbling lakes and steam shooting into the sky—were received with great skepticism and passed off as the result of delirium or lies. That mountain men such as Jim Bridger were known for their exaggerated tales didn't help. Ultimately, though, reports by government expedition parties confirmed what many had refused to believe.

The air was warmer now that I was out of the mountains. I was making good time, the road was flat, a gentle breeze nudged me along. I made the first five miles easily, at about seventeen miles per hour. I was in the Yellowstone of tourist brochures now, the green of the fields, the Firehole River meandering through. I rode over a mild rise, and I relaxed, thinking I would make the campground easily before dark. And then I came around a bend in the road and saw the long line of stopped vehicles ahead.

I pedaled cautiously until the obstacle became apparent. Bison. Hundreds of them. Not crossing but marching right down the middle of the highway.

How do you bicycle through a buffalo herd? The answer is, you don't. Many of the cows had calves. It wasn't hard to imagine what a fifteen hundred–pound mother might do to a bicycle, not to mention the guy riding it. I pulled over to wait them out, but it was obvious they wouldn't be off the road anytime soon, and two issues became distressingly clear. One, I wouldn't make the campground before dark. And two, riding on this stretch of road in the dark was a really bad idea.

At a pull-out two men were standing by their vehicles talking while they waited. One of them was driving an old '70s Pontiac with a canoe strapped to the top. He wore a fishing cap and vest. I asked if by any chance either of them might be so kind as to carry a guy and his bicycle through the bison herd. The man driving the motor home said he didn't have room, but the man with the Pontiac said that, though his trunk was full and there was a canoe strapped to the top of his car and the backseat was crammed with gear and belongings, he was sure he could rope my bike to the top of the trunk.

I was skeptical.

"Trust me," he said. "I once hauled four canoes with this very vehicle." I helped him lift the bike onto the trunk, and expertly, he tied it down with rope. I tested his skill by trying to jiggle the bike to see if it was tight. The bike didn't budge. It had taken him all of three minutes to secure it.

"Let's go," he said.

Inside, the car was loaded with clothes, fishing gear, binoculars, camera equipment, boxes, guides about Yellowstone, about geology, about animals and birds. He moved handfuls of items off the passenger seat and into the already loaded back. And then we were off.

"Name's Joseph Conrad," he said.

Thus it came to be that I hitched a ride through a buffalo herd with a man named Joseph Conrad.

"Heart of Darkness," I said.

"That's the other Joseph Conrad," he said. "I'm the science professor Joseph Conrad, the one you probably haven't heard of until now."

This was true.

"Actually, I'm the retired science professor Joseph Conrad, was a chemistry professor at a university in Wisconsin," he said as we began our slow way through the herd.

A bull looked sideways at us as we passed him, his large eye calm, unconcerned about the vehicle beside him. A calf scampered off to the side of the road. His mom glared as we passed.

"Listen," he said, once we'd made it through the herd, "I can let you off here, but I'm staying at the same campground as you, so I might as well take you all the way there."

"Sure," I said.

"I do want to make one stop, to this new geothermal area they just opened. If you don't mind?"

I didn't mind.

We walked on the boardwalk, past large bubbling pools. A distant mountain stood behind large billows of rising steam. At the edges of the pools ran long striated lines of red. Oxide. Because he was a scientist, Joseph knew the intricacies of the area, and it was like having my own free tour guide. At one point we stopped and looked at our shadows in the steam.

"Do you see that?" he asked.

I looked into the steam, wasn't sure what I was looking for.

"It's an optical effect, a halo."

I looked. Sure enough, there was a halo around my head.

"You can only see your own," he said.

"Just like real life," I said.

"Yes, well. It happens when you look at your shadow in steam with the sun behind."

We finished the walk and pulled back onto the road. I could feel the wind against us as we drove, and I turned to look at my bike. It was still holding steady.

"You ever lost a canoe hauling it like this?" I asked.

Joseph chuckled. "One time," he said, "I was hauling a couple of them with a buddy of mine. The wind got underneath one, pulled it up, and it toppled off the roof. In my rearview I could see it bouncing down the road, end to end. Luckily, it didn't hit anyone."

Up ahead two cars were parked on the road, the international signal for sighted wildlife. We stopped. A porcupine scampered along the edge of a caldera, his quilled spine backlit by the sun. He kept looking back over his shoulder at us, a look not of fear but of disgust. Clearly, the calm of the porcupine's evening had been interrupted.

We returned to the road. That morning, Joseph told me he had been putting in his canoe at Lewis Lake.

"One of the launching sites was open, on the other side of the lake, and I'd originally gone there, but the water was rough and choppy. So I drove to a different site. A sign said closed, but there was a boat dock, so I started to put in anyway. A ranger drove up, told me I couldn't put in there, that I'd have to go to the other side of the lake.

"I argued with him," said Joseph. "The water was much smoother and safer where I was. I told the ranger, 'You want me to be safe, don't you?' But he just said it was closed and if they let me, they'd have to let everyone. What 'everyone' I wanted to know? I was the only one there.

"These government park guys, they get rules in their head, there's no sense of logic can change them."

He sighed. "I suppose you need rules in a place like this, though. No telling what some people might do."

I thought about those bison and nodded. If I had ridden close to the bumper of a car in front of me, could I have made it through? I'd considered it at the time, though I'm not sure I would have actually gone through with it. I was grateful for the ride and said so.

"Just my way of paying back," he said. "You see, not long ago I was walking on Tower Road, which was closed to traffic due to construction. In the evening I started walking back to where I'd parked my car, when I saw a bear cub. Then I saw the sow. They were right on the road, going nowhere, blocking me from getting back. Fortunately, a guy in a water truck came by, gave me a ride."

"So now I owe someone else then," I said.

"Not a bad way to look at it," he said.

We arrived at the campground. I helped Joseph untie my bike. It was 8:57.

"You made it," said the ranger who checked me in to my campsite.

"I got a little delayed, courtesy of a bison or two," I said.

"Didn't want to ride through them, huh? Could've been an experience."

"Would you have ridden through them?" I asked.

"Noooo," he said. "Couple days ago there was a guy on a motorcycle, taking pictures. Got too close to a calf. The cow charged him."

"Was he hurt bad?"

"Luckily, he was okay, bruised up a little. But his motorcycle was completely demolished. They ought to put what's left of it on display. You take one look at what one of those animals can do to a motorcycle, it'll make an impression."

I set up camp and built a fire. Orange and blue flames danced beneath the star-filled Yellowstone sky, and for the first time all day I felt warm.

# Richard I

"LITTLE WARM IN THE SUN, IN'T IT?" asked the pale man who ran the Laundromat. *Warm* was a relative term. It was all of fifty-eight degrees. "You can take one of those chairs from inside, put it in the shade if you want."

"Feels good in the sun," I said. I was sitting in West Yellowstone, on a bench outside the Laundromat where earlier I had purchased a shower and was now waiting for a load of clothes to dry. Simple acts that felt not like chores but welcome tasks.

"Nice and quiet here," I said.

"Ha. Come back in a month," he said.

"What are winters here like?" I asked.

"Cold." He walked back inside. From warm to cold. In a short span we'd covered a lot of ground.

On my ride back to Madison I was again delayed by bison. When it appeared they were well off the road, I waited some more, just to be sure. Sure enough, two behemoth stragglers emerged from the trees. Side by side they moved, slowly, as if on achy joints, like elderly friends on a neighborhood walk. I watched them amble to the edge of a wide stream, and then they swam across it, their chins up, careful to keep their heads above the water. I thought they might shake like dogs, when they got out of the water, and I waited for the dramatic moment. But they simply kept moving forth, up the side of a hill. Roughly a mile farther, a small band of elk stood up to their knees in the same stream.

It was a routine that repeated itself throughout the day. Bison on the road, elk in the forest. Twice I had to stop and wait for the road to clear. Often a bison would stop in front of an RV and turn to face it, as if sizing it up, before continuing on its way across the road. In the grassy meadow near the campground the elk and bison grazed in peaceful coexistence along the Madison River.

Back at the campground a small tent had been pitched in the site next to mine, and an old single-speed bike leaned against the table. Later the man who was camping there walked over and introduced himself. Richard. A self-proclaimed vagabond, he was tan, and even though he was unshaven, maintained distinguished gray features. He was living a lifestyle, he said, that had been validated by the Supreme Court.

"They ruled that a vagabond lifestyle," said Richard, "is one of America's most enduring ways of life, with a long history in this country." As evidence, he carried copies of the decision.

"Sometimes," he said, "I give a copy to law enforcement officials, to remind them of my rights. Amazing how often law officials need to be reminded." He handed me a copy, and I read:

VAGABONDING UPHELD BY SUPREME COURT
*Papacristou vs. City of Jacksonville*
409 US 156, 31 L.Ed. 2d 110, 92 S.Ct. 839

Eight defendants were convicted in the Jacksonville (Florida) Municipal Court of violating a vagrancy ordinance which levied criminal penalties on a variety of persons enumerated in the ordinance, including; rogues and vagabonds, habitual loafers, gamblers, jugglers, and persons wandering or strolling around from place to place without any lawful purpose or object. The Florida Circuit affirmed, and the District of Appeals of Florida, First Circuit dismissed a petition for writ of certiorari (236 So 2d 141). On certiorari, the United States Supreme Court reversed. In opinion by Justice Douglas expressing the unanimous views of the court, it was held that the Jacksonville ordinance was void for vagueness—the absences of ascertainable standards of guilt—and likely to encourage arbitrary and erratic arrests and convictions. The court ruled that the Jacksonville ordinance makes criminal certain activities which by modern standards are normally innocent. These activities are historically part of the amenities of life as we have known them, although not mentioned in the Constitution or Bill of Rights. These unwritten amenities have been in part responsible for giving our people the feeling of independence and self-confidence, the feeling of creativity. These amenities have dignified the right of dissent and have honored the right to be nonconformists and the right to deny submissiveness. They have encouraged lives of high spirits rather than hushed, suffocating in silence.

"It's good to know the Supreme Court decided juggling isn't a criminal act," I said.

"Yes," said Richard. "Or that one doesn't need a lawful purpose to stroll around!"

"How long have you been traveling?" I asked.

"I've been living this lifestyle for some time," he said. "At one time I worked as a social worker, but I got frustrated with that—a system set up to help should help rather than hinder, but hinder it did, and I realized I was part of the hindrance, though I like to think I did some good. I've worked other jobs throughout my life. Now, though, I'm mostly retired."

"Home" for Richard, was Maine, where he returned periodically to catch up on his mail. Mostly, he toured the country on the single speed bicycle. He had no panniers, and he carried only a small backpack and a bivy tent and sleeping bag on his rack.

I looked at his bike. One gear. I couldn't imagine. "Do you have trouble on hills?" I asked.

He shrugged. "Sometimes, if a hill is really steep, I have to get off and walk. But it only slows me down. I have no schedule."

As the evening fell, I again made a fire and invited Richard to join me in a meal of roasted hot dogs.

"I left Arizona a few months ago," he said. "I've been living outside exclusively, rain or shine. I had a lot of rain in Utah. I lived for over a week in a baseball dugout in a town park because of flooding, which made it impossible for me to keep riding. I don't mind the rain, though. People ask me, 'What do you do when it rains?' I tell them, 'I get wet.'" He laughed.

I was wearing all of my warmest clothes, and still I was shivering, so I moved closer to the fire. Richard wore only a light windbreaker, and he didn't seem cold at all. In fact, while I could see the wispy puffs of my own breath, I noticed I couldn't see his breath at all.

"What do you do?" he asked me, and I told him I studied and taught literature.

"Have you read *Illusions*, by Sebastian Bach?" he asked, and I told him I hadn't. "You should read it sometime," he said. "A great book. How about *Ishmael*, by Daniel Quinn?" Again, I had to answer in the negative. Often this happens when I tell people I study lit: I'm faced with all the books I haven't yet read.

I asked him about the Quinn book.

"Here's the thing," he said. "Two of the most common human motivations are to learn and to enjoy," says Richard. "But there is a third, which Americans seem to be obsessed with—security. Quinn talks a lot about how a desire for security encumbers us. It plays in to all our fears, how things are marketed to us, and on and on. To live outside the realms of security is increasingly difficult. But to do so is to live."

That was it, I thought. Exactly it. The paradox of the culture. Our freedom was real and profound. But so was the pressure to buy in.

I boiled water and asked him if he wanted to share my hot chocolate. His eyes lit up, and he walked to his camp. When he returned, he held a Chef Boyardee can, which he used as a mug.

We talked late into the night, about our separate journeys, our love for the West, our ideas on what it means to be American, and where the country was headed. His vibrant eyes shone in the firelight, and his face, outlined by gray whiskers, glowed. He moved, unhurried, luminous, in all that he did. He had developed a life that suited him perfectly, and he moved through the world with an ease that I envied. Suddenly the gear that I carried seemed excessive. What did I need, really? I could have lived without much of it.

We talked until the fire was merely embers. I put it out for good with my water bottle. The night was cold without it, and we each retired to our respective tents.

In the morning Richard and I rode our bicycles out to the campground exit. He was heading into West Yellowstone, and I was going to Mammoth.

"Be safe, my friend," he said, and then we both pedaled away.

Steep and rough, to Gibbon Falls, and then the road flattened through the bogs and marsh of Gibbon Meadows. From a meadow pond croaking boreal chorus frogs announced the arrival of spring. At a picnic area in the shade, a Steller's jay landed on my picnic table and watched as I wrote in my journal.

I walked through the alien landscape of Norris Geyser Basin—red and green algae in bubbling pools and fog-like steam rising in the sun. Water boiled up from Crater Spring, and gnarled trees rose from pools of milky blue water. Occasionally, geysers erupted with a fiery hiss, shooting spouts of water and steam high into the sky.

Geothermal activity was strong in Yellowstone because the earth's internal heat—a molten rock called magma—was closer to the surface there. Magma resides in the earth's mantle, which rests beneath the earth's crust. Over most of the planet the crust is fifteen to thirty miles deep. Beneath much of Yellowstone, though, there is an upwelling of magma plume, and the crust can be as thin as two miles.

The result is an extensive system of geysers, hot springs, mudpots, and fumaroles. Over half of the world's geysers exist here, including, of course, Old Faithful.

But it was a different geyser that caught my attention. Minute Geyser was so named during a time when it erupted every minute, to heights of up to fifty feet. But its eruptions are irregular now, the result of rocks tossed into the geyser by early visitors to the park. Removal of the rocks was impossible without further damaging the area. Minute Geyser served as but one reminder of the fragility of the natural world and the human effect on it. Many of the geyser fields throughout the world have already been destroyed through drilling and other human activities.

I thought about Richard, his Chef Boyardee coffee mug, his sleeping in a dugout in the rain. Extreme, perhaps, but proof nevertheless that our needs are not so great as our culture imagines. Yellowstone, at its best, represents not the idea that a few dramatic landscapes should be set aside for occasional forays into the wilderness but, rather, that often our consumptive desires come with a cost, and such costs must be considered on grounds not purely based on short-term economics.

Friday, May 27, and I was not looking forward to spending the weekend alone. Back in Lincoln the writer Erin Flanagan was getting married, and Joan was at the wedding without me, along with most of our Lincoln friends. I came up over a ridge and looked out over the valley. I tried not to think of that wedding, the people laughing, swapping stories, dancing.

The highway below was lined with cars—maybe a hundred of them, a sure sign of a wildlife sighting. More elk or bison probably, I thought. Seemed like an unusual number of cars, though. I rode down the hill and then onto the valley flat, keeping my eyes open.

Then I saw it, moving across the meadow, through the brush at the foot of the Gallatin Range. Grizzly bear, about seventy-five yards off the road. In all my time in Yellowstone it was the first grizzly I'd ever seen. It was late afternoon, my last day in the park, and it seemed a fitting end. I watched as the bear made its way through the flats, seemingly oblivious to the attention it was receiving. I imagined Erin in her wedding dress, Joan sitting at a table with friends, sipping champagne.

The bear stopped, lifted his nose, sniffed the air, and then he ambled on, disappearing into the trees at the edge of a hill.

I made my way into Mammoth, where I wished the couple well and celebrated the wedding alone with a meal of beef stew at the historical Mammoth Hot Springs Hotel. Outside the restaurant window two bull bison were macho posturing in the park across the street, squared off like boxers in a ring, bucking and snorting, their heads lowered, all much to the restaurant crowd's delight.

Finally, the larger of the bulls gave one angry snort, which somehow seemed to resolve it all, no blood having been shed. The bison moved off together along the side of the village road, and the crowd returned their attention to their meals.

The campground was at the bottom of a steep hill. I checked in and started my ride to my campsite, which was all the way at the far end of the grounds. People were watching me. Then I realized I'd been singing out loud. "Cisco Kid" ("was a friend of my-ine . . ."). In fact, I'd been singing it off and on all day. It occurred to me that maybe I'd been spending too much time alone.

I set up my tent and then tried to call Joan, to no avail. Just then, I determined later, she was dancing with a poet named Naca.

There were few trees in the Mammoth campground and little privacy. At the site next to mine two couples sat in lawn chairs. I heard their laughter, the rumblings of memories, good times past. I came to understand that the couples were old friends, were having a reunion. I wanted to join them, to be included in someone's celebration, to tip a cold one in honor of my newly married friends a thousand miles away. But instead I lay in my tent and settled for the companionship of Least Heat-Moon, who charmed me with this line: "You never feel better than when you start feeling good after you've been feeling bad."

It seemed to fit. I hadn't been feeling bad, really, but all day I'd thought I was bored and lonely. Yet I'd begun the day with a man who drank coffee from a spaghetti can, had walked where the hot thermal guts of the earth were spilling out its side, had seen a grizzly bear cross a field, had dined to the entertainment of a pair of thousand-pound beasts knocking their furry horned heads in a park outside the window, and had caught myself singing old War songs at the edge of America's most famous national park.

I'd been on the road just long enough that it all felt like a typical day.

In the morning magpies landed on my breakfast picnic table and on the grass around my feet. When I feigned a lunge toward one of them, it didn't flinch, just continued its search for food. But when a robin flew at them, they scattered, squawking away. I wonder sometimes if my gentle demeanor doesn't occasionally work against me.

I rode out of Yellowstone, past holiday weekend cars lined up at the park entrance. But the exit lane was empty, and I pedaled down the middle of the road, glad to be out before all of that traffic moved in.

# Montana

# Another Log on the Fire

A NORTHERN BREEZE, the river weaving through the valley, deer on the grass-covered hills, Emigrant Peak in the distance, cows and horses grazing in pastures, a bluebird on a fence post. A large ranch house, the smell of meat on a grill, and a bald eagle perched on a bare tree branch in the yard peers down at people in lawn chairs or standing on the porch, their dinner party laughter carrying in the air. This was lightly traveled Highway 540—East River Road.

Montana. A perfect dreamy land of green and cool breezes. It was the West at its best. Nowhere, on that first journey, had the world been more new to me than in Montana, which seemed exotic to me both then and still. The rain was soft, the people happy, kind, rugged, and strong, not yet jaded enough to have given up on a belief in basic human goodness, despite a history that included vigilante justice and Ted Kaczynski. The scenery was a pristine blend of glacial carved peaks and fertile river valleys.

In my first-ever night in Montana I'd been taken in as one of their own by a group of Montana State students. We'd driven to Chico, where we soaked in the hot springs and danced to a live band in the lounge.

Chico Hot Springs first opened as a resort in 1900. In its early years the painter Charles M. Russell frequented the springs, sometimes trading napkin drawings for drinks. More recent guests included Richard Brautigan, Steve McQueen, Tom Brokaw, Meg Ryan, and Dennis Quaid, whose band sometimes performed there. And yet the hot springs lacked any sense of pretense. One did not have to be famous or even wealthy to feel welcome.

Now the pool was crowded. Children played in the middle, and adults stood at the edges with drinks in their hands. For nearly an hour I soaked in the healing water, and then I ate a fajita meal at the restaurant. Well fed and hot spring cleansed, I rode through a town called Pray.

*Go to the four-way stop and turn right*, the waitress had said. She wasn't sure but thought the campground would be one, maybe two, miles. I rode seven. All I saw were fence lines, private land. It was already dusk before I finally stopped at a small house and knocked on the door. An attractive woman, with a cherubic child by her side, answered.

"I was told there was a campground near here?"

"I don't think so," she said. She looked down at the child. "You go get your book and wait on the couch," she told her. "I'll be there to read to you in a minute."

She called a name, and a handsome middle-aged man came to the door and stood beside her. The house was surrounded by a yard full of soft grass.

"Is there anywhere a guy could pitch a tent nearby?" I asked.

"No," said the woman, shaking her head. "Where's your bicycle?" she asked, looking behind me, mistrust in her voice.

"I left it against the gate up by the road," I said.

I could tell the man was thinking. For a minute I thought they might let me set up my tent in their yard. It was getting darker.

"This isn't really our place," said the man. "We're just staying here for the summer."

"There's a KOA. You have to go back to the main road, and then it's another six, seven, miles," said the woman. "And there's a fishing access just past the turn—you can probably just camp there."

The man looked out into the dusk. He looked at the woman. "I think we have to help this guy find a place to stay," he said.

"He'll find a place," she said. "It's just back down this road. That fishing access, I'm sure you can stay there." She looked nervously behind her to where the girl had just headed, and I realized that she was imagining the worst of what a stranger might do. I was creeping her out. It embarrassed me. I wanted to tell her, even magpies aren't threatened by me.

"I'm sorry," I mumbled. "The fishing access. I'll find it."

"This really isn't our place," said the man.

"No problem," I said.

Twenty years earlier I'd had a roof over my head my first three nights in Montana without even trying. In Gardiner I'd met a woman in a restaurant who lived in Bozeman. She'd given me her number, told me to call when I arrived in town, and then she put me up for the night. In Anaconda a man named Mr. Polakovich greeted me outside a Safeway. He had seen me with my bike and handed me a key to a cabin he owned and gave me directions, told me to help myself and just leave the key on the table inside. The Montanans I'd met now, so far, were no less friendly but not so inviting, and I wondered if it was because I was no longer the boy who looked so innocent or if the inundation of people over the last twenty years had made Montana less open, space less available. Or was it the result of a post-9/11 culture of fear?

I didn't blame the woman at all and fully respected her priority of keeping her family safe. I surely didn't expect to knock on a stranger's door and automatically be extended a welcome into their home or property. It was clear that they had wanted to help me but didn't want to take the risk. Who could blame them?

And it is this, it seems to me, that has changed the most in the past twenty years—maybe in just the last five: a caution, a suspicion of people we don't really know, an undercurrent of fear. This is not a condemnation but an observation. For my own part I too am less inclined now to invite a stranger into my home.

All of which makes the act of generosity that would be extended to me later—by a born-again Vietnam veteran and his wife—an even more profound act of grace. But that comes later, when my journey would come to an abrupt halt and I'd be led to an experience that I can only now think of in terms of the divine.

I made my way back down the dark road, pulling off to the side and letting each car pass whenever I saw headlights in my mirror. I was tense, not sure where I'd sleep. The temperature was dropping quickly, and I could feel the cold through my clothes, chilling my sweat. My hands grew numb. I cursed the waitress who'd given me the directions, cursed myself for getting into this situation yet again. By the time I found the fishing access, roughly ten miles later, it was pitch-dark, save for a large fire burning down by the river. I leaned my bike against a tree and walked down to the site. There was a man sitting in a lawn chair, holding an opened bottle of Jim Beam. I greeted him, asked if it would be okay to camp nearby.

"Yeah, hell, do whatever the hell you want. This is Montana," he said.

I walked closer, saw that there were a couple of other people there and four tents set up, along with two aluminum boats, several coolers. It didn't appear that the others had been drinking as heavily.

"You're sure I won't be invading your space?" I don't know why I said this. I wasn't going to go anywhere else.

"Don't be an ass," said the man, who, it was clear to me now, was drunk. "Set up your tent; come have a beer."

I laughed. I looked over at one of the other men, and he smiled, nodded, seemed embarrassed at his friend's behavior. As I set up my tent, he walked over.

"How far have you ridden?" he asked, and I told him I'd left just over three weeks ago.

"Really, you should come over, get warm by the fire, have a beer with us," he said. I said that I would. Truth is, I wanted their company. I set up my camp with cold hands in the dark. Then I walked down to their campsite.

There were five people in all, two couples and Greg, who still sat in the lawn chair and was taking long sips from his bottle. One of the women, Brigette, graciously gave up her chair and sat on her husband's lap. They were all old friends, they said, who'd gone to college together. Joe was a chemical engineer, Steve was a pilot, and Dorisa was a veterinarian. And then there was Greg, who they only seemed to be tolerating as he rambled on in his drunken state. I watched him, sympathized. Though it had been a while, I knew what it was like to spend time with happy couple friends when you were the only one single. Around the fire the couples sat close. Greg embraced the bottle.

I could see the others were growing annoyed by him, so I engaged Greg in conversation. He told me he lived in Butte, was buying a house there.

"It's a cheap place to live still," he said. "The same house in Bozeman or Missoula would cost almost twice as much."

He was happy about the house, I thought, but there was a hint of resignation about it, as if the house were a letting go of a different dream, or perhaps it felt to him like a vessel for his loneliness.

The others talked about politics politely, the way people do when they don't want to offend. There was a melancholy around the group, and I realized they were at the end of a weekend reunion that they had probably been planning for a while. In the morning they would head back to their regular lives, and who knew when they might see each other again?

Greg cleared his throat, as if preparing for a grand speech. I could feel the others grow tense, not wanting to be annoyed with their friend on the night before they were to say good-bye.

And then he started to sing. "Put another log on the fire." Then, making up the words as he went, he sang about friendship, about being young and meeting people you would know your whole life. "Put another log on the fire," he crooned—about fishing trips, about being on a boat in the river. His voice had a soft twang, a perfect pitch that rang out into the Montana air, and through it he poured all of his longing, his pride, a wailing lament but also a kind of coming to peace. "Put another log on the fire," he sang about love, about rivers and mountains, about deer in the forest. "Put another log on the fire." He sang about warmth, about drunkenness, about not letting the fire go out on this night.

When he stopped singing, we all looked deep into the dying flames. And the night was silent, save for the river lapping gently against its bank.

## Paradise Valley to Ennis

MAY IN MONTANA WAS COLD, and I waited in vain for the temperature to rise with the sun, but instead came a wind that threw cold at my face and chapped my lips as I rode. Whatever layers of warmth I had, I wore, but the cold pierced through it all as I made my way through Paradise Valley, its green hills and fields of horses, the Absaroka Mountains behind. By the time I found a café that was open, I was sniffling, had to blink the moisture from my eyes. I brunched on a sausage and egg burrito and warmed up by drinking coffee and reading about Caribbean vacations from old travel magazines that were piled high on a shelf. It was late morning by the time I finally forced myself to leave. Crossing the bridge over the Yellowstone River, I merged back onto Highway 89.

Livingston was off-season Sunday morning quiet. Downtown shops were closed, and no pedestrians walked the streets. Just after noon it finally started to warm, and I napped in the sun on a picnic table near the old train depot.

Bozeman Pass was a relatively easy ride as mountain passes go, but when I reached the top, my tire went flat, and I filled it with my hand pump, a quick fix to a slow leak, and then I headed down, thinking it would be an easy ride into Bozeman. Normally, it would have been. But road construction had narrowed I-90 to one lane, with temporary concrete walls set up to the right of the roughly six inches of shoulder. I dealt with my fear by trying not to look in my mirror at the thundering trucks approaching and then passing in a blur. I want to say they were so close I could have reached out and touched them, but it's a theory I didn't test. Remarkably, the shoulder narrowed even more, narrowed finally to a state of nonexistence, and this time when I heard an oncoming truck, I stopped and hugged the wall.

I waited until there was no traffic—thank God it was Sunday—and when it was clear, I pedaled like a madman directly on the interstate roadway. Foolish, to not have patched that tire. If there are no atheists in foxholes, there are just as many riding bicycles on single-lane, no-shoulder Interstate 90. I prayed that if any truckers were coming, they would see fit not to hit me. Then I prayed that the tire would hold enough air to get me to the next exit. I wished I knew more about theology—specifically, the efficacy of praying with eyes open wide.

I heard the unmistakable eighteen-wheeler roar, still a distance behind me but bearing down fast. Roughly fifty yards ahead lay the East Bozeman exit lane. I pedaled faster, knowing that if my tire blew, it would be hard not to keep the bike from swerving. I could see the truck in my mirror, leaned forward, low to decrease wind resistance, and I aimed straight for the end of the concrete wall. In my mirror I could see the grill of the truck. It was a race to the end of that wall, and I won it, barely, pulling onto the exit shoulder just before the trucker barreled by, hitting his horn rather than his brakes as he passed me where I stood panting.

Downtown Bozeman, and Main Street was quiet. Spring semester was over, and the college students were mostly gone, or so it seemed. I pulled up to an ice cream shop with no cars in the parking lot, and the two young employees looked up in surprise when I entered, their first customer all afternoon.

Twenty years earlier I'd ridden into town on the edge of a rainbow that had stretched out over Bozeman Pass. In Gardiner I'd met Teresa Deyton, who told me when I came to Bozeman I'd have a place to stay. She was almost thirty, seemed old to me then. I'd ridden to the university, where I played basketball in the gym on a guest pass, played one on one against a left-handed sharpshooter who exposed my defensive liabilities. The game ended quickly, and I showered and rode back downtown. The town had seemed livelier to me then— many of the college students were still in town, music flowed from the cafés and bars. By dusk it had started raining again, so I called Teresa, and she told me how to get to her house. She was in the process of moving to Yellowstone for a summer job, so I helped her pack some boxes and load them in a storage unit. On the way home we stopped and had ice cream.

Now her face was a fading image. Her name, as I expected, wasn't in the phone book.

I sipped a cup of coffee. Teresa would be fifty now, wherever she was, and that didn't seem old to me anymore. Outside the window Main Street slumbered empty in the cool sunshine. Nick Drake was playing on the stereo, that haunting voice, made even more so by the fact that he had died over thirty years before. The girl working behind the counter was perhaps the age I was on my first trip here, and she bobbed her head to the music, which made Drake feel contemporary.

I thought about all that lives on in the world, the recorded sounds of the long dead singer, the fading memory of a woman met on a previous road, the bittersweet nostalgia of the kid I once was. All these years I have dreamed of Montana. I have always believed that I would live in the state, but save for a brief three months studying photography at a school in Missoula, I have long held that dream out, the carrot on the stick, always the place that would be there for me when I needed it most.

I checked into the Imperial Hotel, and as I rolled my bike down the concrete sidewalk toward my room, I discovered that my tire was flat.

Later I walked up and down Main Street in the dark, looking for food, but the restaurants all were closed, and I headed away from downtown, hoping to find a grocery or even a convenience store. Finally, several blocks west, I saw what looked like an old house outlined with strings of light. Tables were set out on the front lawn. I walked closer. The sign above the door said GRANDMA'S CAFE AND ICE CREAM PARLOUR and there was a neon OPEN in the window.

Inside, a large man in an apron sat at a table reading from an old magazine. The house, which had been built over a hundred years earlier, was filled with antique furniture and the tables were covered with flowery country-style cloths. An old piano sat against the wall, and lace curtains hung over the windows.

Grandma's was a one-man operation. He was open, he said, because he was open this late every night. Seven days a week.

"How many employees do you have?" I asked.

"It's just me," he said, "for the most part. I have a couple of students who come in sometimes during the lunch and dinner rush." He shrugged.

For seven days a week he cooked, waited tables, took orders at the cash register, and yet there was nothing about his demeanor that would suggest any form of stress or even frenzy. I ordered a chicken breast in mustard sauce and an orange cream soda. When he brought it to my table, he sat down and filled my meal with lively, and welcome, conversation.

"I used to travel around the country a lot," he said. "I had a motorcycle, and with friends I'd go all over. Every summer for awhile."

"Bozeman is an adventurer's kind of town, isn't it?" I asked.

"I don't know. I guess in some ways it is. But adventure's kind of a controlled world these days. These students today, they come in. They don't have the same sense of adventure somehow. In the '60s, '70s, even '80s, youth culture was a movement against materialism. Today it seems like everyone's concerning themselves with security, jobs.

"The other day there were some kids in here—college kids—and I was listening to them from the kitchen. They were talking about saving for retirement. Going on and on. I was thinking, man, you're only twenty years old. Get out and enjoy the world a little bit."

In the morning I patched my tube, and using my hand pump, I worked until my arm was sore. Then I pumped some more. But the tire wouldn't hold air. I was out of new tubes. I walked outside. It was sunny, but the air was cool. Just a block away there was a sporting goods store with a bicycle shop in the back. I bought new tubes, some $CO_2$'s, a new long-sleeved shirt. I walked back to the motel, changed the tube. I had hoped to leave by 9:00, but by then it was 10:45. Checkout was at 11:00. When I went to fill the new tube, no air seemed to be going in. That's when I noticed a small crack in the pump valve.

I walked back to the bike shop to buy a new pump, but the only one they had was small and cheap and wouldn't fill the tire beyond 80 psi (pounds per square inch). My tires held up to 120. I used the shop's floor pump, but I was nervous about riding without one of my own. I left Bozeman in an afternoon rain. As I approached a casino on the outskirts of town, the rain fell harder. Torrential. It seemed a sign. I pulled into the casino parking lot. Inside, I sacrificed five dollars to the Keno gods.

When I returned to the bike, the clouds had cleared.

The ride west briefly followed the Madison River. The early evening sunshine was warm for a change, and when my tire went flat yet again, I sat on a guardrail and calmly fixed it with one of my $CO_2$'s while the river rolled by. Earlier, as I rode, I thought about how far I'd come in just three weeks. Yampa and Baggs seemed a long time ago.

The School House Cafe in Norris was closed. The morning had started warm, but then clouds rolled in, bringing with them a cold drizzle. I made my slow way over long and steep Norris Hill. There was almost no traffic. It was Tuesday. The combination of gray sky and light-green hills brought to mind images of Scotland. I kept warm by pedaling and thinking about a midmorning breakfast. I remembered the School House because I'd eaten there before. Thoughts of the restaurant sustained me as I rode to the top of the hill, and then, chilled by my own sweat, I fought a side wind as I made my way down and turned left onto Highway 287. I could see the old schoolhouse resting halfway up a hill.

Twenty years earlier it had also been a gray, overcast day when I pulled into Norris. The CAFE sign had seemed incongruous attached to the old school, which then still had a playground in its yard. Once through the door, it was easy to imagine children stomping mud off their shoes, hanging up their jackets. Down a short flight of stairs, the menu was written on a blackboard with chalk. A man behind a counter told me to help myself to a seat at any table.

The man's name was Jack. I was the only customer, and as Jack made my lunch, he told me that as a boy he'd attended school in that building.

"When the school closed," he said, "I bought it and made it a restaurant. It's my revenge against those teachers. No child shall ever be forced to sit still here again."

"Weren't you a good student?" I asked him.

"Naw—I got into a lot of trouble. But I did win a cake baking contest once," he said.

For years I had told the story of Jack, the child who'd sat restless in the classroom, only to later buy the schoolhouse and close it for good, filling it with homemade cakes and pies. Every child's dream.

Then, one summer day in 1996, I again visited the café. I asked the woman working there about that story.

"That Jack," she said, rolling her eyes. "That story's not true. He never even owned the place, just worked here."

So much for oral history.

Now I stood in front of the door, looking in. As a school, the restaurant was closed for good, and as a restaurant, it was closed on Tuesdays. I settled for a single table at the convenience store downhill from the restaurant, where I warmed on bad coffee and appeased my hunger with a small bag of miniature donuts. I lingered long enough to allow the wind speed to increase before heading south into the teeth of it, a very slow eight miles into McCallister. The drizzle turned into rain. I pulled into a place called the Bear Claw and took a seat at the counter. The talk inside was all about weather.

"I heard it's supposed to snow. Up to ten inches in the mountains," said a man who spoke into his lunchtime beer.

"Kinda bad day to be riding a bike, ain't it," said another standing at the bar, looking at me.

I agreed that it was.

I ordered the largest cheeseburger I'd ever seen, and no flavor had been sacrificed for the size. The burger was topped with a thick slice of cheddar—nothing that had ever been singly wrapped in plastic—and an onion slice, tomato, and pickles. It was served with a huge mound of fries. I mention it only because it was the single best hamburger I'd ever eaten. Just because McDonald's sells by the billions doesn't mean they couldn't learn a thing or two.

A man walked in, the screen door banging behind him. He sat down beside me and nodded.

"That your bike out there?" he asked.

I said that it was.

"You might get wet," he said. It seemed a logical conclusion.

I told him I was in no hurry, that I just might wait it out.

"You might be here till July," he said. "That's the month we usually have summer. Last year it was on the eighteenth."

I finished my burger and got up to use the restroom. Two doors were labeled POINTER and SETTER. I stood thinking, which one was I? Finally, I pushed open one door. The urinal inside told me I'd guessed right.

"Turns out I'm a pointer," I said to the waitress when I returned.

"We were taking bets," she said. "A lot a people are confused by those signs, but it's pretty obvious when you stop and think."

I stopped and thought. She was right.

Ennis was a town full of signs.

At an antique store, one sign said OPEN, and another said CLOSED.

A third said FOR SALE. The door was unlocked, but there was no one inside, and I browsed the narrow aisles and shelves alone.

I walked back outside. The building was painted bright orange, and the front yard was full of antiques, cabin-style furniture and cowboy kitsch, including a life-size wooden cowboy, his trigger hand poised by his side. A cow skull hung over a hand painted sign: NO COW TIPPING ON SUNDAYS. Two red cowboy boots sat upside down on a picket fence, between a coiled rope and a small washtub.

Farther downtown, on the wall outside a saloon, a sign stated: COWBOYS LEAVE YOUR GUNS AT THE BAR. There was no such mandate for the rest of us.

I browsed the shops and galleries, and as I did, I believed that I'd discovered the perfect town. A balanced mix of old rancher and artsy, not yet tainted by the trendy.

That night I sat on a barstool at the Silver Dollar Saloon. A large moose head hung over the end of the bar. A bumper sticker pasted behind the bar read, THERE'S PLENTY OF ROOM FOR ALL GOD'S CREA-TURES. RIGHT NEXT TO THE MASHED POTATOES. Another one claimed, MONOGAMY IS FOR GEESE. I hadn't known.

The bartender was a twenty-one-year-old woman trying to save for college. I asked how it was, living in Ennis.

She shrugged. "I've never lived anywhere else," she said. "But I'm 'bout to. A lot of bad stuff happens in this town."

This didn't surprise me. A lot of bad stuff happens everywhere. "Like what?" I asked.

"Like my brother," she said.

And what was bad about him?

"He's just such a bully," she said. "My mom can't do anything with him." She took a drag on her cigarette. She had a slight lisp but only, I realized, because of the stud in her pierced tongue. Her skin was pale, and she wore a black T-shirt. She was just the touch of gothic that every good cowboy town needed.

"He'll probably outgrow it," I said.

She shook her head. "No. It's getting worse. He beats up on my other little brother. I mean bad, not just the usual brother stuff. But it's not just that he's violent. He just has such little remorse."

95

"But, you know, it's a good town, too, in a lot of ways." She moved away, wiping down the bar, and then she stepped outside to finish her cigarette, leaving me inside alone to read more signs. IF YOU'RE NOT LIVING ON THE EDGE, YOU'RE TAKING UP TOO MUCH SPACE. CHAINS REQUIRED ABOVE 5000 FEET. WHIPS OPTIONAL.

The bartender walked back in. "That your bike outside?" she asked. I'd left it leaning against the wall beneath a neon Budweiser sign.

"Yeah, it's mine," I said.

"You oughta bring it in here," she said. "Just to be safe."

"There a lot of thieves in Ennis?" I asked.

"Not a lot. Some," she said.

I walked out to the bike, and when I did, I noticed the rear tire was flat. Again. I carried it inside and leaned it against the wall next to the jukebox.

Throughout the West small towns were dying, all of the young people moving away. But walking around Ennis, I noticed a lot of young people. I asked the bartender about this.

"Yes," she said, "but there's nothing for them to do but drink. And meth's a big problem here, too."

"Do many of the kids go to college?" I asked.

"Some go to Bozeman. Or Butte. But, I don't know, they all seem to end up back here."

"And what about you?" I asked.

"I want to go to college," she said. She took a long drag on her cigarette and blew smoke into the air. "Soon's I can afford it."

A man walked in and sat at the far end of the bar. He was wearing a cowboy hat and a button-down western shirt. He looked up at me, and I greeted him. He nodded but didn't smile, and I noticed his hands were shaking. I sipped my beer.

The bartender walked over and was talking soothingly to the man, who was clearly distraught. He put his head in his hands, and I could tell by his shoulders he was weeping. She put a hand on his arm.

"I know it doesn't seem so right now," I heard her say, "but everything happens for a reason. You'll be better off without her, you'll see." The man ordered a shot of whiskey with his beer. He downed it and ordered another. I looked straight ahead, trying not to let on that I was

listening. A QUAINT LITTLE DRINKING VILLAGE WITH A FISHING PROB-
LEM, said another bumper sticker pasted on the mirror behind the bar.

A group of young people came in and started playing pool. One of
them put money in the jukebox, and suddenly there was music. "Save
a Horse, Ride a Cowboy." Out of the corner of my eye I saw the man
down another shot of whiskey. He wiped his mouth with the back of
his hand. His lips were tight; he shook his head and looked down at
the empty shot glass. I finished my beer and rolled my bicycle out the
door and stood on the curb. I wasn't ready to go back to the campground, though, was restless, in the mood for conversation. I came
to another bar. The Jack Creek Saloon. Once inside, I recognized the
place, though it had changed dramatically.

In 1985 the bar had been darker, its walls of old grainy wood.
Two men in long rain jackets sat on stools talking about their day
fishing in the rain. I was discovering the road for the first time, something I hoped was the beginning of a lifestyle that would never end.
I had spent the day riding in a slow steady rain, an entirely pleasant
softness, unlike the pounding thunderstorms I knew from Colorado.
To be caught in a Colorado thunderstorm was to be pelted with the
stinging wrath of God, but rain in Montana was simply a matter of
being wet, and once wet, it was done. Montana rain had a cleansing
effect, an oddly warm kind of subtle joy that inspired nostalgic yearn-
ings for childhood days of splashing in puddles and racing Popsicle
rafts down street-side curbs.

I had sat in that bar, listening to the rain, happy to be alive, happy
to have made it to Montana under my own power.

The memory of that rainy night flooded back as soon as I walked in
the door. But it was a sad nostalgic memory. Everything had changed.
The bar was brighter, with strings of light hanging above the mirrors
and along the shelves of liquor bottles. One wall had been torn down,
making the bar twice its earlier size. The bar was crowded, not with
ranchers and fishermen but people who were newcomers to the town.
The bartender was a voluptuous brunette, her cleavage revealing just
enough to inspire better tips. Something about her suggested city, and
when I asked her, sure enough, she told me she was from Las Vegas
and had been in Ennis for less than a year.

"Little quieter than Vegas here, isn't it?" I asked.

"Little bit," she said. "It's why I'm here."

The man two seats down from me nodded, welcomed me, and nothing stood more incongruous with my memory than the silk tie he wore. I told him I was from Colorado, and he said he had moved from there himself.

"I'm a contractor," he said. "I came up here from Breckenridge. 'Fore that I was in California. Just about all the contractors up here came from Colorado." California to Colorado to Montana. It was a modern-day migratory route, in the tradition of the West: follow the latest boom. Bison, gold, coal, oil, development. Far be it for me to begrudge a man his living, but I had a brief and horrific image of condos on the hillside overlooking the town, of three-story houses next to the river where stood my tent.

Before long the heartsick cowboy from the Silver Dollar walked in with a drinking buddy. His cowboy hat was resting so far on the back of his head, I expected it to fall off, but it never did, so far as I know. He and the other man were laughing, boisterously, and he was so full of inebriated joy, it was hard to imagine he was the same man I'd seen crying earlier. He saw me and tipped his hat in my direction, a broad smile on his face.

I continued to talk with the contractor, who was pleasant, positive, and a good conversationalist. I found in him common ground in our mutual love for the West, its people and its land. Still, I longed for the dark rotted wood, the old local men, a longing that, surprisingly, the Las Vegas cleavage not only didn't help but actually made worse.

I left my beer unfinished and walked my limping bicycle back to the campground and settled into my tent.

Sometime in the night I woke to the sound of rain. I opened my tent flap and reached my hand out until it was soaked. It was the same soft rain of my memory, something to count on in the Montana spring. I curled up in my sleeping bag and listened to it fall until I finally fell asleep. In the morning the rain was still falling, and I carried my patch kit and pump to the pit toilet, the only dry place to fix my tire. I packed my bike in the rain and spent the morning in a town that I had no right to think of as my own but I'd fallen in love with anyway, and

I made my good-bye a slow one, avoiding the steep climb out of Ennis for as long as I dared. It was cloudy, still raining, and so cold I could see puffs of my breath hanging in the air before me as I pedaled. The wind blew harder as the road wound higher, and the cold reached through my warmest clothes, dampening my skin. Occasional heavy gusts rendered me stationary, or so it seemed. For much of the last three miles to the top of the climb, my speed reduced to two miles an hour. It was pure obstinacy that kept me from stopping and walking the bike, which might have been faster. Just before the top, a cold icy rain blew, stinging my face.

At last I reached the summit, where a truckload of pigs sat parked on the shoulder. Oinking, grunting, and squealing, their desperate cries of horror carried on the wind. If pigs dream, their worst nightmares were probably about to come true. They seemed to know this. I stopped and listened to their cries, not without sympathy. The driver of the truck was nowhere to be found. I didn't see anyone sitting in the cab. All around me, the world felt abandoned.

I considered setting the pigs free, imagined them running joyfully into the nearby hills. But I knew it would only delay the inevitable. Besides, I was craving a Montana delicacy I remembered well, a sandwich called the Monte Cristo, which was partially made with ham.

I turned a deaf ear to the pleas of the hogs, put on a second jacket, and began my descent into Virginia City.

## Virginia City to Opportunity

VIRGINIA CITY IS COMMONLY associated with vigilante justice, the most famous case being the execution of Henry Plummer. Plummer was elected sheriff of Bannack in 1863 and used his power to organize a gang of road agents who terrorized the community through theft and murder. Plummer had an agreeable personality that belied his cold-blooded nature and for a time managed to disguise his corruption. Little did he know, though, that a group called the Vigilantes was conspiring against him. Plummer was brought to justice in January 1864, when he was hung from a scaffold he himself had built.

I remembered the town for a more contemporary incident, which had captured the nation's interest shortly before I'd first ridden into the town.

In 1985 Virginia City had been the site of a bizarre court case in which a father and son—Don and Dan Nichols—were convicted of kidnapping and the father with homicide. The elder Nichols had wanted a woman for his son, so the men abducted twenty-two-year-old biathlete Kari Swenson, who was out on a training run.

Swenson had been missing for less than a day when two friends went searching for her. As they approached the Nichols's camp, they heard a gunshot and a scream. Dan Nichols had accidentally shot Swenson in the chest. The pursuers rushed to the sound. In the melee that followed, Don Nichols shot and killed one of the men, Alan Goldstein. Then the two mountain men fled, leaving Swenson behind. Though the bullet had punctured her lung, she managed to survive. She was ultimately rescued by a search crew.

The hunt for the Nichols men lasted until December, when smoke from their campfire was spotted, and the men were finally apprehended without a fight.

By the time I'd pedaled into Virginia City, the trial had just recently ended, and though vigilante justice was a thing of the past, bars were serving drinks called hangman's specials, with the Nichols clearly in mind. Swenson dealt with the trauma this way: six months after the incident she won a U.S. gold medal in Quebec.

Now I leaned my bike against the side of a concrete wall and walked up stairs that led from the street to a boarded sidewalk. A sign on a window said INFORMATION and the door was open. Fitting the ghost town theme, the shop was full of merchandise but devoid of people. "Hello?" I called out. But no one answered. I kept expecting someone to walk in from the back, but no one did. I walked through, browsing the racks and shelves, rubbing my hands, trying to regain warmth. The store had the usual tourist fare—jarred jellies and jams, trinkets, jewelry, postcards, books about vigilantes, t-shirts, carved wooden animals, cowboy curios.

On a shelf in the back, though, lay a pile of hot-pink women's panties, which on the front had the words VAGINA CITY. I did a double take. Was I reading that right? Or had I been on the road alone for too long? I picked up a pair, held them up in front of me. Sure enough, my reading had been correct. I was a stranger in town, standing in this store holding up a pair of hot-pink undies with less than delicate phrasing across the front. Quickly, I put them down, relieved that whoever was supposed to be working there didn't walk in just then.

Back outside, the cool air felt good and I walked up and down the wooden boardwalks, peering into old storefront windows. A headless mannequin wearing a glove-fitting corset sat on a counter in front of shelves of old dry goods. Farther up, two blue clay chickens rested in a windowsill. An American flag hung from the old wooden storefront, and on one of the boardwalk benches someone had left a jacket. A dilapidated wagon, its tongue dragging, rested in the yard of a stone building at the edge of town. It was hard to imagine such a vehicle once crossed this rugged terrain.

It was not just the legacy of the old West that was gone now. When I'd bicycled Montana before, the Monte Cristo had been offered in nearly every small town café, but so far on this trip, I had yet to see it on a menu. There was one open restaurant in town. From outside I recognized it, had eaten there before. Virginia City was a town where the past lingered. Surely I could find the sandwich there.

A Monte Cristo begins with two slices of bread dipped in egg batter and fried, much like French toast. Generous hunks of ham and Swiss cheese are placed between the slices of bread. It is best eaten covered with maple syrup and sprinkled with powdered sugar.

My mouth was watering at the very thought, but when I sat down and looked over the menu, there was no Monte Cristo listed. There were three people working in the café, two teenage waitresses and a middle-aged woman I took to be the mother of one of the girls. When I asked the girl who took my order about the Monte Cristo, she shrugged. She'd never heard of such a sandwich. When the woman came from the back kitchen, I asked her.

"Sure," she said. "I remember them."

And what had happened to them?

"I don't know," she said. "I guess they were just too messy for people. No one could decide if it was for breakfast or lunch."

That it defied such categorization, I thought, was part of what made it so special. What had become of that sandwich and why? All across Montana I would inquire, time and time again, to be met only with shrugs and a disappointing lack of concern. What was once a Montana staple seemed lost, faded silently away, like 3.2 beer and Tears for Fears, Rubik's Cubes and Van's tennis shoes, just another memory left unpreserved in that semi–ghost town. That it was unavailable made me crave it more, and I grumped over a club sandwich with fries.

The road through town continued downhill, along the railroad that ran through willows and bogs, and past the old wood buildings of Nevada City, past horse pastures, and weather-stained homes, some crumbling to the ground. And then I was in a valley surrounded by mountains. Sporadically, it sputtered soft gentle rain. It was an easy ride, a tailwind pushing me through the towns of Alder and Laurel, where I stopped to take pictures of an old church that reflected the sun but stood before dark gray storm clouds. The air was filled with the scent of freshly cut grass and rain. When the clouds lifted, the snow line on the mountains was lower.

The clouds moved swiftly, and the sun was a flirt, shyly moving in and out of its nimbostratus cover until, finally, the clouds dissipated, leaving behind a strip of rainbow in the eastern sky. A red-winged blackbird watched me from one fence post and a western kingbird from another. In a field of willows stood a mule deer, and then another, and I didn't realize there were actually several until, seeing me, they all sprinted, tails held high, into the hills of green.

I pulled into Sheridan just before dusk. I wanted to stay at an old inn I remembered, which stood in the center of town. The inn had a bar downstairs with rooms up above. I walked down steps leading from the street into a basement bar with a dungeon feel. The room was long and narrow, with a dance floor at one end. I asked about a room but was told the inn was no longer an inn; the rooms were all monthly rentals now. I stayed long enough to finish a Sprite, and then

I walked through town, found a different motel with clean rooms. But there were no phones. When I asked about this, I was told there was only one pay phone in operation, at the other end of town. So I delayed my dinner and walked to the pay phone, which was outside a café that claimed to be closed. But I heard raucous music inside, the building a beating heart of thrumming bass, so loud I had to holler into the phone for Joan to hear me. At one point a country song I didn't know came on, and I heard voices that seemed too young for what I assumed was a bar crowd singing.

A woman pulled up in a car.

"I hope you can hear okay. Eighth grade graduation party," yelled the lady, pointing to the building, and suddenly it all made sense.

The ride into Twin Bridges was easy, the day cool with a tailwind, and then into Silver Star, where I'd once camped discreetly on the outskirts of town. I was feeling confident, thought maybe I could make it to Butte or even Anaconda. But riding out of Silver Star, my tire went flat, and I fixed it with the last of my $CO_2$'s. My pump was still broken. One more flat, and I'd be in trouble.

I stopped at a café for lunch. My wait service was shared by a four-year-old girl, who served my food with a quiet formality. The other waitress, a teenager, watched the child closely as she carried the plate of food to my table, but she didn't spill a thing. I made sure to hand her a tip when I left, and she looked up at the teenager with a big eat-your-heart-out smile.

Outside, it was starting to drizzle. Four miles later my tire again went flat. I walked the bike to the Highway 41 intersection, the turn-off to Butte, and I stuck out my thumb and waited. There was little traffic, and though several cars stopped, none of them had room for my bike.

Finally, a white van pulled over, and I lifted my bike into the back and sat on the floor between shelves lined with a large assortment of handyman's tools. The van was driven by a chatty man, his wife in the passenger seat. They had just moved to Butte from South Dakota, he said. They knew a bike shop in town, which was run by the brother of a Tour de France rider. They told me all about the rider, whom I'd never heard of, and the man talked about living in Montana, about the animals and wilderness. He had hunted moose for the first time the previous fall. But my listening drifted in and out, and mostly I was watching what little I could see of the blurred landscape out the windshield. The road was curvy, with rock outcrops and lush, dripping forests. I watched with sadness, wishing I was out in the air. When raindrops began to fall on the glass, I wanted to be wet. I wished the man would slow down, though he wasn't speeding. I felt claustrophobic, needed to be outside, listening to the singing breeze, smelling the damp soil.

Then we were in Butte, suddenly surrounded by strip malls and traffic. The couple dropped me off in the parking lot at a sporting goods store called the Outdoorsman. The man helped me unload the bike, shook my hand, and wished me well.

The Outdoorsman was run by a man named Rob Leipenheimer, the brother of the cyclist Levi. Levi's presence was everywhere—posters, newspaper and magazine clippings, autographed team jerseys. When Rob asked me if I followed the tour and if I'd heard of his brother, I had to sheepishly admit the truth. Probably like many Americans, my knowledge of professional cycling didn't extend far beyond Lance Armstrong.

Levi Leipenheimer, I learned, had been riding in the Tour de France since 2002, when he had finished eighth. He had since finished as high as fifth. Later, in July, he would finish again in the top ten (sixth), and in August he would win the Tour of Germany.

The Outdoorsman was well-stocked and clean, but the service I received was what made it perhaps the best shop I experienced in my ride through the West. When my pump broke, I assumed that I'd have to wait until Missoula to replace it, so I was thrilled to discover otherwise. Rob left me in the hands of his employees, while he went to lunch with his father. The head mechanic was a pleasant man with a shaved head and a tattoo on his arm. I told him about all the flats I'd been having.

"There's a lot of glass on western highway shoulders," I said.

"I know it," he said. "I used to be one of the jackasses throwing bottles out my windows. Now I curse those people."

Meticulously, taking his time and explaining it all to me as he went, the mechanic fixed the tire and attached the mirror. I bought a new pump and several $CO_2$'s. When Rob returned, he rewrapped my handlebar tape, work that was so professional and tight I would never again need to rewrap it on the trip. When they were done, the bike was like new. When the Tour de France began in July, I assured Rob, I'd be rooting for his brother.

In that van I'd barely been able to take in the scenery, had felt disconnected from it, both by speed and by confinement. It felt good to be pedaling again. I merged onto I-90 and rode the interstate until the exit at a place called Opportunity.

## Anaconda to Missoula

THREE MILES FROM ANACONDA, and I turned into a stiff cold wind toward Lost Creek State Park. The temperature was dropping, my hands were numb, and the stinging headwind blew dust in my eyes. At first I took it as a challenge. Wind, though, is not a foe to be beaten but a warning to be listened to. Go back, it screamed. It took me five miles of struggle before I took its point. On the road ahead, which rose steadily upward, I could see thick flurries of snow. Wherever the state park waited, it was socked in by low clouds and a promise of a shivering night.

I turned back. Now the wind was behind me, and it took only about one-fifth the time to get back to the highway. In Anaconda I checked into the first motel I saw. Later, at an all-night casino diner, I sat at the counter and looked at the menu.

"You ever heard of a Monte Cristo sandwich?" I asked the waitress.

"No," she said, shaking her head, her ready pen a signal for me to get on with things. I ordered a chicken fried steak, my fallback meal. Several minutes later the waitress brought my plate. I took a bite. The meal went far to disprove my long-held theory that chicken fried steak was a meal that couldn't be botched. I finished it anyway, every bite.

Morning, the first Saturday of June, cold and gray. The coffee shop was mostly a drive-through, though there was a single table inside.

A young college woman worked behind a closet-sized counter, and a line of cars waited outside. She took time to talk to the people, all of whom she seemed to know. The table was covered with a pile of old magazines, which gave me something to do while I waited. When she finally brought my coffee, I asked if she'd worked there long.

"Naw," she said. "I just started—just moved back to town."

"Where from?" I asked.

"I was working at Old Faithful," she said. "There were three rapes just during the little time I was there. I had to walk a mile from my work to the dorms. At night. I told my dad—he's a sheriff—and he made me come home, which was fine with me."

I asked her about camping, and she said there were lots of places to camp between Anaconda and Missoula. Then she told me about her own recent camping trip.

"At the end of the night there was just one tent for me to sleep in, and that was with Adrian." She said his name with a roll of her eyes that seemed habit, as if she'd never spoken his name any other way. "He'd been drinking beer, like the rest of them. He gets handsy when he drinks. And then he pukes."

"Nothing worse than a handsy puker for a tent mate," I said.

"No," she said. "So I came home."

"You come home a lot," I said.

She nodded. "I keep thinking I need to get away from here. I leave. My mind changes. I come back."

Sounded like every home I'd ever known. Hard to leave, hard to stay. The West was full of us: restless spirits in constant search of what we already had.

Around the turn of the twentieth century Anaconda was home of the most productive copper industry in the world, and the mining operation was the largest employer in the state. The company was founded by a man named Marcus Daly, whose contributions to the town included a trolley line and amusement park. Later Daly sold out to the Anaconda Copper Mining Company, which maintained its status as a copper giant until the 1970s. The company closed its Anaconda operations in 1980. It was one more example of boom gone bust.

I spent the afternoon doing laundry, reading, eating lunch at a family diner, where a two-year-old in a pink dress stared at me while her mother smoked cigarettes and talked on a cell phone. I walked through town. An old brewery had been converted into an antique store, one of its many rooms filled with old gasoline pumps. I managed to stretch the day and didn't leave town until nearly five o'clock, and then I rode all of twelve uphill miles to Spring Hill Campground. The campground was empty, save for the host and a single van parked in one of the far sites. The lower sites were a swamp of standing water, and the flat grassy area by the outhouses was ankle deep in flood. I pitched my tent up on the hillside. I was cold from the damp air. I'd been cold for days. It was June already, but summer was lost, somewhere on its migratory trail. The camp host had stacks of split wood, and he gave me an armload for free, but it was wet, and my attempts at a campfire were a dismal waste of a book of matches. I followed a short trail up the mountain and hung my food from a tree. When I returned, the couple from the van were walking on the gravel road. They were middle-aged, maybe in their fifties. The woman had short hair. The man was an amateur photographer, whose favorite expression was "Bless you." He wore a ball cap with a cross on the front. They were heading to Phillipsburg to search for gems, and then were heading home to Coos Bay, Oregon.

Later I was sitting at my table reading, when the man came walking toward my site. He was carrying a brown paper bag.

"Do you eat meat?" he asked, and I told him I did. From the bag he took a plastic platter full of food—baked chicken, a salad, a small container of tapioca pudding.

"We couldn't eat ourselves," he said, "until we knew your needs were taken care of. I'm Randy, by the way, Randy Randall. And my wife's name is Carolyn." He handed me a slip of paper with home and cell phone telephone numbers. "When you get to Oregon, you'll have a place to stay if you need it," he said. "Do you mind if I pray a blessing over you?" I didn't mind. He didn't ask about my own personal theology, and he didn't seem to be pushing one of his own. He put his hand on my shoulder and prayed for me. He prayed for my safety, my health, my warmth and comfort as I continued my journey. When he was done, against my skepticism, I believed that I would indeed be safer.

"Please do call when you get to Coos Bay," he said, before he left me to my meal. I told him I would think about it. I was grateful, but I had no intention of ever calling. I placed the slip of paper in my wallet, though, and I watched him as he walked gently down the road, back to his wife and his camp. Such a gentle man. There was nothing in his walk or in his demeanor then that would suggest a past I would learn about later—the war trauma, the drug use, the standoff with federal agents that nearly ended in a fury of violence. And then the slow conversion, the solace finally achieved through faith.

I slept well, waking and rising once in the night. The sky was clear and full of stars, the Big Dipper tipped at a slight downward angle. Inside my sleeping bag I stayed warm through the night. When I rose the next morning, the Randalls were already gone. I didn't expect that I'd see them again.

The road rose to a crest and then skirted Georgetown Lake. The air was cool, but the sun was up, and I knew I'd have a day of mostly downhill and flat riding. I had been struggling through a sort of traveler's melancholy, which was, in large part, the result of missing Joan and probably also because of the days of cold and wind and gray sky. It seemed to me, though, that this feeling occurred most when I was in the places I loved. It was hard to force the elation I thought I should feel upon revisiting places I remembered most fondly. It felt like Christmas afternoon, when the gifts were all open and you realized, through all of the anticipation, how fleeting was the moment.

At Dentine's Point I sat inside the café by a side window, where light streamed through the glass, warming me. It was the first time I'd seen the sun in a cloudless sky for over a week. On the first trip, when I'd ridden this stretch, it had been pouring down rain, and I'd stopped at the same restaurant, with its large wood-stained patio. I had ordered a bowl of Texas chili and hot tea. Sitting in that lodge now, it occurred to me that every weather-induced misery I'd ever endured had been worth it, just for the slow, creeping warmth that came afterward.

Part of my mood came from the tension that arose from my desire to drift into both time and solitude. I felt regret for not reaching out to others more. But this regret was not out of loneliness so much as out of what I felt was my responsibility to seek stories, drama, adventure. The truth was, bicycle touring was peaceful, simple actually. The real point was not adventure—a word that was imbued with frenzy and high energy—but a means of slowing down, of finding solace and peace. I felt I should be an investigative reporter, rewriting the contemporary history of a changing West. But I was really just a guy on a bicycle, moving through a space that I wanted to melt into. My journal could be a distraction, a burden, and I wanted both to fill it with words and to throw it away.

The Flint River flowed into a green valley, with horses grazing in the fields and mountains on every horizon. This was the western side of Pinter Scenic Route 1.

The Granite County Museum in Phillipsburg had displays of the town's mining history. Downstairs was an exhibit that showed what life was like in the mines—a model of the worker's quarters and a small railroad that carried ore from the mine. The basement was filled with the cool below-earth damp smell of soil.

A man I knew in Phillipsburg once ran a small but well-stocked photography shop on Main Street. When I'd studied photography in Missoula, I'd often driven there for supplies. Now, though, the shop was gone. A sign on the door gave a new address, on a different street, which led up a steep hill lined on both sides with wood frame houses and a small church. Steve's shop was now in a detached garage, next to his house. He had expanded the business to include a nursery of potted trees and plants.

Steve was wearing old overalls and a ball cap—I'd never seen him without one—the bill skewed slightly to the side. He talked in a monotone mumble and rarely looked you in the eye, except when he made a joke, and he'd glance up with mischievous eyes, just to see that you got it.

Boxes stood in haphazard piles, and rows of metal shelves were stocked with gear—developing chemicals, photographic paper, tripods, camera bags. Behind the counter he had lenses and cameras old and new. Shelves were lined with rows of film. It was perhaps the best-stocked photography shop in Montana, if not the most organized.

Steve's demeanor and appearance could be misleading. His knowledge of camera equipment was unparalleled, and he kept up-to-date. Though shy, he wasn't afraid to share an opinion. I asked him if he ever saw anyone from the photography school in Missoula, and he shook his head.

"I'm not real happy with them just now," he said. "They made a deal with a New York company that is offering their students a discount. They must be getting some kind of kickback—I can still sell to their students cheaper." He said this without ever raising his voice. Though the anger was real, it was wholly contained in a Zen-like calm. I changed the subject, asking him about Phillipsburg. He bemoaned the growth.

"The reason I moved from the downtown store was because the rent on my lease was raised. I don't even know anyone who lives in town anymore," he said.

Steve had an old-fashioned combination of business savvy and ethics. I bought five rolls of film.

He handed me a card as I started to leave. "You decide you need anything else," he said, "just call me."

At a local tavern I sat down next to an old graybeard who was drinking beer as he waited for the kitchen in back to prepare his family's bucket-of-chicken meal. He called the town "P-burg" and said that it had indeed changed a lot in recent years.

"It's getting harder and harder to afford to live here," he said.

I told him that Steve had said the same thing.

"Steve Neal?" he said. "Man, I didn't even know that guy was still alive."

Alive and well, I was happy to report. Phillipsburg might have been growing, but so far it retained its old mining charm. It was a place where the entrepreneurial spirit could still allow a man to compete with Internet chains.

At Drummond a frontage paralleled Interstate 90, and I rode down the middle, not having to worry about traffic or trucks or exhaust. There were old wooden barns, semi-collapsed in the fields of green between me and the interstate, and cliffs that rose to the north. Beavertail State Park was a quiet spot, save for the occasional train that ran on the nearby tracks and the honking geese that flew overhead. In the morning I emerged groggily from my tent, only to find a mule deer doe eating from a tree not twenty yards away. I thought she would run upon seeing me, but she just gave me a sidelong look, as if mildly annoyed that I had interrupted the solitude of her breakfast. By all rights I should have shooed her away. I had, after all, paid for the site. But that look was enough to spur my guilt, so, meekly, I sat in the grass outside my tent and waited for her to finish her meal.

It was an easy ride into Missoula on Interstate 90, the Sunday morning traffic light, the shoulder wide, a cloudless sunny sky. I took the Van Buren exit into town and then passed the apartments on Greenough Street, where Joan and I had once lived. I crossed the bridge over Rattlesnake Creek and then made my way over railroad tracks. Though I'd only lived in Missoula for three summer months, it was one of the handful of places I thought of as my own, a bustling western college town with an artsy emphasis on outdoor recreation. It was the cultural center of Montana—the liberal yin to the general yang of the rest of the state.

Higgins Street was lined with cafés, galleries, sporting goods shops, bars, office buildings. I headed south and ate a vegetable sandwich with a bowl of tomato, lime, and tortilla soup at a place called Catalyst. Hanging from the walls were color photographs by a local artist named Susanna Gaunt. She'd titled the series "Recto/Verso." The photos were haunting images of ghostly reflections and lurking shadows. One showed narrow windows reflected in two glass doors, an abstract design of lines and color. At first glance it seemed to portray a skewed reality, but upon a closer look the reality wasn't skewed at all—just uniquely observed.

Outside I stood beneath the storefront canopy, waiting. Rain droplets plunked onto the pavement, and a steady drip rolled off the canopy overhang. Traffic swished down rain-soaked Higgins. The water was a percussive symphony playing lightly over the afternoon. I walked, staying close to the storefronts, trying to stay dry, stopping once at a used bookstore, where I browsed the dusty aisles, my wet feet squeaking on the wood board floor.

Night at the Oxford Saloon and Café. A sign behind the diner counter proclaimed: AS OF 2/28/05 WE HAVE SOLD 146,891 CHICKEN FRIED STEAKS. So that's what I ordered. When I was done, I shifted the few feet from diner perch to barstool. Above the shelves of booze, high on the wall, hung a glass display case with twenty-four rifles, mostly Remingtons and Winchesters. A sign advertised PICKLED TURKEY GIZ-ZARDS, $1.50.

"Are they any good?" I asked.

"People tell me they taste like roast beef," said the bartender. I took her word for it.

Behind me, in the front of the bar, next to the street window, eight men were playing live poker.

"How long's poker been legal in Montana?" I asked.

"It became legal in the '70s, I think," she said. "Before that they played down in the basement."

In the morning I went to get a haircut. The barber was sitting in the single chair of his small shop reading the day's *Missoulian*. When I walked in, he stood, greeted me warmly. He was thin, friendly, and there was a sense of active, almost youthful energy to him, which was entirely undiminished by his graying hair. He asked me how I wanted mine cut, and I told him to take it all off.

"You mean your hair, right?" he asked.

"You're a barber, aren't you?" I said.

"Well, I'm definitely not a surgeon," he said.

As he worked, we talked about grizzly bears. The Sunday before, *60 Minutes* had aired a report about grizzly problems in Cody, Wyoming. The barber said that he lived up in a canyon, close to the forest. Bears had once destroyed his bird feeders.

"You know what—," he said. "When you live in bear country, you have to accept that there're some things you just shouldn't have. It wasn't the bear's fault—I never should have put those feeders there in the first place."

We talked about the conflicts between those who wanted to develop the land and those who wanted to preserve it. I told him that all along my route I'd encountered people whose love for the West centered on the landscapes—there was talk about fresh air, open space, room enough to breathe. But time and again, I encountered a host of paradoxes—a support of development for economy but a range of disapproval that ran from concern to contempt toward the outsiders who fed that growth; a love for the land but disdain for the environmentalists who wanted to conserve it; a flag waving patriotism but a distrust of government officials.

"It's true," said the barber, laughing. "I'm the same way. I mean, I don't want them to dig for oil, but I drive a car. I don't want to cut down all of the forests, but I live in a wood house. I do what I can, though. Recycle. Ride my bike to work. But this is Missoula. We don't exactly represent the ideas of the rest of the state here."

He turned me around so I could look in the mirror. He hadn't cut it all yet. He'd left a very short crew cut. "Now, we could stop here. Are you sure you want me to shave it all? Some people say that's what they want, but when it's too late, they change their mind."

"Cut it," I said, and after he did, we both looked at my reflection in the mirror, leaving unsaid the obvious truth: mine was not a head suited for the aesthetics of baldness. A good lesson to learn. Luckily, I had a hat, and Montana was not the kind of state that would expect me to remove it. My prayers were not usually inspired by vanity, but silently I asked for a speedy regrowth.

"Good luck to you," said the barber, and I wasn't sure if he'd sensed my plea or if he meant it toward my journey.

# Face-planting on Highway 2

A TRUCK STOP JUNCTION AT HIGHWAY 93 and a warm bowl of rainy evening soup. Men in greasy hats with callused hands, their shirts stretched at the gut, revealing lives spent eating in greasy spoons. At a table by a window a young boy spoke loudly to his hard-of-hearing grandmother. Gently, he helped steady her as they made their slow way out the door and to the parking lot.

The old waitress had mammoth arms, could have moonlighted as a bouncer at the strip club across the parking lot. But she carried the coffeepot with a practiced grace, and her head turned in conversation with a man at the counter as she filled a perfect cup, never once turning to look, not even when she was done pouring.

"You eatin' tonight or just having coffee?" she asked a man sitting at the booth in front of me.

"Just coffee. I'll eat at your house later," said the man, winking at her. She never even flinched or rolled her eyes.

"My house, hell," she said. "Ain't nothin' but Ding Dongs and Twinkies there."

I was only about twenty miles out of Missoula when, once again, I heard the hiss of leaking air, a slow leak, not bad enough to keep me from riding. But I wasn't sure where the next campground might be, and it was getting dark. So I turned back, decided to camp at one of the commercial campgrounds I'd passed, a place called Jellystone Park RV Campground.

The campground store had video games in back, next to the guest laundry room. I asked the man behind the counter how much, and when he said, "Twenty-seven dollars," I asked again. Same answer. Only a fool would pay that price to sleep in his own tent.

I handed the man my credit card.

In the actual Yellowstone I had paid five dollars to camp. Granted, the national park campground didn't have a miniature golf course or a playground with swings and a slide. It didn't have a swimming pool or a Laundromat or cabins to rent. In Yellowstone I hadn't been given the opportunity to camp on DAZZALATION DRIVE, and perhaps that was the touch that gave Jellystone its "award winning" quality.

I pitched my tent on a plot of grass next to a picnic table. There were nearly thirty-five RV's parked neatly in paved parking spots. No annoying trees to keep them all from being neighborly. Remarkably, mine was the only tent. It was hard to imagine why.

A man who had rented one of the cabins with his wife and five-year-old daughter walked by, watched me set up my tent.

"You need a buddy," said the man. I wasn't sure if he meant for company or to help me set up the tent. I really wasn't sure what he meant at all. But I nodded, as if in agreement. He and his daughter walked to the playground. By the time they walked back, I'd replaced my old tube and was pumping up the tire. It was then I saw that the tire had a hole in it.

"Looks like that takes a while to blow up," said the man. I said that it wouldn't take that long, and the man and his daughter watched me, as if to see for themselves just how long.

That hole was a problem. Should I go back to Missoula, get another tire? I wondered. That would set me back another day at least. I was already behind schedule. It was June 7, and I was scheduled to meet Joan on the 24th in Friday Harbor. I finished filling the tire.

"See," I said, looking up at the man. "All finished."

"You could use an air compressor," he said, and then he and his daughter walked away.

Yes, I thought. And maybe a generator, to plug it in.

Kalispell was just a day's ride away, if all went well. There would be a bike shop there. I thought the tire would last until then.

The tire didn't last.

I made it easily to Ravelli and then to Arlee, on the Flathead Indian Reservation. The sky was gray with intermittent rain, and mists of fog wove through mountainside pine. Dots of dandelion dotted green fields where horses grazed. Outside Arlee road construction resulted in very narrow to nonexistent shoulder. But the traffic was light, the drivers courteous.

At the intersection of highways 93 and 200 the road began a steep rise. The skies were clearing, and I stopped to remove my rain jacket. My tube was now protruding through the hole in the tire, a node-like bubble of air. All I could do was pedal and hope, but I'd traveled only about fifty yards up the hill before I heard the popping explosion and the steady hiss of escaping air. I had extra tubes and $CO_2$'s. What I didn't have was a spare tire, and no matter what I tried, I couldn't keep the tube from stretching like a tumor out the tire. I tried replacing the tube but only made about twenty yards before the new one blew.

I walked the bike up the hill. I had already hitched three rides so far, one in each state. Each time I swore it would be my last. I didn't want to hitch and vowed not to. But when I heard the shifting gears of a pickup starting up the hill, I stopped and stuck out my thumb. The driver didn't stop. I tried this several more times. No one stopped, save for a young college student returning home for the summer, in an already fully loaded small blue Pinto. He had no room for me, much less my bike. He seemed genuinely regretful that he couldn't help, and I thanked him, happy for the charitable attempt and then watched the car sputter up and over the hill.

It was a slow walk to the top, where I sat down at a rest area picnic table and contemplated my next move. I ate and read from *Blue Highways* and came to this maxim: "I can't take anymore comes just before 'I don't give a damn.'" My grumpiness had sought validation, and in Least Heat-Moon I had found it.

I had the whole rest area to myself and was exercising my self-pity when a green Ford pickup pulled up. A man got out. He was probably in his early fifties, wore thick glasses, had a pockmarked face. He was built like a man who knew the joy of sizably proportioned meals. I nodded hello and he jovially returned my greeting. When I explained my predicament, asked if he'd consider giving me a ride, he said, "Sure, why not."

The back of the pickup was full, and I helped the man move some boxes and tools to make room for the bike. Then I lifted the bike into the bed. I offered to sit in back with it, but he told me there was room in the cab. But when I opened the passenger door, there was a woman sitting there. Again I said I'd be happy to ride in back, but the man said it wasn't a problem, that she could sit on one of the seats in the extended cab, and she moved to do so. I felt bad, but the woman smiled at me, assured me it was not at all uncomfortable back there.

"I'm Rob," said the man, "and this is Anita. We live in Missoula."

Anita had brown eyes and long dark hair. She spoke with an accent, and I asked her where she was from.

"The Philippines," she said.

"How long have you been in the U.S.?" I asked.

"About three years," she said. "I like it here. Very much."

"Are there mountains in the Philippines?" I asked.

"Yes," she said. "But you can't go into them. Because of the guerrillas."

Rob looked over at me. "The kind with machine guns," he said.

We drove through St. Ignatius, and I was sad that here was one more stretch of road I wouldn't ride. We passed the small brick mission, and I could see the steeple rising into the sky. I knew that inside the muted light would be streaming through the stained glass windows, shining on the biblical scenes portrayed on the light-blue walls. As I ruminated on the simple beauty of that architecture, Anita told me about the antigovernment rebels who hid in the mountains of her home. Though not the same, I thought about Montana's own history of antigovernment rebels: Ted Kaczynski, the Freemen.

"When she first came here," said Rob, gesturing toward Anita, "we went up to the mountains to go fishing. I loaded the four-wheeler, including a rifle. She wanted to know if it was safe. I had to explain to her that the rifle wasn't to protect us from guerrillas, that we'd be fine." They both laughed.

"She's the best thing that ever happened to me," he said, and the smile that had yet to leave her face grew even larger.

"Where did you meet?" I asked.

"Online," he said, gauging my reaction.

"I have good friends that just got married," I said. "They met online. They lived in the same city but had never met."

"Well, we were living half a world apart," said Rob. "A friend taught me about computers—had to tell me everything, even how to turn them on. Then, the first time I got on, I got into a chat room. It was all gay men. I didn't try that again for a long time. Then, when I did, I got into this other chat room. There was an empty room, just Anita. No one was talking to her. So I just started chatting with her, and we got to know each other that way."

In the back Anita beamed. Their mood was contagious, and whatever grumpiness I'd nursed at the top of that hill disappeared in their presence. When we arrived in Polson, I offered to fill their tank.

"You know what," said Rob. "Don't even worry about it. I'm just happy to help someone out."

There was no bicycle shop in Polson, but at a True Value I found a cheap tire, just the size I needed. It was heavy and held only 70 psi, which slowed me down considerably, especially on hills.

I rode along the west side of Flathead Lake. On my original trip I'd ridden the east, but due to mud slides, that route was closed now. Just as well. It was on that road that I'd nearly been hit.

It had been at the end of an eighty-mile day. The sun was already behind the trees, and the highway was entirely in shadow. I glanced lazily in my rear-view mirror, and, not seeing or hearing the oncoming car, I turned left onto the highway, heading toward the road that led to Finley Point State Park. Suddenly, I heard the screeching of brakes, and the car swerved into the oncoming lane, just missing me. Fortunately, there was no car coming from the opposite direction. The car moved back into the lane in front of me and had to adjust quickly, slamming to a stop just in time to prevent going off the edge. The driver, a teenage girl, had jumped out of the car and justifiably scolded me, an unnecessary reinforcement of the lesson I'd already learned.

Now I made my way to Big Arm State Park. There were only a handful of other campers, and I found a site near the lake. In the morning I sat on a rock at the lake's edge, listening to the water lapping against the shore. I could see town lights across the water, through a thin layer of fog. Distant mountains and hills stood in striated shades of blue.

The ride into Kalispell was flat. The town had grown considerably since I'd been there last, such that by the time I saw the ENTERING

KALISPELL sign, I'd already been riding through four miles of new outskirts.

Just past four-thirty, and traffic was heavy. I found a sporting goods store with a small bicycle shop in the back. I couldn't find the tire I needed, and there was no one on the floor to help. I saw a young man with a mechanics apron working on a bicycle on a stand. I called out to him, asked if they had any twenty-seven-inch tires. Without looking up, he simply said no.

"Are there any other bike shops near here?" I asked.

The man mumbled a name, which I didn't hear.

"And can you tell me where that is?" I asked.

He gestured vaguely with his hand, without saying a word. It was getting close to five o'clock, and I was afraid the other bike shop would be closed.

"Is that north or south?" I asked.

The man stopped, glared at me. "Actually," he said, "it's that way," and he pointed west, a different direction than he'd gestured previously. Then he returned his attention to the bike on the stand, turning his back to me as he worked.

I left and found the bike shop downtown and bought the tire I needed, along with some tubes. At a picnic table in a parking lot across the street, I replaced the True Value tire, which, in a pinch, had served me well.

A restaurant on Main Street was fine dining—white tablecloths and cloth napkins folded accordion style at each setting—with prices to match. Across the street there was another restaurant. I looked at the menu. Meals were running nearly $20 a plate. Twenty years earlier I'd eaten at an all-you-can-eat restaurant here for $2.95. I walked down a side street until I found a third restaurant. From the outside it seemed like nothing fancy, but inside, again, it was fine dining, the tables set with more silverware than I'd know how to use, the glassware spotlessly clean.

A hostess looked at me, paused before offering to seat me. I told her I'd sit at the bar. In the restroom I looked at myself in the mirror. There were bags under my eyes and my cap was splattered with mud. My clothes were dirty, covered with grease and mud spots. I needed a shower. I washed up the best I could and walked back to my seat at the bar. There were only a handful of other patrons sitting there. Several people were working—waitresses and servers walked behind the bar to get drinks. The bartender filled glasses. He didn't look at me. I tried to make eye contact. Finally, I called out to him, asking for a menu. The bartender set one in front of me, never looking at me, never asking me what I wanted to drink. A young couple came and sat on the barstools beside me. The bartender immediately handed them menus, smiled, greeted them. They ordered beers, and he filled two glasses from the tap, set them in front of the couple.

I waited for him to take my order. Nothing. Message received. I rose and left, grumbling to myself as I walked out the door.

For the last several days I'd been struggling with tire problems, cold and rain, loneliness. What was I doing? Suddenly the whole journey seemed as ridiculous as the stubbles growing on my bald head. I'd been riding for over a month. It would be two long weeks before I'd see Joan in Friday Harbor, if I even made it there in time. I missed her, and I masked it with a slow, seething anger leveled toward the rudeness I'd encountered at the sporting goods store, at the restaurant. I was also angry at myself for my own attitude, my inability—or was it unwilling-ness?—to go with the flow, to take the minor adversities in stride and just enjoy the natural beauty of the landscape. Maybe it wasn't my appearance that was inspiring rudeness in others. Maybe it was me.

I'd once longed to live in Kalispell, considered it the perfect western mountain town. The day I'd arrived there twenty years earlier had been my first ever century ride and one of the best days I'd ever spent bicycle touring.

I had left St. Mary's campground on the east side of Glacier National Park at five-thirty in the morning. By rule, bicycles needed to be to the top of Logan Pass by noon in order to avoid the afternoon traffic. Logan Pass, also known as the Going-to-the-Sun Highway, was a steep road, with many switchbacks. I expected a difficult ride.

But just before sunrise I stopped to watch a small group of elk swim across St. Mary Lake. The lake reflected a lavender sky, and the elk swam through a pastel shade of purple, their heads back, the velvet of their antlers just skimming the top of the water. Seeing those elk made the uphill ride feel effortless, and I rode between glacier-carved mountains spotted with patches of snow. Water seeped down sides of roadside cliffs, and the green meadows were dotted with Indian paintbrush.

I made the summit by ten o'clock, and then it was an easy ride down, past Lake McDonald, through Apgar and West Glacier. I rode easily into Kalispell. It was my first one hundred–mile day, and I had slept in the forest, never even bothering to set up a tent.

My memory held that day as one of the best of the entire journey. I'd been young and free, moving effortlessly through the country's most rugged wilderness, sleeping on the ground. And yet a look back in my journal revealed that I had struggled then also. I had foolishly run out of food and cash and hadn't eaten at all between Lake Mc-Donald and Kalispell, where I could get money at a bank. Then I had also ridden on a bad tire, for over two hundred miles. What I had then was a kind of blind faith, a belief that no bad could come to me. Where now I grumbled, earlier I had bought into an optimism that came from something larger. Call it God or karma or simply chance, but for each of those two hundred miles I had prayed for that tire to last, knowing that it was bound to blow. Which it did.

Six blocks from the bicycle shop in Kalispell. It had not been merely a matter of luck.

I'd fallen in love with Kalispell, had ever since idealized it as the perfect town, with a palpable friendliness. How disappointing, the rudeness I encountered now, like looking up an old friend only to be shunned.

But there was another side too, a generous Kalispell spirit that still existed, as I would discover later, on my return through town.

I headed toward Columbia Falls. It was late, but the road was flat, and it felt good to ride. I was still angry, and I rode with a fury. The rain had ended, and the sun broke through the clouds. I fell into a comfortable rhythm, an easy twenty miles per hour. The shoulder was wide, and the rain-soaked pavement was drying in the cool air. In the distance, I knew, lay the mountains of Glacier, and I felt their draw, pedaled faster. I started to cross a railroad track. I thought back to the sporting goods store, the bartender who hadn't served me.

Suddenly, my front tire caught on the indentation around the rail. I felt the bike lean, and I tried to right it, but it was too late. I heard the sound of my panniers skidding along the pavement and then my helmet, and I felt the impact against my jaw, my side, my knee, my hand. My face scraped along the pavement.

I lay stunned. The traffic was light but steady. Nobody stopped. Finally, I stood, cursing, and I lifted the bike, surveyed the damage. My panniers had fallen off. I reattached them to the bike. My knee was scraped and stiff. I placed my hand on the bone beneath my eye, and my fingers came back with blood. My back was sore, and my hand, the same one I'd broken the previous January, was so stiff I couldn't make a fist. I feared I'd broken it again. My mirror was shattered, and the handlebar stem was crooked. The handlebar bag mount had snapped in half. My rain pants and jacket were both torn.

I flexed my hand. It was stiff but not swollen. I made a fist. It wasn't broken. I stood, breathing deeply, and something lifted inside. I felt the anger and self-pity dissipate, like the wisps of fog moving through the trees on the mountains in the distance. Suddenly I was filled with a new surge of energy. I readjusted the handlebar stem and started to ride. Several miles later, when my front tire went flat, I laughed. I fixed the flat and rode on.

At an RV campground in Columbia Falls the woman behind the registration desk asked about the scrapes on my face, and when I told her what happened, she knocked five dollars off my fee. The tent sites were on the back side of a wooden fence. In the night it rained, and I lay awake in my tent, my back stiff, a mild throbbing pain in my hand. I smiled. I felt alive.

# Glacier National Park

A RISING MIST shrouded the Flathead Range, and my shoe imprints dotted the dew-covered grass. At the campground office, a large room with free coffee and tables covered with tourist brochures, a man was scolding two women—the desk clerk and the maid. The desk clerk was clearly rattled, but the maid seemed entirely unfazed by the man, as if she'd heard it all before and knew she'd hear it again. The man looked at her.

"Are the rooms all clean?" he asked.

"No one's checked out yet," she said.

"No one?" he asked.

"No."

"Number eleven's gone," said the man.

"No. Their truck's gone, but there's a dog still stayin' in there." She said this slowly, as if explaining to a child.

"What are you doing?" he asked the desk clerk, who was shuffling papers near the register in a feeble attempt to look busy.

I was standing, drinking coffee, looking at a book of photographs on a table beneath the window. I admit it fully: while the two women legitimately had nothing to do, I was just being lazy. My back had stiffened in the night, and my hand cracked every time I flexed it. The man turned, as if just noticing I was there. He looked me up and down.

"Something I can do for you?" he asked.

"I'm good," I said holding up my coffee.

"He's a camper," said the desk clerk.

The man turned back to her. "You make sure you get those receipts done," he said. The maid looked at me, gestured toward the man, and rolled her eyes. I smiled back at her and returned to the photographs on the table.

My wreck had left me with one unsolvable problem: my handlebar bag. The attachment system was a hard plastic plate to which the bag attached by sliding it between two grooves and then locking it into place with a lever. The plate had snapped entirely in half. I relied on that bag to hold my maps, my sunglasses, my camera, snacks, my journal, all the items I liked to have readily accessible. I spent the rest of the morning doing laundry and trying to think of a fix for the bag.

I folded my laundry and loaded it into my panniers. Perhaps there was a bike shop in Whitefish, which was only about five miles west, and I could buy a new bag there. I stopped back at the office. The boss and the maid were gone. The desk clerk looked up at me.

"Could I borrow a phone book?" I asked.

There was one bike shop listed. I asked if I could use the phone.

"No," said the woman, "you'll have to use the one down the road, at the convenience store."

"Okay," I said.

"It's not worth losing my job over. If my boss calls and the line's busy . . . it's just not worth it."

"No problem."

"Like that woman came in, wanted to use the restroom. He said, 'I ain't paying water bills for anyone's sewage that ain't a customer.' I'm sorry. I'm just not going to lose my job over it."

"It's fine," I said. "Not a problem."

Once on the bike, I decided just to keep riding. Using bungee cords, superglue, and duct tape, I managed to get the handlebar bag to stay, a very temporary fix I hoped would last until my return to Kalispell.

The west side of Glacier National Park was a lush and damp world of green. A bicycle trail ran from West Glacier to Apgar, through western red cedar trees, lodgepole and western white pine, rocks covered with yellow and orange lichens, and the rich black forest floor covered with mushrooms and thick ferns.

I set up camp in a small site at Apgar Campground and unloaded my gear, storing it in the bear box provided at my site. The bear boxes were an improvement. Twenty years earlier I'd stored all my food in one of my panniers and had hung it from a tree with a nylon cord. The next morning the bag was gone, the cord having been cut with a knife.

Now, my gear secure, at least from bears, I rode back into West Glacier through a soft, comfortable drizzle. I came around a corner, and the trail dipped slightly. At the bottom the trail was covered with standing water, but there was enough trampled dirt beside the trail to ride around the puddle. I slowed, not wanting to slide in the mud.

I looked up. Roughly thirty-five yards ahead on the trail stood a black bear, watching me. I skidded to a stop. The bear started to move, and at first I thought he was coming toward me. But the bear veered off the trail and into the forest. I expected to hear crashing through the trees and brush, but he disappeared silently.

I felt the hair on my arms rise. There is a mystical elegance to the black bear, and I liked thinking of them living among the ferns and moss and flowers of this primeval forest. Twenty years earlier I'd seen a different bear chomping grass in a dandelion meadow. When it had seen me, it jumped, turning in the air, its four legs churning even before they hit the ground. My heart pounded, and I stood straddling my bicycle, unnerved by how quickly the bear had moved.

Always with bears it had been like that: a brief glimpse and then gone, fleeting spirits with a bouncing gait.

Now I stood looking down the empty trail, and then I pedaled past where the bear had been. I stopped and gazed into the forest. Nothing but rainwater dripping from the branches of trees.

In West Glacier, as if on cue, the bartender was talking to another man about a grizzly bear study that the park service was conducting. Someone had been sabotaging the study, he said, by destroying some of the bait sites.

"So they had this meeting. The meeting was advertised as an educational talk to explain the bear study, because there'd been a lot of controversy about it. So I went, and once there, it was clear the whole meeting was really just an attempt to find out who was responsible for the sabotage. They tried to say that whoever was doing it was really hurting the bears."

"Why would anyone want to do that?" I asked.

"Well, there's a feeling among a lot of people that the study was manipulated, not for preservation but to delist the grizzly from the endangered list. Whoever destroyed the sites probably at least believed they were helping the bears."

"What do you think?" I asked.

"I'll tell you this," he said. "The people running that meeting had an agenda that had nothing to do with research or conservation."

That night, in my tent, nearly asleep, I heard something shuffling in the dirt, moving closer. Then quick, panting animal breaths and sniffing, just inches from where I lay. I tensed. Was my food carefully packed away inside the bear box? The breathing continued. It was no bear. Something smaller—a raccoon or fox. I barked, slapped the ground.

And then silence. A breeze through the trees. Whatever had been there was gone.

I waited out a morning rain at the Apgar Café and pored over two newspapers with related headlines. The *Daily Interlakes*, the Flathead Valley paper, read, "Delisting for Yellowstone Grizzlies to Be Sought," and the *Hungry Horse News* proclaimed, "Too Many Grizzlies Dying, Advocates Claim." In the nineteenth century the grizzly bear population in what is now the lower forty-eight states had been somewhere between 50,000 and 100,000. Now, according to the first article, the population in the eighteen million acres of the greater Yellowstone area was around 600. In the same paper a completely separate article described a different style of habitat: outside the courthouse in Santa Maria, California, a tent city housed twenty-two hundred reporters covering the Michael Jackson trial.

Logan Pass was closed due to rockslides and snow. I could still ride the southern part of the park, but there was no guarantee that the pass would be open by the time I arrived in St. Mary, in which case I'd have to return the way I'd come. I was already behind schedule, and even if the pass opened, the route would add a minimum of four days to my trip.

So, I decided not to retrace that leg of my route. Instead, I would head west in the morning. That afternoon I rode to Lake McDonald Lodge, stopping along the way to look out over the lake and to walk through the ferns and forests. Back in camp I sat at my table and watched a deer munching on leaves pulled from a nearby bush. To be a deer, it seemed to me, meant a life lived in a constant state of fear, always on the alert for predators. And yet they seemed to live in a state of grace, alert, but with a Zen-like calm. Maybe it was resignation, an acceptance of their role in the chain.

The deer watched me as it chewed, as if gauging the threat. Or maybe I had that wrong. Maybe the deer watched me for the same reason I watched it. Curiosity. A desire for a glimpse into an existence that was so entirely different from its own.

# Kalispell Again

KALISPELL. I rode into town and leaned my bike against a wall. A man rode up on a mountain bike and then, shortly after, another. They were older than I. Though they weren't together, they knew each other—locals, both of whom had toured some on their own. One of them had gray hair, though he was hardly elderly. He looked at the helmet I held in my hand.

"I never wear a helmet," he said. "Never have, never will."

It was an act of defiance that had everything to do with not letting others dictate rules and nothing whatsoever to do with common sense.

"Do you pay when you camp?" he said.

"Sure," I said.

"I absolutely refuse to pay to sleep on the ground," he said. "I use to sneak campsites in ditches, behind old stores."

I laughed, and the other man, who wore a helmet and an army-green shirt tucked into a pair of jeans, turned and looked down the street. The grayhair said good-bye and rode away. I wasn't one to sleep in ditches. Still, I determined to seek out more free places to sleep. The seed had been planted.

The other man waited with me. He was soft-spoken and kind. He told me about the road ahead, what I could expect. I was hungry, and I remembered my experience at the restaurant, just three days earlier. I asked if there was an inexpensive place to eat.

"You picky at all about decor?" he asked.

"No," I said.

"Sykes," he said. "It's a grocery store too. Food's good. Got ten-cent coffee."

Sounded perfect.

Sykes was not fine dining. No well-dressed hostess greeted customers at the door or led them to a chair. Instead, one could seat oneself, either at the counter or at one of the several tables, which sat haphazardly on an old linoleum floor. Napkins weren't cloth but paper.

Smokers were in the majority, and most of the patrons were elderly. The men wore beards and timeworn flannel shirts with suspenders. A group of women wore bowling shirts.

I took a seat at the counter and was immediately handed a menu. My coffee cup was filled the second I turned it over. The waitress was friendly, courteous. I splurged on the $7.95 Prime Rib Special, which was delivered on a platter with steak sauce and gravy for my mashed potatoes. I listened to the old-timers give each other a hard time. They teased the waitresses, a small crew of women who could dish it right back while making sure the service they gave never wavered. The restaurant, like the clientele, was old but clean and entirely lacking in pretense.

Later, at a Main Street stoplight, a teenage boy in the passenger seat of an old Plymouth van waved, smiled, and looked over my gear. He gave me a thumbs-up.

So, I thought, this was a Kalispell different from three days ago. And, I realized, no moment in time could accurately portray any given place. How much of what I perceived on either day was an accurate portrayal, untainted by preconceptions, expectations, the fickleness of mood swings? I knew this: twenty years earlier I had considered Kalispell the perfect western town, and now I was feeling that way again.

It had rained every day for over a week, and my gear, my bike, and my person were covered in mud. That evening, against the spirit of my ditch-camping friend, I checked into a cheap motel. I emptied each of my panniers, spreading out the gear on the bed, and I cleaned the bags in the shower, streams of dried dirt turning to muddy water as it swirled down the drain. I hung the bags to dry and then washed each of my stuff sacks. Most of my clothes were damp, if not soaked, so I put them in the single washer in the guest laundry room. I bought a small box of detergent and emptied most of it into the wash, saving a small handful, which I carried back to my room and dumped into the empty plastic wastebasket.

I took the wastebasket outside and filled it with water, turning the detergent at the bottom into suds. Then I borrowed some old rags from the woman at the front desk, who thanked me for not using the room towels. With the rags I cleaned the bike, wiping the dirt and mud and grease from the derailleur, brake pads, cables, pedals, chain and chain rings, the frame.

Back in the room I rinsed my tent and tarp in the shower and hung them up along with my sleeping bag. I went through all of my gear, cleaning whatever needed it.

I went to check on my laundry. The wash cycle was complete, but there were someone else's clothes in the dryer. I waited, reading in my room, checking the dryer every fifteen minutes or so, but the clothes remained. On my fourth try I decided I would take the clothes from the dryer and leave them on top. But the dryer was empty. I deposited the required three quarters and pushed START. Nothing. I tried three more quarters. Nothing. So I took the clothes out and hung them in my room.

I was almost asleep when the phone rang.

"This is the front desk. Were you doing laundry earlier?" asked a male voice.

"Yes."

"Did you take some clothes from the dryer by chance?" he asked.

"No."

"Are you sure?" Then he explained that the woman who had left the clothes in the dryer had gone back to get them, and they were gone. I was bothered, both by the idea that a person would steal another's clothes and the possibility that anyone might think I was the thief.

"I'm sure," I said.

The next day I asked the morning clerk about the clothes.

"All I know about it is from the note left by the night clerk," she said. "Far's I can tell, they were never recovered." The mystery of the missing clothes remained unsolved. It bothered me then. It bothers me still.

My handlebar bag was my most immediate problem. I decided to buy a new one. I rode to the downtown bicycle shop.

"I don't have any bags now," said the owner. "But I am expecting a shipment this afternoon, if you want to wait."

So I waited by browsing a couple of downtown galleries, a bookstore, sipping coffee at an Internet cafe. In the *Daily Interlake* "Law Enforcement Roundup" I read about a man named Goat Boy, who had been following women and telling them they were pretty. He'd been asked to leave the premises. A typical American town, I thought, with its laundry thieves, its flirting goat men.

When the bike shop shipment came that afternoon, there were no handlebar bags. The bike shop owner was as disappointed as I, and he apologized profusely.

I walked outside. I took the old bag and looked at it. If I drilled two holes through the plastic plate inside the bag, I could attach screws to the bracket. This would make the bag permanent so that I wouldn't be able to take it on and off, but it would at least be usable until I could get replacement parts. I walked to True Value and asked if they had a drill I could use.

"No," said the man inside. "We sell them, but we're not set up to let you use them. You might try one of the repair shops." He directed me to one nearby.

"No," said the man at the repair shop, "but you might try the pawn shop across the street."

"I had one about a week ago," said the man at the pawn shop. "You might try the carburetor repair shop next door." If this doesn't work, I thought, I'll just strap the bag to the rack. I was anxious to be back on the road.

The carburetor shop didn't have a drill.

"You might," said the man inside, "try the machinist shop across the street and down a block."

Against my own impatience I went there. Inside, long tables were covered with old tools. The shop had the feel of an old barn, damp and cool, with dots of dust dancing in the light stream shining through a side window. There were several people working inside. I walked up to a man in a green and blue button-down shirt with rolled-up sleeves, his hair parted on one side and combed over neatly. I showed him my bag, explained what I needed. Without a word he took the bag and held it in his hand, examining it thoughtfully. Then he cocked his head, a nonverbal "follow me," and we walked into a separate room in the back. He took an old drill, from where it hung on a mount on the wall, and then a bit from a drawer.

"Where do you need it drilled?" he asked.

I took a screwdriver from the counter and marked two spots.

"Can you see the marks?" I asked him.

He looked at me and smiled. "I don't have to," he said, and he handed me the drill. And then he left me alone to my work. His demeanor calmed me, and I drilled the holes easily.

I walked back to the front of the shop, found the man.

"How much do I owe you?" I asked.

"That's not necessary," he said.

On my ride into Marion I stopped for chicken fried steak at a bar/restaurant/casino. The TV behind the bar was turned to Fox News, and commentator Bill O'Reilly was having a contentious discussion with Michael Jackson's spokeswoman. Jackson had just been acquitted on molestation charges.

"That man likes a good fight," said a man sitting at the end of the bar.

"He's kinda conservative, ain't he?" asked a different man.

"Thinks he is. He don't speak for me none," said the other man.

"He's just a nut job," said the bartender.

I looked up at the TV. O'Reilly was speaking about the accuser's mother. "She's a despicable human being," he said. Even Jackson's spokeswoman seemed taken aback.

For my part I had no opinion about any of it. After days spent outside riding, I felt entirely disconnected from shouting heads on the small screen. I found it disturbing, stressful. At home I watched TV all the time, but having been separated from it, I could immediately sense the tension that it caused. I wished the bartender would turn it off, but his eyes were glued to it, and I ate hurriedly, anxious to be back out in the cool air, where the only chirping came from birds.

At Moose Crossing, just past Marion, I pulled into a campground and walked into the office/store. A middle-aged woman with long blonde hair stood behind the counter, and a man leaned comfortably back in a chair.

I asked how much to camp, and when she told me, I paid.

"It's a good place," said the man. "Big sites, private, quiet. You'll be comfortable here."

And I was, even though the night temperature dropped to twenty-four degrees. I slept huddled deep inside my sleeping bag.

Morning, June 14. Joan would be in Friday Harbor in eleven days. Inside the campground store I sat at the only table, where I was joined by a woman with a Swiss accent whose automobile tire had gone flat. She was waiting for AAA. She had lived in the area for nearly thirty years. I was thinking about the comment in the bar the night before: *kinda conservative, ain't he?* and I asked her about the local political leanings.

"Montana's a red state, isn't it?" I asked.

"Less so all the time," she sighed. "I was on the election commission. For a long time we feared Kerry was going to win."

During the course of our conversation she said that she was an environmentalist. Later she spoke derisively of those "environmentalists" who "come in and dictate what people have to do." This was a familiar conversation in the West, where the term *environmentalist* took two forms, spoken both with pride and derision. I pointed out the contradiction to her, and she laughed.

"It's true," she said. "The people here, we all love the forests, the animals. There was a house not far from us. Recently they cut down two beautiful lodgepole pines. For years I had looked out at those pines from my window. It broke my heart when they cut them down."

"So what's the difference between a good environmentalist and a bad one?" I asked.

She sighed. "It comes down, I think, to people coming here from the West Coast or the East Coast and telling us how we should live with the land. We were going to build a guesthouse near our house, so when our children and grandchildren came to visit, they'd have a place. This kid came out to inspect, make sure it was up to code. Fresh out of college. He said he'd have to check—wasn't sure if it was too close to wetlands. Well. The wetlands are on the other side of the acreage. We know that. It took nearly two weeks for him to get back to us—to tell us what we'd already told him.

"I'll tell you where the real wisdom is," she continued. "It's the old people who grew up here. There's a man lives near us. He's eighty, has lived here all his life. He taught me to understand wolves by watching elk. When the elk are lying in a field, spread out, there are no wolves in the area. But if they huddle together, you know there's wolves close by. There's so many things like that you can learn from people. That kind of learning can be lost on the educated."

"Has a lot changed here in the last thirty years?" I asked.

"Oh my, yes," she said. "Twenty years ago there was one real estate agent in Kalispell. Today there are at least a dozen."

We talked about the mountains in Montana versus the Alps she remembered from her childhood. She said, with a wistful tone of nostalgia, the Alps were something extraordinary, that I should visit them someday. I wondered, were she to return, how true to her memory Switzerland would be.

"Do you miss Europe?" I asked.

"Sometimes," she said. "But you know, they really don't like us there. We ordered the German news on our satellite. It's so biased against us."

Interesting, I thought, how easily she distinguished "us" from "them" when she was, in fact, both. In thirty years she had developed an American patriotism yet had retained her European accent.

Through the window we watched the AAA truck arrive. The woman rose to leave, wishing me a safe journey.

The store was empty then, except for the blonde woman at the register and another younger woman with long brown hair and wearing a light-green sundress. I listened to them as I took two cold drinks from the cooler to fill my water bottles. The woman at the register was from California. Everywhere I went, I'd heard people speak of "Californians" with the same derisive sneer they used for "environmentalists" and "liberals." I asked the woman if people held it against her.

"Naw," she said. "When I first got here and bought this place, people told me not to say I was from California. They said no one would shop here. So I started saying I was from Minnesota because I did live there for three years. But then I'd ask the people who came in where they were from—half of them said, 'California.' You know, people here really get along pretty well, despite our differences."

"I went to Evergreen College," said the other woman. "We didn't even have grades. You don't get more hippie-dippie than that place. I'm left of just about everyone else here. But people accept me. A friend of mine, a logger, asked me the other day, 'How many trees did you save today?' I said, 'I don't know.' I wasn't sure what he was gettin' at. He said, 'I saved a bunch.' I said, 'What do you mean?' He said, 'Well, I looked at a tree and said, you know, you're a good-looking tree. I'm not gonna cut you down today. Saved maybe ten, twenty trees. Cut down others instead.' I thought, Oh my. But we can joke about it. We all know where we all stand."

"People do blame Californians for driving the prices up," said the blonde-haired woman.

"Of course," I said, "it's the locals who sell at the higher prices."

"But no one wants to say that—at least not very loud. There was a couple here. The woman hated the influx of people, raged about it all the time. Said she couldn't stand to see how the place was changing, couldn't bear the rising costs. So she and her husband decided to move. But they sold their place for half a million dollars. I thought, you're doing what you're condemning others for." She shrugged. "That's progress, I guess."

It was raining, a good steady cleansing rain, which gave the lush forests a healthy green shine. Mist formed on the pine-covered hillsides, ghosts dancing between trees. I felt good, pedaled effortlessly. I thought back to my first day, over a month ago, how I had struggled my way up those Colorado mountains. I was in such a steady rhythm from the ride that I almost didn't see the moose standing up to its knees in the creek by the side of the road.

In the afternoon the rain slowed to a drizzle and then stopped. The clouds cleared, and I squinted in the newly found brightness of the day. It was one of life's most simple and pleasant joys: to be drenched by morning rain and slowly dried by afternoon sun.

# Libby to Troy

LIBBY, MONTANA, had always been a company town, at least since 1910, when a Wisconsin lumberjack named Julius Neils bought a local mill and made it into the most productive lumber mill in the state. And it was a good town, full of decent people and small-town life, where its unique identity was celebrated with Logger Days and Nordic Fest. A good place to raise a family, relatively safe, surrounded by mountains and seemingly clean air, away from the crime and violence and decadence of cities.

But for years Libby held a secret, kept suppressed, beneath the ground. Or maybe it was denial, an unwillingness to face the awful truth. Because the secret really wasn't a secret at all. Certainly, the powers to be at the W. R. Grace Company knew. State and federal officials knew. Doctors knew. Even the miners—some of them—knew. But who would dare to speak out about a company that paid so well? There were profits to consider and jobs and the economy of a whole community. Maybe it was just the price a family man paid for wanting more, wanting a good life for his family. So the secret stayed beneath the surface, festering, spreading. It took a reporter from the *Seattle Post-Intelligencer*—Andrew Schneider—to unearth the truth for all to see, to point out the asbestos elephant in the room. By then nearly two hundred people had already died from either asbestosis or lung cancer, caused by the toxic Zonolite vermiculite mine. And not just the miners. Family members, too, were dying, people who had never even been in the mines. Such was the toxicity of the poison.

Now the mine was closed. And still people were being diagnosed, even as I rode into town and my tire went flat.

The town was eerily quiet, with little traffic. It was nearly 7:00 P.M. A building that had once been a drive-up burger joint stood empty, the windows boarded up, the parking lot crumbling, full of puddle-filled potholes. I walked my bike to the picnic table that was sitting crooked on the lawn in front, a bowing shade roof overhead. I felt my tires and realized they were, in fact, both flat. I replaced the first tube but, in my rush to fill it with the pump, broke the valve stem. For good measure I repeated the mishap on the other tire. I re-replaced them both, using my final $CO_2$'s. I walked to the sidewalk and peered down the street. A sign ahead said, RV CAMPING. I left the bike and walked toward the sign.

There were a few RV's parked in some of the campsites, but except for the smell of charcoal burning, there was no sign of life. I knocked on the office door. A middle-aged woman with long blonde hair answered. She was talking on a cell phone. "Just a minute," she said into the phone, and then she put her hand over the receiver and asked me what I wanted.

"Do you have tent sites?" I asked.

"The tent sites are all very wet right now," she said. "I wouldn't pitch a tent on them." She thought for a minute. "I'll call you back," she said into the phone. She clicked it off and turned to me.

"There's the lean-to sites, but the ground's pretty rough for tent stakes." She looked behind me. "Where's your car?" I told her about my bike trip, that I'd left the bike a couple blocks back. She walked to the edge of the porch, peering around the corner.

"How much are the sites?" I asked.

"Fourteen," she said. "Do you have a ground pad?"

I told her I did.

"Tell you what. You can sleep in the room attached to the laundry room." She walked to a sliding glass door and opened it. The room was small, about ten square feet, with a concrete floor.

"Least you'll stay dry. It's supposed to rain again tonight," she said. "I'll let you stay there for ten dollars." I told her I'd take it.

"You know what," she said. "You've been riding in all this rain—you can just sleep in there for free. I'll take you to go get your bike."

"It's just a couple blocks. I don't mind walking," I said.

"I'm happy to give you a ride." She already had the keys and was walking toward her pickup truck. "Get in," she said.

"I live most of the year in Carson City, Nevada," she said, as we drove. "I'm just running the campground for some friends over the summer. My husband and I, we have eight kids, all adopted. One of my sons, Shawn, just died of brain cancer. He was only thirty-four."

"I'm sorry," I said.

"In my family," she said, "we believe that there's a better place than this one you go to after you die."

"I believe that too," I said.

She pointed to a black-and-white photo of an attractive woman clipped to her visor. "That's my best friend," she said. "She died of the same thing, about a month later. I guess I'm still mourning, kinda. That's why I came here. To spend some quiet time in Montana."

"Montana's a good place for that," I said.

"Yes, it is." We drove in silence then. She pulled into the parking lot of the old abandoned burger hut, and I loaded the bike into the bed of her pickup.

As we drove back, the woman pointed again at the picture of her friend. "I think she died so Shawn'd have someone he knows up there. I think they're up there together, looking down at us right now, laughing their asses off."

I nodded. I believed it.

"You know," she said. "You kind of look like Shawn. I thought that when you first knocked on the door. If I looked at you funny, that's why. Maybe that's why I'm being so nice to you," she said.

"How long has it been?"

"He died almost four months ago now," she said, "on February 18."

I didn't tell her, but that just happens to be my birthday.

Later that evening, after I'd rolled out my ground pad and sleeping bag and stored my bike in the little room with the concrete floor, I walked through Libby in the last remnants of the light of dusk. I thought back to that long-ago summer, when Libby had been a vibrant town, full of tourists and a summer sense of excitement. I'd camped in a city park, where I met a man named Steve, who told me about rock-and-roll rivers playing deep in the mountains.

The campground had been nearly full, and I felt lucky to get one of the last sites. I was sitting at my picnic table when he walked over and sat at my table, not waiting for an invitation. He wore crooked black-frame glasses and an old ragged T-shirt. His teeth were yellow, his curly brown hair uncombed.

"I'm Steve," he said, sticking out his hand.

I shook it. "I'm Daryl."

He was from upstate New York but now lived in Idaho. He spoke loudly and occasionally broke into raucous laughter for no apparent reason.

"I usually don't camp in places like this—I like to go alone into the hills," he said. "What did you say your name was?" he asked.

"Daryl."

"Sometimes I get a little spacey because of my past with drugs," he said. I could smell alcohol on his breath. "When I go hiking alone," he said, "I hear rock and roll in the creeks. I swear it. And I don't have acid on my head. But you have to go way back into the mountains, thirty to fifty miles from nowhere. Now, what was your name?" I repeated it again.

"Some creeks play the meanest rock and roll—sounds just like Jimi Hendrix." He said it as if hearing music in a creek was a profound religious experience, and, who knows, maybe for him it was.

"You have to be miles from nowhere," he repeated. "The hardest rock and roll you've ever seen."

Again, he asked my name, and when I told him again, he exclaimed, "Oh! Just like Daryl Hall and John Oatey!"

"Sara Smile," I said.

"You're a bitch girl!" he whooped, giving me a high five.

He rose then, about to leave me in peace. "Remember," he said as he walked away, "camp by the creek. Camp by the creek!"

Twenty summers later I walked back into that city park. The campground was still there, but it rested empty, not a single camper. It was smaller than I remembered, and there was a cemetery beside it. I found the exact site where I had stayed, where Steve had introduced himself. I had forever linked Libby to that man and his mystical rivers playing screeching guitars to their audience of one.

Now I knew I would remember Libby for the kind woman from Carson City whose son had died on the day I turned forty.

The ride out of town was steep but short, and then it leveled off into an easy flat. I wasn't on the road long before I felt a slight thumping in my tire, and I rode it that way into the town of Troy.

The best side of Troy rested two blocks off the highway—an old downtown with wooden storefronts. At the volunteer fire station a group of men sitting in chairs on the shaded lawn greeted me as I passed.

I browsed a small used bookstore that was run by a man from Portland. It was my last day in Montana, and I marked the occasion by purchasing an anthology of Montana writing called *A Big Sky Reader*, edited by Allen Jones and Jeff Wetmore. I asked if there was a bike shop in town, just for conversation. I fully expected him to say no.

"Sure," he said, and he gave me directions.

I came to a street at the edge of town. There was no sign on the house, but the address was the one I'd been given, so I knocked on the door. A jovial man with thinning hair and a round face answered. I told him about the thumping of my tire, and he nodded, told me to remove the tire from the bike. His bike shop was run out of a residential garage. Bicycles hung from the roof, and there were parts and accessories suspended from the walls. The man took the tire and diagnosed the problem—the tire hadn't sealed properly—and he showed me how to fix it. He took his time, worked meticulously with practiced hands. He said he was sixty but seemed much younger than that. In addition to running the bike shop, he taught fourth grade. He'd been teaching in Troy for over thirty years.

"The district would like me to retire so they can pay someone less," he said. "But I don't want to retire. I don't need the money—I just really like the kids. And what else would I do?" There was no hint of bitterness as he said this. In fact, he seemed to revel in the fact that his work had become an act of defiance, both against age and administration. I thought about other cultures that revere the wisdom of elders. How strange it was, all that was sacrificed in the name of economics.

I told him that I'd been having a lot of flats, so he put liners in each of my rims. Then he wished me well, and I rode away.

The day was sunny and warm, my tires were fixed, my belly was full from the strawberry-covered French toast I'd eaten at the local café. The mountainsides were lush with green, the sky a vibrant blue, and thick ferns grew by the side of the road. The hills were steep, but I was now conditioned for them and rode without stopping until I arrived at a sign with snow-capped mountains painted purple beneath a blue sky and bright-yellow letters reading: WELCOME TO IDAHO.

# Idaho

# Karaoke Night in Bonners Ferry

IN BONNERS FERRY two children, a boy and a girl, were walking a dog in the lawn adjacent to a parking lot. The boy was about seven and wore thick glasses. The girl was slightly older. She wore a dirty dress and a red Kool-Aid mustache. They walked up to me when I stopped, an unofficial welcoming committee.

"Are you getting pizza?" asked the boy.

"What?" I said. I reached down to pet their dog, whose whole body was wagging along with its tail.

"My mom's coming back," said the girl.

"I'm sure that she is," I said.

"We're getting pizza," said the boy.

The girl looked at him. "We always get pizza when we come here," she said to the boy. Then she turned back to me. "We're not supposed to talk to strangers."

"That's probably a good idea," I said.

The two children stood looking at me as if considering this. Then they turned and walked away.

I parked my bike. Main Street was vacant, but I could hear laughter and voices coming from a bar and grill at the end of the block. I walked closer. The sign said MUGSY'S. Inside, I sat on a barstool. "Dude, jail sucks," said a voice from behind me. It didn't seem like a paroled kind of crowd. I turned to look, but I couldn't place the voice.

The bartender was young, with blonde hair and a tight pink shirt that said NEW YORK in glittery letters. The bar was crowded, an after-work festive atmosphere. It felt like Friday, but it was Wednesday. It was happy hour, according to a lime-green sign behind the bar. Two young men sat on the barstools to my left, friends out to have a good time.

"Something to drink?" asked the bartender.

"You should order a Hefeweizen," said the man two seats down from me.

"That good?" I asked.

"Only the best beer ever."

I shrugged. "Hefeweizen," I said to the bartender.

"You want lemon?" she asked.

I looked over at the man, deferring to his judgment in the matter.

"Hef's not Hef without lemon," he said, so I ordered it with and a chicken wrap sandwich with fries. The waitress brought my meal. A sign on the wall said, BEAUTY IS IN THE EYE OF THE BEER HOLDER. I looked over at the man who'd recommended the Hef.

He was drinking Budweiser.

"The hell?" I said, pointing to his beer. The man's buddy, call him Ken, laughed.

"What?" said the man.

"I thought you said Hefeweizen was best," I said.

"It is. I'm not drinking for *good*. I'm drinking for *cheap*," he said.

I finished my meal and rode out to the fairgrounds. I'd been told I could camp down by the river nearby. There was a little league game being played in the park, and I could hear the chatter, the clang of the ball against an aluminum bat, the cheers of parents in the crowd.

The riverside wasn't set up for camping. The weeds were high and beer bottles lay scattered at the edges of the cul-de-sac of a road, which was really just two tire tracks in the weeds. It was the kind of location you might use for the discovery of a body were you filming a detective movie.

I returned to the fairgrounds, where there was a fenced picnic area with a roof, and I thought if it rained I would be fine just sleeping on one of the tables. Once the ballgame was over, the families slowly emptied out of the parking lot, and I had the park to myself. It was just past six, plenty of daylight left.

I heard water from across the parking lot. There was an RV dump station. The water hose had been left on, and water was flowing out across the gravel. Seemed wasteful. I walked over to turn it off but accidentally flipped the lever the wrong way, and the hose went berserk, dancing around in a looping rhythm, spraying everything—including me—within a ten-foot radius. I shuffled back out of its range. But

I couldn't just leave it. So I jumped back into the water stream and flipped the lever all the way off. It was the first day in over a week that I hadn't pedaled in rain. And now I was soaking wet. I dried off by walking in the sun.

When dusk settled in, I stashed my bike inside the fence and returned to Mugsy's. The bar had emptied, save for the bartender and her coworker, who was sitting at the bar sipping a cola. Happy hour was over.

"Hef?" asked the bartender when I sat down. It hadn't been my intent, but I said sure.

She brought it with lemon, and her coworker shook her head. "What kind of man puts fruit in his beer?" she asked me.

"It was your brother suggested it to him," said the bartender.

The coworker shook her head. "Lord, I wouldn't take man lessons from him."

"You find a place to camp?" asked the bartender. I lied and told her I'd found a spot by the river. I wasn't sure sleeping on top of a picnic table was legal. Plus, the fewer people who knew the better.

"You're camping?" asked the coworker. Her hair was dyed black, and she had a silver stud in her nose.

"Sure," I said.

She pointed at the beer. "Really roughing it, huh?"

It was a fair point. Real Idaho camping probably didn't include happy hours. Or lemon slices.

Or, for that matter, karaoke. Yet on the way back to the wilderness of my caged picnic table, I saw the sign in the window of the Last Chance Saloon. The night was warm and I was restless. I walked inside, expecting it to be nearly empty, but it was as if the whole town had been hiding there all along. The Ken look-alike recognized me, and he walked up, shook my hand in greeting.

"Where's your friend?" I asked.

He rolled his eyes. "We're not really friends," he said. "We just work together."

I sat at the bar. A clock made from green felt and pool balls showed it was nearly 9:30. A sign on the wall said: IF YOU APPEAR INTOXI-

CATED, WE WILL REMOVE YOUR DRINK. I glanced around the room. It was clearly a policy not strictly enforced. The border was only twenty-five miles north, and a large American flag stood behind the stage, along with two smaller Canadian ones. A man was singing a surprisingly skilled version of "Friends in Low Places." Two women worked behind the bar. Ken leaned against the bar beside me. He was handsome, soft-spoken, the kind of guy you'd cast as the young partner of the cop who first arrived on the scene of the body down by the river. There was a sadness to him. He'd grown up in this town, and yet in a room full of celebrating fellow locals he'd buddied up next to me.

"See her?" he said gesturing toward one of the women behind the bar. She wore a low-cut peach-colored blouse and tight blue jeans. She looked about twenty-five, probably the same age as he. I wondered if they went to high school together.

"She owns this place. She's married to the man running the karaoke machine."

I looked over at that man. He had gray hair, thinning on top, and a mustache. I looked back at the woman.

"He's sixty-some-years-old," said Ken. He said this with a sad loneliness that seemed to me mired not in disapproval but disappointment, and he eyed the woman, with a longing that the cleavage she was doing nothing to hide probably wasn't helping. I looked back at the gray-haired man. Seemed to me that if Ken were patient, she'd eventually be widowed. But I kept it to myself.

One song ended, and another began, to a loud cheer. A new singer had taken the microphone. The song was "Save a Horse, Ride a Cowboy." When the singer got to the verse, everyone sang along, and then all the women hooted and hollered.

On the corner of the dance floor one woman danced alone. She danced no matter the song, no matter the singer. She was very thin, and her brown hair swung around her face as she moved. Ken watched her, shook his head.

"Ain't a lot there," he said, "but she sure uses all of it."

One by one, local singers took the stage. There was a surprising level of talent. You can learn a lot about a community in a small-town karaoke bar, just by how the crowd reacts to each singer, how they hoot and holler at the ham who likes to tease or how they clap politely for the shy person's rendition of "Smoky Mountain Rain," even if it's a little off-key. It also struck me that, despite opinions and differences, there's a library of American music that unites us. When a middle-aged woman in a gray sweatshirt sang "Sweet Home Alabama," the whole bar sang along.

The music stopped, and there was a sudden buzzing of the multiple voices, rising to the ceiling with the smoke.

I turned back to the bar and started writing in my journal, and as I wrote, I sensed someone walk up to the bar to my left. I glanced over. It was the woman who'd been dancing alone. She ordered a drink, and while she waited for it, I could feel her eyes reading my words. I turned to her and smiled.

"What are you saying in there about us?" she demanded.

"Only good things," I said.

"Let me see," she said.

I handed her the journal. She read and then looked at me. She seemed neither offended nor impressed. She set the journal down in front of me, leaning close as she did. I could smell her shampoo.

Ken turned to look away from us. I had the feeling that he knew her. The music started, and she walked to the back of the room, set her drink on a table, and played a game of darts. Soon she was dancing again. All of this she did alone. For reasons I wouldn't be in town long enough to ever know, there was a space around her that no one invaded. I figured that space had a man's name around it, and I wondered where he was.

I finished writing, looked around. I felt every cell of the stranger I was. I said good-bye to Ken, shook his hand, wished him luck.

Outside the sky was clear. I could see Orion and the Big Dipper. I walked back to the fairgrounds and rolled out my sleeping bag on top of a picnic table.

Predawn, just light enough to see across the grounds, and I rose, paced, blew into my hands. I was still groggy, rubbed the sleep from my eyes. I walked to a downtown café. The sign in the window said

CLOSED. But a different sign said the place opened at six. I looked at my watch. 6:05. I peered in the window. Nothing. Then I realized I'd crossed into Pacific Time. I was an hour ahead.

I walked across the empty highway to a hotel/casino. Speakers outside played oldies, and my walk across the parking lot was soundtracked by Harold Melvin and the Blue Notes's "If You Don't Know Me by Now."

Inside the casino, and the music continued, along with the electronic beeping of the machines, the occasional clinking of coins. A yellow glow filled the room. A handful of people stared blankly at the machines in front of them as they pulled levers. It was not yet 5:30. I wondered whether they'd risen early or had been playing all night.

In the hotel lobby a woman in a blue blazer was walking toward me. She said something, but I couldn't make it out.

"Excuse me?" I said.

She looked startled, as if she had just then noticed me.

"I wasn't talking to you," she said. There was no one else around. Then I realized she was wearing a tiny earphone, a handless radio.

I read a paper and left the casino. From the parking lot speakers Manfred Mann was singing. "There she was just a-walking down the street." Back downtown the café was now open, and I ate a slow breakfast, warming my hands with a full coffee cup.

I spent the morning browsing gift shops, a small but well-stocked bookstore, a gallery, where I saw a painting by the western artist Tom Ryan: a cowboy is riding a horse down the side of a hill. It's dusk. The cowboy has a slight smile on his face. He holds the reins in his left hand. In his right he carries a bouquet of flowers and under his arm a six-pack. The painting was titled "Six-Pack Saturday Night." It was a picture of such pure optimism; had I the money, I would have bought it on the spot.

I would see Joan in just over a week, and I could feel her pull, willing me to the coast.

Sandpoint, Idaho, in 1985, had been an artsy outpost, a friendly town with galleries and shops. Now, though, it was a horror of traffic. Highway truckers, exhaust, and impatient motorists were being diverted through downtown. Though bigger, the town seemed a shell of its former self, and while some of the same shops were there, others had been replaced with real estate offices, which posted in their windows flyers showing exorbitantly priced homes and properties. It was difficult to cross the streets, such was the traffic, and I was eager to leave almost as soon as I arrived.

In the evening I set up camp at Mudhole State Park, and then I rode into Priest River, which had been settled by Italian immigrants who had come to work the local mill. I rode past the mill, past a strip mall, and through the downtown, where most of the shops were closed. It had grown dark and not only on account of night. Suddenly the sky filled with what I thought was distant thunder and lightning. I pedaled back toward the campground, unconcerned at first. But the storm moved swiftly, and soon the dark clouds above me exploded with flashes of electricity.

The race was on, and I sprinted frantically, reaching the campground and diving inside my tent, just as a loud crash of thunder roared and the sky unleashed a torrent of rain. Lightning flashed so bright and frequent, I could have read by its illumination inside my tent. The storm raged through the night, its racket reverberating around me. The tent was pitched in sand, and the rain fell so hard and fast that it pooled beneath me, transforming my tent floor into a waterbed. When I woke, the rain was still falling, and I waited, hoping it would slow, but finally I rose and packed my gear wet, the tent covered with leaves and mud that had splashed onto its sides.

When the rain slowed to a constant drizzle, I started to ride, but by the time I arrived back in Priest River, the downpour was pelting me mercilessly. I parked my bike beneath a storefront overhang and sprinted toward a restaurant with a lit neon OPEN sign.

Inside, paneled walls were covered with old license plates and digital paintings of horses running through purple lightning storms. I ate a plateful of biscuits and gravy, while a man who sat with his wife the next booth over told me that this area had the largest population of mountain lions in the country. His wife was very concerned about this. They had just moved from Cody, Wyoming, she said, to get away from grizzly bears, and now she had to worry about wild giant cats.

I told them I'd ridden through Yellowstone, and the man asked if I'd seen bison. I told him I had.

"One time," he said, "I was there with some friends. One of them dared this friend of mine to run up to a bison and poke it. So he did. The bison jumped toward him, and he ran, and we all told him the buffalo was chasing him. 'It's right behind you,' we yelled. But it wasn't really. Had just gone back to grazing." He laughed as he told me this. I tried to laugh, too, to be polite. Every year in Yellowstone bison kill people who get too close. The man's friend had been lucky. I wondered if he realized it. Here was a couple, I thought: the woman scared of a cat she'd likely never see and the man entertained by the harassment of a thousand-pound beast.

I finished my coffee. Outside the rain calmed to a soft drizzle. I browsed the downtown antique shops, where human pasts were stored on shelves, stacked in corners, displayed beneath glass. By noon the rain had stopped. I was out of the Rocky Mountains now. Washington was less than an hour away.

# Washington

# Fire Trucks and Rodeo Queens

AN ABANDONED BARN stood in a field of tall grass surrounded by barbed wire fence, with leaning wooden posts. The loft was open, and though the paint was fading, the rain had darkened the wood, a stark garnet red against a backdrop of mountain fog. Such was the effect of the gray, post-rain dampness. The effect was a softening of contrast and dimension, and I felt a part of it, a small figure in a yellow raincoat in the foreground of a pre-impressionistic landscape.

At an intersection stood an old wooden building, the Tiger Store, which was a small art gallery and historical center. Twenty years earlier the paint had been faded, and the store appeared like a last remnant from an Old West storefront town. Now the store had a fresh coat of paint and a new wooden deck built with large wooden benches.

From here Highway 20 led all the way to the coast. But first there were mountains to cross. I started the uphill climb, shifting into my lowest gear, and suddenly my pedals locked. I looked down. My chain was stuck in the derailleur. I thought at first it was because of the mud and grease and grime, but even after I stopped to clean it, the chain stuck, so I was forced to climb in my middle gears.

Dusk at Leo Lake. The state forest campground was primitive, with pit toilets. And yet the cost was twelve dollars. It was odd, the rates to camp. National parks, with their clean restrooms and full plumbing, had charged me five dollars. In Washington the state parks, with their full showers and clean facilities, only charged three. The national forests, though, the most primitive of all the campgrounds, and the least maintained, charged the most.

No one was stopping me from sleeping in ditches, though. I paid the fee.

With all the rain the lakeshore had risen above the boat launch. A NO PARKING sign stood three feet deep in water. Yet the water pumps ran dry, and my bottles were empty. I started to boil water from the lake, but I ran out of stove fuel. So I feasted on a meal of carrot sticks and plums before falling asleep to the throaty calls of frogs and the quacking of ducks. And then I was awakened by the familiar percussion of rain, building to a steady crescendo. How odd, I thought, to be thirsty in this land of perpetual wet.

The map of Highway 20 was worth the look, if only for the music of names—Twisp, Tonasket, Wauconda, Okanagon, Fidalgo, Winthrop.

Saturday morning I rode through the lush Selkirk Mountains. At a small store and café a man walked in through a door in the back. He had a large beard and wire-framed glasses. I took my time, and I could sense his impatience. What I really wanted was coffee. There were several tables, with menus, in an adjoining room.

"Something I can help you with?" he asked, finally.

"I think I'm just going to sit down and order breakfast," I said.

He glared at me. "The café is closed," he said.

"When do you open?" I asked.

"Eleven." It was clear he wanted me to leave.

"You don't have coffee then?" I asked.

He said that they did indeed have coffee and pointed to a small room beyond the café, where there was a coffeepot and several mugs resting on a tray. I walked back and poured myself a cup.

"It's okay if I sit here?" I asked.

He hesitated. "I guess." He seemed annoyed.

"You'd rather I didn't?" I asked.

"It's fine. It's just I have other things to do," he said.

Must be hard, I thought, to be inconvenienced so. But the sign outside had said OPEN. I sat down, determined to stay, no matter the level of welcome.

Oddly, the whole episode did nothing to sour my mood. Outside the sky was clear. My legs had grown strong, and even in my middle gears I easily climbed the steep hill past Old Dominion Mountain, and then it was down, into Colville, where I rode past a barrier blocking off a Main Street lined with people—children with balloons, heavy-set women in lawn chairs, men standing in groups laughing. One man leaned against a street post. He wore a cowboy hat and red suspenders.

"What's going on?" I asked him.

He looked at me, surprised by the question. The answer should have been obvious from the large banner hanging over the street: PRCA RODEO PARADE.

"It's a parade," he said. "Fire trucks and rodeo queens."

A woman wearing a red, white, and blue shirt, with stars and stripes, carried an American flag as she rode down the street on a brown horse. Following her was a group of women in cowboy hats, riding side by side, stretched all the way across the street. They each wore a white shirt, with a single red letter. In order the shirts spelled AMERICA. A rodeo clown rode a mule with a deer's antlers strapped on. Miss Rodeo Washington and Miss Omak Stampede, each with perfectly straight teeth and blonde hair flowing Farrah Fawcett style beneath their hats, waved as they passed.

At the funky Cafe del Mundo I ate a curry Madras burrito and washed it down with fresh raspberry lemonade. The waitresses all wore tie-dye; the woman behind the counter had a yin-yang tattoo, and though a contrast to the cowboy hats and boots, there was no sense of irony. My kind of town—a healthy mix of cowboy and granola. People decked in their identity of choice.

That evening I walked through the fairground mud and took a seat in the rodeo stands. The rest of the crowd wore blue jeans, cowboy hats, and western-style shirts, and they clapped for each of the calf roping and barrel racing contestants. In between events they all stood and removed their hats for the playing of the "Star Spangled Banner," the same AMERICA seven women from the parade, now all of them carrying American flags, circled the arena, to the delight of the patriotic crowd.

The loudest cheers, though, were for the children who bucked mutton bustin' out of chutes bull riding style on the backs of sheep. Fathers aided by holding their sons and daughters on and running beside before the sheep finally dumped the children to the ground. This was followed by a competition in which teams of teens took turns placing items of clothing on bewildered goats.

Bull riding headlined the event. The competitors had come from all over the West, but not one of them stayed on their bull long enough to get a recorded time. Most were already airborne even as the chutes were still opening, the final rider landing so hard that the paramedics were still attending him as the crowd slowly dispersed.

I walked back to Main Street, where I ducked into a dark bar. A young group of friends were drinking beer from pitchers and playing pool. On the TV the Mariners were playing the Mets.

I ordered a Fat Tire, a Colorado brew with a bicycle on the label, and the barmaid delivered it cold, tipping her cowboy hat—a gesture of good old-fashioned western chivalry—as she set it down on the bar in front of me. A cold sweat ran down the sides of the brown glass. High on the wall, opposite the bar, hung an old painting of a nude woman, lying comfortably on a couch. Baseball, rodeos, Madras burritos, beer, a Saturday afternoon parade. It was June 18, 2005. The Fourth of July was over two weeks away but I was filled with a wave of patriotic pride, and Colville, it seemed to me, was the perfect place to celebrate all that was good about America.

The welcome sign entering Kettle Falls claimed: "1,550 FRIENDLY PEOPLE AND ONE GRUMP." In 1985 a more rustic sign had said the same, except there had been only 1,224 friendlies then. Now the sign also advertised a Walleye Tournament and Town and Country Days. It also boasted Kettle Falls as home of Miss America 1992 and two high school softball state championships. The Rotary Club had added a greeting of its own, as had The Seventh-Day Adventist Church.

I felt welcome.

Still, I wondered, who was the town's lone grump? Was it the same person whom it had been in 1985? Or was it the sort of title that was passed along to the next generation, like British royalty? Did the grump live in town or up in the nearby hills, like the Grinch? When I asked in town, I received chuckles, but no one offered answers to the question they must have been asked before.

Finally, a clean-shaven man with a limp offered this: "Might be my brother-in-law. But if you asked him, he might say it's me." I thought I was onto something, but then he said, "Naw, I'm just playin'," and he got in a pickup and waved as he drove away.

I looked closely at the people I passed as I rode through town, searching their faces for identifying frown lines. But the grump of Kettle Falls was nowhere to be found.

The temperature was in the mid-70s, it was sunny, wildflowers were in bloom. I looked down as I pedaled and diagnosed the problem with my gears—the sprockets on my smallest chain ring were bent. I would have to make do without my lowest three gears, and I had a series of very steep climbs the next few days. But I wasn't worried or even irritated.

And this was something new, I thought, this lack of panic or frustration. I felt calm, relaxed, self-sufficient. In time the problem would be fixed. It was as if by searching for a grump and finding none, I had extinguished the one inside me. I realized, too, that the cold spring that had seemed as though it would never end was nearly gone.

Canyon Creek Campground was a musical feast of chirping birds and running stream, performed in an arena of cool, damp forest. A trail led through fir trees and lodgepole pines. Tiny berries dotted bushes with dollops of red and orange, and the forest floor was filled with wildflowers—Indian paintbrush and purple lupines and dashes of pink. I felt the air against my skin and through it a unity with the trees that produced the oxygen I breathed. In return I willingly shared my own exhalations. How easy it is, due to its invisibility, to forget that air connects all life.

The ride up Sherman Pass was sixteen steep miles. A deer sprinted noiselessly into the brush. Logging trucks passed, perfuming the air with the aroma of freshly cut pine. The lush green gave way to a sudden open dryness on the other side of Wauconda Pass, where the soil was sandy, with sparse vegetation of sagebrush and golden grass, a color theme of light brown, wheat, and olive green, with scattered pine and rocky outcroppings jutting out from the hills. A group of black cows stopped grazing to watch me, and when I stopped to watch them back, they trotted away.

Outside of Riverside a plume of black smoke filled the air. I came over a rise and saw fire on the dry hillside, orange flames, shimmering in the distance. Traffic was diverted through the town, as firefighters worked to douse the flames.

By the time I reached Omak the sky had clouded considerably. I walked my bike through the downtown streets and to the library, where a small farmers' market was being held on the lawn. I bought a bag of Bing cherries and then went inside the library to check my e-mail. I came back out to a slow drizzle and walked quickly to a bar and grill on Main Street.

Inside, the bar was mostly empty, save for the bartender, one waitress, and the grill cook, a young man with curly brown hair and a tattoo on his bicep. A couple sat in a booth in the back. One other man sat at the bar.

Four rough-looking men came in, clearly intoxicated. They walked to a booth and took a seat, laughing and loud.

"They're back," said the bartender. She was visibly nervous.

"Don't serve them," whispered the waitress.

"What should I tell them?" asked the bartender.

"Just say you can't serve someone who appears intoxicated," she said, pointing to a sign above the register that said as much. Then the waitress moved to the back room. I could feel the men's impatience behind me.

"Sure wish we could get some service," said one of the men, but the bartender ignored them. Finally, he walked up to the bar and stood beside me.

"Hey," he said. "Can we get a pitcher of Bud."

"I'm sorry," said the bartender softly. "I can't serve you guys. I have to cut you off." I could see that she was shaking.

The man cursed at her. I felt my grip tighten around my glass. The cook walked out from the kitchen, the door of which was behind the bar. The man turned to his friends and told them they weren't going to get served. They rose from the booth. I could see their reflections in the glass behind the bar. They glared at the bartender and the cook.

"This is America," said one of the men.

"I'm sorry," said the bartender.

"C'mon," said one of the other men. "They'll want our business down the block."

"We're coming back," said the first man, with a threatening tone. Finally, they left.

"You handled that good," said the cook. The bartender shook her head and took a drink of ice water from next to the register.

She came to refill my Sprite. "You okay?" I asked.

"I could have taken 'em, if I had to," she said.

## Okanagan to Friday Harbor

A TRUE OUTDOORSMAN MIGHT suggest that if the ground upon which you sleep has a sprinkler system, it's really not camping at all. My contention is that adventure and adversity can take many forms. When you awaken, for example, to a sudden, rattling, helicopter noise and then the thumping jet of water shooting against the side of your tent. My watch said it was 2:00 A.M. It took me a few minutes to diagnose the noise. Luckily, the sprinkler head was just outside my tarp. Had it been inside, I would have a better story to tell. I'm glad not to tell it.

The sprinklers stopped after about twenty minutes. Wide awake, there were new sounds to keep me from sleeping—alarms, sirens, coughing from inside the tent pitched in the adjacent campsite. Fairground RV parks were no hymns to silence. I rose early and was happy to leave.

It was a short ride to Okanagan. Without my low gears I was dreading Loup Loup and Washington passes, steep climbs, the memories of which still lingered after twenty years. So, I was happy to see the sign above the storefront across the street: BICYCLE SHOP.

I walked inside. The shop was open and fully stocked. It was a large, showroom-like space, sparkling clean, all merchandise meticulously organized, evidence of a kind of care, pride taken in the work done there. I determined right away my bike troubles were over, and when a man in a blue mechanic's apron greeted me and listened attentively as I described the problem I'd been having, my determination was confirmed.

The shop, though large, was a one-man operation, and I had no doubt he had a full day ahead of him. Yet if my appearance added to his stress, he didn't show it. When I explained that I was scheduled to be in Friday Harbor in three days, he nodded, said he'd get me in right away.

"Is this afternoon soon enough?" he asked. I almost kissed him.

When I returned later that afternoon, not only was the bicycle fixed, it had been spotlessly cleaned. He had replaced the small chain ring and the chain and then had carefully cleaned the grease and mud, had checked the brake cables and pads, had looked the bike over for any other possible problems. He had me ride it around the block a couple of times, just to check it out, make sure it was okay. The shifting was smooth, all gears intact. The bike rode like new, and I told him so.

"Nice day," he said, looking up at the sky. "You'll have a good ride now. I should get out too."

"Do you ride a lot?" I asked.

"When I can," he said.

"Maybe tonight you can go for a good ride," I suggested.

He shrugged. "I'll be here until ten, at least." I realized my intrusion had set him behind schedule. I apologized, but he seemed not at all put out.

"I close at six," he said. "Then it'll be quiet. I can just listen to music and work. Peaceful."

Reinvigorated, I stopped at a fruit stand at the edge of town for more cherries and plums, and the woman who rang up my purchase was friendly. A palpable goodness flowed, and I felt a lifting, tingling sense, an electric rise of the hair on my arms—that feeling I've known enough to realize that all that mattered led to it. If bodies and lives are intended as vessels for spirit, as surely they must be, I felt full.

It was a twenty-mile uphill climb to the top of Loup Loup Pass, and I wasn't sure I'd make it over before nightfall, but it didn't matter. Time, like the uphill climb, was no longer a foe to be conquered but an ally I was slowly becoming a part of. I could ride in the dark or stop and disappear into the forest, where I could sleep beneath a canopy of trees. I was realizing a slow dissolve of any distinction between human and nature. *Pattica samuppada*, a Buddhist term, suggests that all life relates interdependently, that none of us—plants, animals, humans—leads a separate existence. Atmospheric scientist James Lovelock's Gaia hypothesis, which he sets forth in his book *Gaia: A New Look at Life on Earth*, says something similar: "The entire range of living matter on Earth," he writes, "from whales to viruses, and from oaks to algae, could be regarded as constituting a single living entity, capable of manipulating the Earth's atmosphere to suit its overall needs and endowed with faculties and powers far beyond those of its constituent parts."

Not only is all life related, but in Lovelock's words, we live in a "world that is the breath and bones of our ancestors." Past and future are also related. A Native elder in New Mexico once explained it to me this way: "When you consider every human being in the history of the world who has died and been buried, you can see why we call the earth our Mother." The idea of Earth as ancestor is not just metaphor—it's literal.

My father says: "Everything we have comes from the soil." All time is carried in that soil, all hope.

A country is first and foremost a landscape, and this one deserved both care and reverence. This is not left-wing radicalism. It's self-preservation.

Daylight was fading, but from the summit it was an easy eight-mile ride. My eyes watered, and for a moment the world became a Monet-like impressionistic blur. When I blinked my eyes clear, I felt a mad joy toward the fresh air and the efficiency of bicycle gears, my lost weight, and improving cardiovascular health. Mostly, though, it was a joy that came from being outside.

Twisp. The very name suggested whimsical joy. I parked my bike and walked through town. It was dark and starting to get cooler. On Main Street I heard music and followed it until, once again, I was seated in a small-town karaoke bar, where enthusiastic effort sought to make up for lack of talent. A man wearing tight jeans and a cowboy hat sang, "Save a Horse, Ride a Cowboy." That his rendition was off-key mattered not a wit to the women in the place, who cheered as if the singer were a bona fide star. I'd seen it twice now: that song somehow inspired frenzy in western women.

I skimmed through the black notebook in front of me, a song list for the karaoke machine.

"You gonna sing?" asked the bartender. He had long dark hair, an exotic, Polynesian kind of handsome.

"No," I said.

"Well you oughta try," he said.

"I'll tell you what. It gets near closing time, and you need people out of here, I'll get up there. That'll clear the room."

He laughed and moved away to help other customers. A man came in and sat at the barstool next to me. He was slight of frame, with leathery skin, and he wore a black leather Harley Davidson vest.

I looked at the man, at his jacket.

"You ride a Harley?" I asked.

"Sure," he said. "You?"

"Trek," I said.

He nodded. "Better gas mileage, hell on hills."

"You ever go to Sturgis?" I asked.

"Naw," he said. "There's too much weather between here and the Dakotas to go that far without a roof over your head."

In the time I sat next to him, nearly everyone who came up to the bar to order, upon seeing him, walked over and shook his hand. They all seemed to hold him in a kind of reverence.

"How long have you lived here?" I asked.

"About sixty years," he said. The answer surprised me. I didn't guess him to be that old. Breaking my rule to never talk politics to a stranger in a bar, I took a chance and asked him about Twisp political leanings.

"It's conservative," he said, "mostly. 'Cept for the city assholes who move in more and more all the time." This was said deadpan, with no hint of anger or malice.

"So, when they say Washington's a blue state, do they mean the coast?" I asked.

"Yep. That's it exactly—two entirely different worlds here to there," he said.

"Why do you think that is?"

"In the city, people work, have retirement benefits—they're working to not have to work. Out here we scramble day to day, just do what we have to to get by. It's harder living in a way. But a city's expensive to live in, and people live above themselves—everyone's in debt. Out here you can live pretty cheap, and people pay for things. If the economy ever tanks, the city'll be in trouble. People won't know how to take care of themselves. But here we'll just keep doing what we've always done. City folks want this as their playground—don't want logging, don't want ranching, don't want hunting. But for us that's how we live, how we get by."

"So, you think that whole blue-red divide is an urban-rural thing?"

"That's exactly what it is," he said. "Two different worlds."

Onstage a man was butchering a country and western song I didn't recognize. We each winced and leaned our heads away from the sound.

"Oh, that's what that song is," said the man beside me. "Hell, took me three verses of his singing just to recognize it. My hat's off to him, though. Takes a lot of courage to get up in front of people and sing like that."

It was nearly eleven, and still I hadn't procured a place to sleep. The night was warm, and the stars were out. I didn't want a motel. I fought the urge to ride on toward Winthrop. Earlier I'd noticed a small park across from a swimming pool. The park had a stage and a small playground. A sign had said NO CAMPING, which I appreciated. It meant there would be no crowds or RV's.

The playground slide had a child's fort at the top, with wooden planks for a floor. Twenty years earlier I'd slept in just such a place, in an Oregon state park. A policeman, seeing my bike parked against the ladder that led to the fort, had climbed up and shone a flashlight in my face, waking me. I thought he would make me leave, but he had simply apologized, said he'd seen the bike and wanted to make sure everything was okay.

Now, in the Twisp city playground, I pulled my sleeping bag from its stuff sack and laid it out over the planks. It was a perfect fit. I reveled in the simplicity. It got old sometimes, the procuring of each night's sleep. On a clear night all I needed was a picnic table or a base-ball dugout or some bleachers. It was easy. Ride into town, wait for the concealment of darkness, and then you could sleep anywhere.

I lay on top of my sleeping bag. The night was silent. With my growing confidence came boldness, a lack of fear. Soon, on a similar night, such boldness would have repercussions. But for now I felt comfortable and safe.

In that time of dawn before sunrise I woke and sat up, the slick of the vinyl of my sleeping bag beneath me, just at the edge of the slide. I stretched and yawned. Unbeknownst to me, the sleeping bag was creeping over the edge, and suddenly, with a whoosh, I was moving down the slide. I landed on my side with a thud in the sand, tangled in my sleeping bag. I had ridden a bicycle two thousand miles, over mountains, through rain and wind. And yet here I had been unable to gracefully negotiate the simple dismount from a child's playground slide.

I stood, looked around. In the trees at the edge of the park a single deer had been watching. She must have wondered how a species such as ours ever made it to the top of the food chain. When I dusted myself off, the deer turned and disappeared into the trees.

I packed my bike quickly, shivering in the cool morning, and found a café, two doors down from the karaoke bar. It was just past five-thirty, and already there was a man seated at the counter, sipping coffee. I took a seat in a corner booth. The door opened, and a man whom I recognized smiled and greeted me. He was the bartender from the night before.

"Hey," he said. "You're up early. You did well last night." At first I didn't know what he meant—I hadn't sung—but then I realized he simply meant that I'd limited my drinking to a single beer and had left early. The waitress looked at me closer and then gave him a quizzical look.

"He was at the bar last night," he explained.

He seemed to me rather awake and refreshed. I was still wearing the same clothes he'd first seen me in. I wondered if he noticed.

"How late did you work?" I asked.

"We closed at two. I got out of there about two-thirty."

"What in the world are you doing here so early?" I asked.

He shrugged. "The breakfast shift. I'm the cook." I thought back to my conversation from the night before about people here scrambling to get by.

Johnny Cash's "Ring of Fire" and the bakery scent of cinnamon rolls, sweet rolls, bagels, donuts, gourmet coffee. Twisp was awake now, cars on the road, the sun rising over the hills to the east. I sat at a small table and read from the *Methow Valley News* police blotter. The writer had a quirky style, with small dollops of commentary added on. Here's a small sampling:

> "An intoxicated person in Twisp was yelling and swearing, which isn't very nice."

> "Twisp resident said the neighbor threatened to kill his dogs, so the cops were going to contact the neighbor and tell them they can't do that."

> "An upside down pick-up needed to be picked-up and put upside up. No injuries."

> "A Twisp landlord has been bothering a tenant and it is bothersome. Apparently he threatened to make the tenant's life miserable if she got a restraining order against him. Ultimately they both got restraining orders against each other. That should work."

And what the paper referred to as the "Blot of the Week":

> "A plastic triceratops was successfully removed from a road in Twisp."

A small boy, maybe four years old, and a woman in a fleece cap and an orange cotton dress had been sitting at the table across from me. Now they were standing at my table.

"My son wants to say hi to you," said the woman. The boy stepped forward, shy but determined.

"Hi," he said. I returned his greeting and asked his name.

"Shilo," he said, and before I could ask, he added, "I'm two." He smiled broadly, and his mother thanked me. Then they left me to my paper.

Outside the window a bicycling couple dressed in yellow and black jerseys and black Lycra tights carried bright-yellow waterproof bags. They wore black helmets. With their dark sunglasses they looked like bees, and they hovered around my bicycle, which was parked across the street. The man pointed at my bike, and the woman nodded.

A boy named Shilo in a town called Twisp and bee people on the walk. It all seemed to fit a morning that had begun with a tumble down a playground slide. I could feel the coast in the air, taste Seattle in the coffee, feel the lure of San Francisco in the mom's orange flowered dress. The Pacific was just a day's ride away.

I rode through Winthrop, past the pseudo-western storefronts, an ode to the old West, newly done. At Mazama I stopped at a lodge, where a group loaded kayaks onto the roof of a van. I felt healthy, ready to conquer the final push over Washington Pass through the Cascades.

Twenty-six switchbacking miles, jagged peaks, springwater runoff dripping down the sides of cliffs, cooling pockets of air. A stream ran so clear, I could see through to the rocks at the bottom. From the top of Washington Pass there was a quick and brief descent before the road rose again to the summit of Rainy Pass, then a downhill rush, past Ross Lake, its turquoise-blue water, the stream rushing beside me, and then over the Ross Dam Bridge. I stopped briefly at a campground to fill my water bottles and then continued through the damp air along the Skagit River, through Diablo and Newhalem.

I stopped at a temporary traffic light planted at a road construction site. The road had been reduced to one lane. I waited for the light to turn green then rode forward, thinking of Joan, trying to make good time so I could get to the ferry early the next day. The road was lined with temporary concrete walls on each side.

I came around a curve and hit my brakes hard.

An suv was headed directly toward me.

The driver glared at me as I squeezed by, but my light had been green. Unnerved, I slowed, careful around the curves. And then I was out of the construction zone and moving past the thick ferns that lined the road. It was growing dark as I passed through Marblemount, but I kept riding, finally stopping in Rockport, where I set up camp at a city-run campground by the river.

Adjacent to the parking lot was a bar, and I walked inside, thirsty, hoping for a grill. Heavy metal played on the jukebox. I had to holler my order of orange juice and Sprite.

The bartender scowled at me, a look of such bitter disgust that I actually edged back on my stool. "I can sell you an orange juice, and I can sell you a Sprite," she said. "But you have to pay for both, and you gotta mix them yourself."

At the end of the bar a young woman, maybe twenty, was unleashing a profanity-laced tirade that would have made Quentin Tarantino blush. An elderly woman listened and tried to provide counsel with words that were slurred.

"It's one thing to treat me like that at home, but he does it in public," raged the young woman. I tried not to turn to look at her, but one sideways glance revealed a bruise beneath her eye.

"What you do, you don't put out for him when you get back home," said her mentor. "For a long time."

Or, I thought, you don't get back home at all.

I finished my drink quickly and slipped quietly out the door.

Joan was already in her hotel room in Seattle. In the morning she would take the shuttle to Anacortes and the ferry to Friday Harbor. I had sixty miles yet to ride.

After a short, steep climb the road flattened into an easy highway, the shoulder wide, the sunshine cool, and clouds drifting lazily across the sky. I rode into the hillside town of Concrete, where I stopped at a small café. The dining room was small, with four booths against each wall and a handful of seats at the counter. I sat at one of the booths, looked over the people, the old bearded men, their shirts worn and faded, a large bald-headed chef, a pear-shaped waitress. A young woman rose from her seat at the counter and, with an exaggerated limp, moved behind the counter, helping herself to coffee. Three men wearing ball caps and old T-shirts entered and sat at a booth. The limping woman brought them menus, even though, she told them, it was her day off.

The screen door squeaked open and closed with a bang, and a squat man wearing a faded orange T-shirt that said WHO'S YOUR DADDY? waddled in and sat at the counter.

The woman's limp was pronounced, and when no one commented, she said, "I'd like to turn in this body for a new one."

"How old are you?" asked the waitress, who was probably pushing fifty.

"Twenty," said the limper.

The waitress walked away, shaking her head, mumbling under her breath. She brought me coffee and then walked to the booth, where the three men greeted her by name.

"Can I get you anything else?" she asked, filling their coffee cups.

"A blonde, a brunette, and a redhead," said one of the men.

"I don't think I can do that," she said.

The man sighed. "Guess I'll have to say I'm fine then." The waitress walked back toward the kitchen. After a while the limping woman brought coffee to two old men sitting in the booth adjacent to mine. She told them she had thrown out her hip.

"What you need to do—," started one of the men, "do you have a washer machine?"

"Yeah," she said.

"What you do is you sit up on that machine. Fill it up with clothes first and run it. And then sit up there, just so, at the edge, so your rear end's hanging over. It'll throw that hip right back into place."

The woman looked at him blankly.

"I'm not kidding, it works," he said.

Politely, the woman said, "I think I'll stick with the chiropractor."

"Works wonders," said the man to his buddy, after the woman walked away. "I 'bout got the paint rubbed off on mine."

I continued west, taking in the sites, could feel the population changing, one town running up against the other, and the thick salty sense of ocean in the air. I rode into Burlington, the highway filled with traffic and stoplights. I was anxious to see Joan, knowing that she was

167

already on her way to the ferry terminal, but I tried not to hurry, not to look at my watch or cyclometer.

Across the bridge into Anacortes a side wind blew so strong off the water that I had to work against it in order not to swerve into the roadway. It was just past five, rush hour, and it was clear to me that I wouldn't make the 5:10 ferry. I stopped to check my schedule. The next ferry wouldn't leave until 8:25. Suddenly, there was no need to hurry.

Then I rode to the ferry landing and waited, trying to read. I wanted to see Joan, but rather than feeling anxious, I felt a sudden sense of calm. Over the last two days I had ridden over 173 miles. Maybe it was the impending culture of island time or that the ferry schedule put things outside my control. But after seven weeks of riding away from her, I was filled with the calm sense that everything would happen in its own due time. Whenever I got there, she'd be waiting, and she was just a ferry ride away.

It was already dark by the time the ferry landed in Friday Harbor, and I rode out of town, past the library. I had vague directions to the Juniper House, where we'd be staying, but it was too dark to see signs, so I rode blindly in what I hoped was the right direction. It was already past ten. Light shone from the windows of a house on a hill, and I rode forward, stopping in front. It was too dark to read the sign, so I walked to a window and peered in. She was there, sitting on a couch, watching TV. I moved to the door and walked inside.

I had lost thirty pounds since she'd seen me last, and now my hair was cut short. At first she didn't recognize me. But then her eyes got big, and she jumped up to hug me. I had never before been to the Jupiter House, but I was home.

# The San Juan Islands

THE PIG WAR was not really fought over a trespassing pig—it was just that the pig brought to a head what had already been brewing. The true cause was a vaguely worded document that delineated a strait as the international boundary. The confusion rose from the fact that the document didn't specify which strait, of which there were two. The British assumed the Rosario and the Americans the Haro. In between lay San Juan Island, and both sides laid claim. It was June 1859, and tensions had already been running high when the British pig in question wandered into an American garden and started feeding on potatoes. When American Lyman Cutler saw the unwelcome pig in his American garden, he shot it. To his credit he offered to pay for the pig, but when the owner asked ten times its worth in compensation, Cutler stalked angrily away. It was the last straw. In the days that followed, ships and soldiers from both camps stood armed and ready. Ultimately, though, cooler heads prevailed, and the governments agreed on a joint occupancy, which lasted for twelve years. All said and done, the pig was the lone casualty of the aptly named war.

The Juniper Lane Guest House sat on a hill overlooking fields of green. The air was filled with the scent of freshly cut grass. The house had neither the communal lack of privacy of the hostel nor the isolation of the chain motel, and unlike many bed and breakfasts and guesthouses on the island, it was reasonably priced. The house was full of art from the Middle East, Africa, and the Native people of the Pacific Northwest. Our room, the Pine Backpacker, had high ceilings, polished wood floors, and brightly painted purple and green walls.

"Whoever painted this room can't be grumpy," I said.

"Wait till you meet her," said Joan. "She's traveled all over, and she's so inviting and artsy, enthusiastic about everything. I think she genuinely lives to make people comfortable here. You're going to love her."

She was right. The next morning Juniper joined us for coffee. She had grown up on the island, and upon returning after years of traveling and staying in every style of accommodation, she had purchased the property from a good friend. The world had taught her what it meant to make others comfortable, and along with friends and family members, she had remodeled the buildings on the property, which was now filled with her eclectic spirit.

Joan and I spent the day in Friday Harbor, visiting the small gift shops, art galleries, coffee shops. At a farmer's market we drank lavender lemonade. That evening we shared a meal of chalupas with

Thai curry and shrimp curry noodles and Argentinean wine. With the sun setting and the green fields shimmering orange in the evening light, we returned to the Juniper House, where we joined other guests in the backyard by the fire pit, listening to their tales of travel. One couple had recently traveled to Botswana, and another told of a trip to Costa Rica.

Long I had dreamed of a life of travel, had once ached to see the world. But more and more, I have settled for the armchair approach, have lined my shelves with works by Pico Iyer, Paul Theroux, Tim Cahill, Mary Morris. The older I get, the more I find myself drawn closer to home. The West, perhaps, was exotic enough for me, and I would never tire of exploring it.

We listened to the other couples as they swapped tales of grand adventure, and after they left, Joan and I stood alone by the fire and watched clouds moving across the moon, the stars.

In the firelight I watched her and felt love, not rediscovered but a fresh awareness of what was already there. Spending time apart had been difficult, but from our distance we had grown closer. Was it nature, the days spent pedaling through the forests, the mountains, the feel of wind on my face, the cold on my skin, the sound of streams, the awareness of the weather, the rhythmic shifting of morning to afternoon to evening to night? Over the past twenty years how many days had I spent not knowing the phase of the moon, not sensing the shift of a changing weather pattern? How many days had I walked out after a day inside a windowless office, unprepared for rain or cold?

In *Arctic Dreams* Barry Lopez writes about an Arctic journey taken by the artist Rockwell Kent. Kent and two other men are shipwrecked on a fjord in Greenland during a storm. When the storm finally ends, Kent writes, "we stand there looking at it all: at the mountains, at the smoking waterfall, at the dark green lake with wind puffs silvering, at the flowers that fringe the pebbly shore and star the banks."

And then one of the men says, "Maybe we have lived only to be here now."

I thought of that quote and thought of those days spent pedaling, both twenty years earlier and over the previous two months. What was time but those stars, those planets, that space expanding infinitely outward from where we stood by a fire on an island that, rather than being isolated, perhaps better represented a harmonious blending of land and sea and sky? Twenty years since I'd last been here, and all I had wanted then was someone to share these islands.

The next afternoon Joan rented a bicycle and a carrier, and we rode out of town, past the small airport, and then up several very steep hills, before the road skirted along the rocky coast. It took us about two hours to ride the thirteen miles to San Juan County Park, where we set up our tent. From our perch on a low hill we could look out at the water, where two couples were kayaking. The skies were gray, and a single ship glided along the horizon. Before long it started to sprinkle, a misty drizzle so soft it was felt only in its cumulative effect. Pods of orcas swam in the distance, an attraction that caused whale watching boats to appear from nowhere and circle around the animals.

Camping in the site beside ours was a man named Richard, a wiry fifty-nine-year-old, 135-pound bundle of raw energy and opinions, who lived in Portland, where he worked in a bookstore. Later Joan invited him to join us by the fire.

"It's the only way to travel," he said. "Bicycling. I hate gas and cars, what the oil companies have done to the earth."

I asked if he didn't own a car, and he said he did not. "I ride my bike to and from work, take the rail when it gets too cold." He did admit to occasionally renting a car but for the most part managed to live without one. "Of course," he said, "that's Portland, where there's a rail, and life without a car is easy."

He said he'd been working at the same bookstore for twenty-five years, ever since he moved to Portland from his home state of New Jersey.

"I grew up in the worst place in America," he said. "Now I live in the best."

He looked out at the whale watching boats, which had circled yet another pod of orcas. "I wish those boats would just leave the orcas alone," he said. When a foghorn blew, he stopped in mid-sentence to bellow right along with it.

"I don't drink," he said, when he was done, "in case you were wondering. I used to, had a bad drinking problem. I was drinking two twelve-packs a day. One day these two women that I work with took me upstairs, had what's called an intervention." He laughed. "They sat me down, told me it was ruining me. They saved me. Haven't had a drink since. Cold turkey." That night, as we lay in our tent beneath the rain, we could hear him singing himself to sleep.

In the morning the three of us waited beneath a picnic shelter. Richard shared his food and stove fuel, and we drank hot chocolate together. Finally, the rain slowed, and Joan and I packed up, said good-bye.

"Maybe we'll see you again," I said.

"More than likely," he said. "It's a small island. And if I don't see you here, it's a small world."

We rode along the southern end of the island, past lush forest and lavender fields. In the early afternoon the sun came out, and we stopped at an Alpaca farm where hand-woven clothes made from Alpaca hair were sold. At Roche Harbor we parked our bikes beneath a tree and walked down a steep hill into the town. We walked along the docks, and I overheard one yachtsman telling another about a recent encounter he'd had with the border patrol.

"So the border guys, they come on my boat, and one of them, he sees the clip, so he knows I have the .33 Magnum on board. They went through everything, left a mess for me to clean. But hell, the gun's registered."

"Piss you off?" asked the other man.

"Naw, hell, it was good. They found stuff I thought I'd lost a long time ago."

Always the bright side. This was the spirit of the San Juans.

In the morning we would leave on a three-day kayaking trip to Stuart Island.

Somehow, despite our unsynchronized paddling form and my dyslexic rudder work, which was moving us forward in an awkward pendulum-like motion, Joan and I managed to maintain a northern direction, along the coast of San Juan Island. We had spent our first two days on land, looking out at the marinas, distant islands, ferries crossing the calm channel. Now we were on the water, looking toward the land, moving slowly past Snug Harbor, Mitchell Bay, past the private cabins that stood in solitude among the island pine. We paddled past Kellett Bluff and along the west side of Henry Island.

We had launched that morning from San Juan County Park. Our destination was Stuart Island, where we would set up camp for our three-day excursion. In all there were twelve of us, in seven kayaks, beginning with our guides, Steve and Sarah, both of whom lived in Seattle. In addition to guiding kayak trips, Steve taught junior high school. Sarah had studied Spanish in Guatemala and once led trips in Peru. The Carghills were a family of four from Cincinnati. Greg and Patty were both engineers, and Allison and Jeff were fourteen and twelve, respectively. The family lived a modest lifestyle, explained Greg, so they could travel together. Jennifer, who was from Iowa, had once lived in Colombia. She shared a kayak with Kate, who was a nurse administrator from New York. Mark and Melanie, from Kentucky, were getting married in September. They had planned this trip as a break from wedding planning. Melanie had never been camping before, and Mark was an outdoorsman. Unspoken was that this trip was, for them, a compatibility test.

It took time, but eventually Joan and I synchronized, and, though slow, we began at least moving in a direct line. After nearly two months on the bicycle it felt good to be moving again, this time powered by paddles rather than pedals. Together the group moved north of San Juan and into Speiden Channel. In the open water we struggled against a wind, which was slowing us considerably. At first it was fine. The kayaks bobbed in the water, a meditative motion that was enhanced by a watercolor-blue sky, muted by cirrostratus clouds. Distant islands, their hills covered with pine, dotted the view. But the wind was strong, and the crossing grew tiring.

"When's lunch?" asked Jeff.

"We'll stop just around the corner," said Steve, pointing toward a landing in the distance. But the corner never seemed to get closer. We would tease him later, and "just around the corner" would become the group's code phrase for famous last words. Now, though, we had all begun to drag.

"Did you mean that corner that's not getting closer?" asked Jeff.

"That would be the one," said Steve.

I focused on the view around us, the Olympic Mountains to the southwest, Vancouver Island to the west. I sensed Steve and Sarah were nervous, wanting us to have a good experience. A landscape that appears not to be getting closer can play havoc on the mind. Struggle, whether on bicycle or in kayak, was a mental exercise. Though slower, the physical work really was the same. The depletion was not of physical energy. We needed what happened next.

"There's a whale," said Sarah.

"No. No way," said Steve.

"I'm sure," said Sarah.

"I don't think so," said Steve. Normally, he would explain later, when there are orcas you know it because there will be whale viewing ships gathered. It's rare for kayakers to see them first because the whaling ships sit up higher. But there were no ships.

"I don't believe it," said Steve, and suddenly the orcas were clearly visible, moving through the water directly toward us, our own private viewing. Steve had us gather—"raft up" he called it—and form a tight group by holding onto each other's paddles. Two of the orcas, a female and a baby, came to within one hundred yards from where we sat. We could hear them, could see the white spots on their nose, their fins moving through the water. And then they jumped and dove. They must have swum directly beneath us.

The sighting gave us a new burst of energy, and we moved easily across the water, the excitement of seeing the orcas sustaining us. Suddenly the paddling seemed easier, and it wasn't long before we could see the landing.

"Is this the corner now?" asked Jeff, as we approached the small cove, and everyone laughed.

We ate lunch and talked excitedly about the orcas. Then we pushed on to Stuart Island, entering the long harbor in late afternoon, through a few scattered skiffs. Together we carefully carried the kayaks above the high-tide waterline and hauled the gear to our camp sites. The tents that had been provided were huge, or so they seemed after the small tent I'd become accustomed to. It was like moving from an apartment into a house.

Before dinner I walked up a primitive road, through the lush forest, cedar trees, and pine, ferns up to my waist. The forest was damp, cool, its effect calming, meditative. Much about these islands felt that way.

The new Stuart Island schoolhouse sat at the top of the hill. It had been built for fifty-nine thousand dollars in 1980, entirely with volunteer labor. The old schoolhouse was a museum now, full of old photos and stories. There was also a library. The museum and library were open, though no one was around, save for a cat that stood in the museum doorway and meowed at me in greeting. In the library homemade postcards made by the students, were for sale. Outside, a large chest was filled with T-shirts and notecards for sale. All purchases were on the honor system. You could leave the money, or, if you didn't have the correct change, there were envelopes included that could be used to send the money later. There was a basketball half-court. A basketball rested at the foot of the pole, for anyone who might want to use it.

Stuart Island had no electricity. Residents used either a generator or, more commonly, solar and wind power.

By the time I returned to the campsite the sun was setting. Sarah and Steve had prepared salmon fettuccine and apple crisp—far and away the best camp food I'd ever eaten.

In the morning Steve pulled out a map and tide charts and carefully explained our options for the day, making sure to involve us all in the decisions. He explained the advantages of each option.

We decided to paddle back out the harbor and then skirt the southwestern edge of the island, an option that took best advantage of the ebbs and flood and current.

We left midmorning, paddling back out of the harbor, where two osprey flew just overhead, and then making our way along the southern edge of the island, landing once at a small cove. Steve, Jennifer, Kathy, Joan, and I paddled to Turn Point Lighthouse, which stood in yellow grass at the edge of the rocky cliff at the island's northwestern point. The sun was warm, the thin clouds nonthreatening.

"Did you guys read the weather report for the week?" asked Steve. We hadn't.

"Well, it didn't say it would be like this," he said.

After lunch I lay on the beach and closed my eyes. Holding a warm, ocean-smoothed rock in each hand, I listened to the lapping of the water on the shore. I could feel the sun on my face, the rocks in my hand. I drifted into a peaceful sleep. When I woke, Jennifer was sitting not far away. She was stacking small rocks into artful sculptures and then taking photos of them.

She had taught English when she lived in Colombia, and I asked if she had felt safe there.

"Mostly," she said. "Like anywhere, you had to take precautions. But people were very kind to me.

"One night," she said, "I was with some friends at a bar, when Pablo Escobar showed up. When he came in, they locked the bar. No one could come in, and no one could leave. That way no one could tip off authorities he was there." The infamous Escobar, she said, made up for the inconvenience by buying all the patrons drinks.

That night, as we sat at the picnic table, we listed the life-forms we had seen: seals, river otters, blue herons, eagles, osprey, Dall's porpoise, anemones, barnacles, jellyfish, purple feather duster worms. In all we counted over forty different species. Though the orcas were a highlight, we all agreed, the trip would have been worth it even without them.

Steve and Sarah, as it turned out, were not just coworkers. They were engaged. This they informed us as together they made enchiladas in a Dutch oven. Mark and Melanie sat together, laughing. Looked like they had passed their compatibility test. For dessert we ate chocolate fondue, imbued with Sarah's secret ingredient: red wine. We stood around the fondue pot, taking turns dipping fruit into the chocolate. Greg, a large man with a voice that sounded just like Clint Eastwood, was smiling like a boy at Christmas. Romance was everywhere.

Earlier that evening Joan and I had walked through the forest, and I thought about lying on the beach with the sun-warmed rocks in my hands. How large the world was. You could spend a life in the Puget Sound and never experience it all, its endless world of complexities, the various interactions of sun and wind and water, the islands and marine life.

In the twelve years we'd been married Joan and I had lived in nine different states—New Mexico, Montana, Michigan, Mississippi, Connecticut, New Hampshire, Oregon, Alaska, Nebraska—each full of experiences I wouldn't want to relinquish. Still, sometimes I envied those who had spent a life connected to a single place. I had been fortunate over the last few years to study with the writer Ted Kooser, a man who could see the world just by looking outside his front window, could explore the variances of human nature in a downtown Dwight, Nebraska, café.

Whatever I was feeling about never settling down, it wasn't regret but yearning. Regret was a word that implied an emptiness, while yearning was an avenue toward fullness, a form of dreaming, of longing for all that we'd yet to do. Our lists were long. We had yet to study Spanish in Costa Rica, to hike in the Arctic wilderness, to buy a house or have children. But the truth was, since I'd met Joan, our days had been filled, and the problem was simply that we had so few. It was yearning that drove us, a continuous engagement with the imagination that I hoped would never end. I looked at Joan. We lived in difficult times but also times rich with possibility, with hope. The world, more and more, was accessible in ways unimaginable even twenty years earlier. An island could represent not alienation but integration, not a place separate from other land but one connected to water. Cultures were becoming hybrids, and admittedly, in the process something would be lost. But the world seemed fuller if seen not as isolated parts but as an integrated whole. The world was not getting smaller, as technology brought us closer; it was expanding, growing exponentially large. You could sit on an island in the San Juans with a woman from Iowa and discuss an encounter with an infamous Colombian drug lord.

"Do you think you could live in a place like this?" I asked Joan.

"I think I could live anywhere," she said.

We would probably never live on Stuart Island, the small community without electricity, where people volunteered to build a school and the library and museum were open to all who entered them. I would long for this island when I left it, like so many of the places I'd seen in the West. But I would carry this journey inside, where it, too, would continue to fill me.

The last day of our kayaking trip, and we were packed and loaded early, wanting to take advantage of the currents. We paddled past Roche Harbor, aiming for San Juan County Park. But the water grew rough, and we paddled slowly into a stiff wind. We turned, skimming the edge of Henry Island, where we had a very rough and difficult landing. Sarah and Steve huddled, debating softly among themselves, and then they suggested to us all that we go back and land at Roche Harbor, which we did, careful to stay close to one another to increase our visibility in the high traffic area of sailboats, fishing vessels, and yachts. We landed without incident and unloaded our gear, loaded up the kayaks on the back of the van that was there waiting for us, and within minutes we were back in Friday Harbor.

The only room available at the Wayfarer Inn was dorm style, which Joan and I shared with four strangers we would never formally meet and would know only through their snores. In town we ate dinner on a balcony from which we could look out over the harbor.

The next days were spent browsing shops, walking around town, visiting museums. On our last night on the island together, we moved from the community bedroom to a room called the boathouse, which was made from an old boat. In the evening we ate at a Thai restaurant, and then we walked to the pier, where we watched the sunset. The next evening we would ride the ferry to Anacortes, and Joan would board the bus that would return her to Seattle. We didn't talk about that now, though, as we stood on the pier. In less than a month we'd be together again, in San Francisco, and we talked about how fast the time would go, how it would really seem like no time at all. But despite the cool summer ocean air and the lazy bobbing of boats in the harbor, we could both feel our impending separation.

On the day of Joan's departure the bus was graciously late, and the driver helped load her bags and then waited patiently. The trip had treated us like newlyweds, and we acted in kind, prolonging our good-bye as long as we dared. And then I watched the bus roll away.

In Anacortes I checked into a cheap motel. That night, from the room next door, I could hear the sounds of love.

# Anacortes to Port Angeles

THE ROAD FROM FIDALGO TO WHIDBEY ISLAND was narrow with no shoulder and traffic was heavy. But drivers were courteous, waiting patiently behind until it was clear to pass. "God bless you, man," said a man in the Deception Pass State Park Visitor Center parking lot, after he asked me where I was headed and where I'd come from. The population of Washington had grown, but one thing hadn't changed from twenty years before: the friendliness of the people.

It was a sunny Sunday, the third of July, and the cheer of the impending holiday was palpable. I passed through Oak Harbor and then climbed the road past the outskirts of town. From there the road was smooth, and a tailwind nudged me into a steady feel-good rhythm. Tall bunches of light-green grass grew from sandy soil and swayed in the cool breeze. I passed a sign that said U-PICK-EM STRAWBERRY PATCH, and suddenly the scent of the ocean air was infused with the sweet smell of strawberries, and I watched families with small children picking the berries and filling small paper bags. A holiday tradition, I presumed, and I imagined those children, a night later, the skin around their mouths stained red from the berries as they watched firework displays. For the rest of their lives they would remember those Fourth of Julys, would always associate fireworks with the sweet berry taste.

A cure for depression, perhaps, this Puget Sound, where the people all were happy, kind, healthy. Was it only temporary, this geniality, a result of the short sunny season in a place known for its rain? Having only been here during summer months, perhaps I was like a man in Plato's cave, seeing only the shadows dancing on the cave walls and never the fire behind.

179

The sun was still high in the sky, though it was early evening, when I rode up to the ferry landing near Fort Casey State Park. It was five o'clock, and I bought a ticket for the six o'clock ferry to Port Townsend and then rode on, past the preserved buildings of the old fort, which had been named after Brigadier General Thomas Lincoln Casey. Fort Casey, along with forts Worden and Flagler, served to guard the entrance to Puget Sound during World War II. I returned to the terminal. Across the water the Olympic Mountains stood capped with snow as I loaded my bicycle onto the ferry.

I like to walk in a seaport town early in the morning, when the shops are all closed and the boats bob easily on the calm water. It was the Fourth of July. I walked along the pier. On a skiff anchored not far from shore, a man mopped his deck. Two women practiced aikido on the dock, their slow, gentle movements silhouetted against the gray-blue water. I walked through a bed of flowers—bursts of red, orange, blue, pink, purple. On the pebbly shore a woman in a straw hat gathered shells.

Slowly the shops began to open. Port Townsend is a friendly arts town, full of galleries and antique stores. One gallery displayed a series of local artisan work—watercolors of sea scenes, oils of fields of flowers, handcrafted ceramic bowls. In the back a small shed housed even more displays, including a marionette titled "Dancing Dubya." There was a small crank, and when I turned it, the wooden caricature of President Bush wobbled, his arms and legs moving awkwardly. I watched him dance. How little rhythm our president has, I thought. But then I realized: it was I who controlled the strings.

At an antique store I skimmed through a box of old postcards. One displayed a hand-colored photograph of Sequim Bay, circa the 1940s. On the back, in pencil, written in carefully legible cursive, the sender had written about a friend who had just had a baby. "I wonder," she wrote, "who the father is." Another postcard, from roughly the same era, showed a black-and-white photo of a large rectangular building with rows of evenly spaced windows. The building was labeled STATE MENTAL HOSPITAL, INDEPENDENCE, KANSAS. I read the back.

"It sure gets lonely in here," it said. "Do you think you might visit some time?"

A roadside café, and inside it was dark, a shift from the sunlight I'd been riding in, and I stood disoriented, waiting for my eyes to adjust. There was a long counter and tables and booths pushed closely together. Two men with beards and black leather jackets sat at one end of the counter. I moved to the other. The woman working behind the bar wore a gaudy straw hat with red, white, and blue stripes and various silver charms hanging beneath the brim—an eagle, Uncle Sam, flags. I ordered a plate of fish and chips. Hanging on the back of the drink dispenser, a photo printed on computer paper displayed a road-killed opossum splattered on a highway. A sign beneath it said the animal was for sale. Tuna-sized cans stacked on top of the nearby cash register had homemade labels: possum. I suspected a peculiar sense of humor at work but wasn't getting it. It seemed to me an appetite suppressant that was bad for business. Taped to the back of the register was an e-mail print-out explaining "the truth" about John Kerry. Another e-mail, with a General Patton caricature, explained the necessity of war to those who would understand "if only they'd put their Starbucks down and stop watching reality TV."

Two women and six children were sitting at a table behind me.

"Can we get our hamburger cut in fourths?" asked one of the women.

The waitress—who was standing behind the bar drinking soda from a straw—looked at her, shook her head. "We don't do that here," she said. She walked back toward the kitchen. "Geez, there's a knife right on their table," she said loud enough for all to hear.

A man in an apron came out from the kitchen and set a plate of deep-fried fish in front of me. The tarter sauce was a dark shade of beige. I forced down two bites but couldn't get the opossum out of my head. I paid quickly and left, squinting in the sunlight outside. American independence was two hundred and thirty years old.

That night I camped at Sequim Bay. In the dark I followed a trail down to the water and out to the tip of a long dock, where the sky filled with fireworks from four different shows. The streams of light reflected in the smooth water, such that I was standing both below and above the display. It felt like I was floating in space.

In the morning I walked back down to the bay. It was low tide, and I studied the variety of shells, barnacles, moss, seaweed. A single crab crawled sideways through the shallow water.

Twenty years earlier I'd stopped at a Finnish restaurant in Sequim called Hilka's Kitchen, where I'd met Hilka's daughter Kiki. It was the middle of the afternoon, I was the only customer, and when Kiki brought my food, she sat down across the table from me. She had blue eyes and a perpetual smile, and she asked me questions about my trip.

"How old are you?" she had asked.

"Nineteen," I lied. "How old are you?"

"I'm almost sixteen," she said.

Hilka invited me to pitch my tent in their backyard, so I rode to their house, using the directions and description she'd given me. The house was easily identifiable by the animals they kept—dogs with puppies, cats with kittens, roosters, and rabbits in a cage. I pitched my tent. Kiki's father walked outside. He was kind but stern. Camping in the yard was fine, he said, but I was not to enter their house.

That evening Kiki and I had sat in the yard and talked about school, about travel, about all that life after high school could be. I told her stories about the West I'd seen, of waking amid a herd of elk, of seeing bears by the side of the road. She talked about living near the ocean's edge, of exploring tide pools. I told her about the mountains of Colorado. We talked until there were stars in the sky, and her father called out to her that it was time to go inside.

We had stayed in touch, and her letters continued, even after her return address had a different last name and included pictures of her new baby son. I hadn't heard from Kiki since 1988.

Now I pedaled downtown, parked my bike. In 1985 the population of Sequim had been around thirty-two hundred. Now it was approaching five thousand. Kiki's parents had divorced. Hilka's Kitchen had long since closed for good.

Inside a small bookstore I asked the woman behind the counter if she'd ever heard of the restaurant. She hadn't. I asked others. Even those who said they'd lived in Sequim their whole lives had never heard of Hilka's Kitchen.

For lunch I ate at a downtown café. The waitress was young, attractive. She had brown hair and green eyes. She was dressed in black, with turquoise earrings. I foolishly tried to engage her in conversation, tried to think of questions to ask. She indulged me, out of nothing but professional courtesy, but she seemed distracted, ready for her shift to end. And I knew that whatever I'd felt once was gone. Sequim, for me, had been not a place but a memory. Now it was just another town.

But I would remember her, the flirtatious fifteen-year-old who drew hearts on her notes, who sat in the grass and shared her dreams. And wherever she was, I hoped she remembered me too, as the stranger who pedaled into her town one day and had slept in a tent in her yard.

A raccoon scurried across the highway in front of me as I pulled into Port Angeles, a harbor town with rain-worn buildings. In the night I walked in the rain, stopping at a small bar near the ferry terminal. For nearly an hour the jukebox played Eagles songs. Two men sat at the end of the bar. One of them was explaining how he'd received the purple and black bruise around his eye.

"We were drinking, and Warren started picking on Louis. Well, you know, Louis never does nothin' to no one. So I told him to cut it out."

"Geez. So have you seen Warren since?"

"Oh yeah. I talked to him today," said the man with the bruise. "We're cool."

"How did he end up?" asked the other man.

"It was a pretty even fight. But—," and with this the man smiled mischievously, "his shiner was bigger. And I think I busted his nose."

To good friends, I thought silently to myself, and raised my glass to my lips. It felt good to be sitting in this dimly lit oceanside bar, the door open to the sound of the rain falling on concrete, the frosty cool of the glass against my lips, "Peaceful Easy Feeling," "New Kid in

Town," "Tequila Sunrise." The Eagles. Just one more reason to feel patriotic on the day after the Fourth of July.

Three days removed from my good-bye with Joan, and I felt myself drifting into a familiar solitude. I had just been riding, letting the scenery flow by as I moved. It was my only chore. I wasn't concerned about the fall semester, for which I still hadn't ordered books for the classes I'd teach. A part of me pretended I wouldn't return to school at all. Graduate assistantship teaching was long hours with low pay—the work of a professional with the status of a student. Maybe it was time to move on, get a job that paid a full salary. The point was, there were options—and so many places in this West I loved where I wanted to live.

The bar grew lively. People were playing pool, all the barstools were full, the bartender was filling pitchers rather than glasses. I sipped my beer slowly, not wanting to drink a second one but not wanting to leave. The Eagles gave way to Tom Petty, zz Top, Sugar Ray. Finally, I emptied my glass and walked outside to my bike, which was leaning against a brick wall. Nearby, a group of rough-looking boys smoked cigarettes. The orange glow of the streetlight and the red and blue neon of the bar signs were reflected in the rain-covered street and sidewalk. Two of the boys held skateboards. A younger one had a fishing pole. They watched me as I pulled my rain jacket from my bike bags.

"I don't mean to be rude," said one of the boys, "but isn't this a bad night to be biking?" He was tall, with blond hair peeking out from beneath a black knit cap, and he was wearing a black T-shirt. The other skateboarder wore a black jacket. His hair was dyed black, and he had a silver ring in his lip.

"I biked here from Colorado. There's been a lot of these nights," I said. This was meant to impress them. If it worked, they didn't show it. I turned to the kid with the fishing pole.

"You catch anything with that?" I asked. The other boys turned to look at him.

"Yes," he said, an edge to his voice. "I caught a fish today."

"Just one?" I asked. I couldn't help myself.

"How many did you catch?" he asked. But before I could answer, he leaned back against the wall and looked the other way, a pose so full of forced angst I wished I'd taken his picture. Touché, I thought. I hoped his buddies were impressed.

I walked across town, not yet ready to return to the small motel room. I followed the sound of music to a small plaza and then down a flight of stairs to a room filled with a variety of multicolored lights. It was very crowded, people spilling out onto the streets. I went inside and sat at a tall table by the window. It was a young crowd, lively, the smell of perfume, everyone working hard to look naturally cool. Oddly, it was karaoke night, and from what I could tell from the dearth of talent onstage, this was no way to impress members of the opposite sex. I stayed just long enough to hear an unfortunate rendition of Queen's "Bohemian Rhapsody." When I left, the resonance of the botched melody was still stinging my ears.

In the morning I would leave for Victoria.

## A Side Trip to Victoria

A MERMAID WITH LONG GREEN HAIR sat holding an accordion. She wore a green bikini top and had a scaly green tail. She sat still as a statue, and if not for the slight rise and fall of her chest, I would not have believed she was real. But when a young girl placed coins in the case by her stool, the mermaid began to play, the accordion suddenly coming to life.

I was standing on the Victoria Pier. Earlier that morning I had rolled my bicycle through the customs building in Port Angeles and then onto the ferry, where I had locked it to a rack on the deck of the boat. So strong was the wind as we crossed the Strait of Juan de Fuca that when I went to retrieve the bike, it was lying on its side. A man standing nearby told me that it had landed hard when it fell. I picked it up. Luckily, the bike had survived unharmed. I wasn't surprised. Twenty-one years with me as its owner, a bicycle had to be able to withstand a crash now and then.

Now I stood watching the mermaid, entranced by her beauty and music, like a man who'd been too long at sea. And then, as abruptly as it began, the music stopped, and the mermaid froze in place. The little girl and I stared at her, but the mermaid looked beyond us, a dreamy longing in her eyes.

Twenty years earlier I'd sat at a table with a group of people in Alberta who—when pushed, and having been assured they wouldn't offend—admitted to an impatience with Americans, who they considered arrogant and self-centered.

"One time," said one of the women, "I was working the register at a McDonald's in Toronto, and I gave an American customer change in Canadian bills. The woman shoved the bills back at me. 'Don't give me this Monopoly money garbage,' she said. I thought, Lady, you're in Canada. This is what our money looks like."

Everyone at the table laughed. They'd all had similar experiences. And yet they'd all been to the United States and spoke glowingly of their travels there.

I walked farther along the pier. Artisans were hawking their wares of jewelry and watercolor seascapes. Vendors sold cotton candy, sodas, popcorn, and coffee drinks. Two bushy-haired men in dirty T-shirts played Celtic tunes on a fiddle and guitar. It wasn't until early evening that I rode down Government Street, past the many downtown shops and cafés, and then to the motel where I'd made my reservation. The man at the reservation center in Port Angeles had said that my bicycle wouldn't be allowed in my room—I'd have to store it in a garage provided by the motel.

I checked in. "Where should I store my bike?" I asked the woman behind the desk. She gave me a quizzical look, as if this was a most peculiar question.

"Well, in your room," she said, as if the answer was obvious. And I guess it was.

I spent the evening walking, past the strip malls, the highly trafficked roads, the various motels, the large shopping mall, fast-food restaurants. It felt like any U.S. city. Maybe city loneliness was due to the feeling of invisibility that stemmed from the way that people didn't make eye contact. Because of this, cities could seem unfriendly, but that wasn't necessarily so. It was an easy barrier to cross really. Just start a conversation.

I walked all the way back to the downtown. In a small café I talked to the waitress. I only had American money, and I apologized for this. I told her I didn't want to be one of those Americans, didn't want her to think I believed my money was better.

"I know our reputation," I said.

"Oh? What reputation is that?" she asked.

"You know. We're arrogant."

"Actually," she said, "my father grew up in Arkansas." She laughed. "You know, you Americans are always so concerned with what we think of you. Truth is, we don't think that much about it—a lot of Americans come here all the time. We just don't understand," she said with a teasing tone, "how you could have voted in that president you have."

I laughed. "A lot of Americans are scratching their heads about that too."

The next morning I walked through the city. It was different than I remembered. In 1985 it had seemed to me touristy and crowded and the people cold. Now it felt more metropolitan, and as a paradoxical result, the people less harried, more laid-back.

I sat at a sidewalk café, sipping coffee, when across the street I saw a man and woman carrying backpacks. Their backpacks were ragged, their clothes dirty and patched. They each had dogs, malamutes on leashes. They sat down on the sidewalk, against a wall. The man had a dark goatee and wore beige fatigues. The woman wore cut-off jeans and a red tank top.

I watched them with respect and envy. I felt like a fraud, me with my motel rooms, my wife's airline visits, my credit cards, my use of organized campgrounds. I was just a tourist, the bicycle mere novelty. I hadn't exactly been roughing it.

The man pretended not to notice the disdain with which he and his partner were held by the passersby, who averted their eyes. I wondered what stories they had to tell, what knowledge they had gained that I would never know, what they had learned of themselves and the world they were living in. The people who passed probably saw them as transients, homeless. And maybe they were. What is the line between transient and traveler, vagabond and bum? Hard life and adventure? Failure and success? Was my romantic envy as misplaced as other people's disgust? Probably. Still, I couldn't help but wonder how their experiences on the road might differ from my own.

I decided to approach them, to talk to them. I paid the waitress, but by the time she returned with my change, the couple was gone. I hurried across the street, walked around the block they'd been on and then the next block over. For over an hour I searched for them. But I never saw them again.

Earlier that morning, in my motel room, I had turned on the TV. There had been a terrorist bombing in London. Several people were killed, and many were injured. The United States was on heightened alert.

When I arrived at the ferry terminal early, I was surprised to see that already the line to board stretched out the terminal door and along the sidewalk to the street. The line moved slowly, while each passenger was searched. The crowd was subdued; a quiet tension filled the air.

Suddenly there was a loud bang, and all in line jumped, alert. The origin of the sound was quickly determined: the engine of an idling taxicab parked on the curb had simply backfired. We all laughed, releasing some tension.

"This is the wrong day for that to happen," said the man behind me in line.

After a day off the bike I felt the need to move, and yet it was that movement that kept me on the surface of things, never in any place long enough to get at its depth, to scratch below. What had I accomplished by going to Victoria? Foolish, to spend two days in a Canadian border town, informally talk to a handful of people and think that their ideas somehow represented the country as a whole. And it was arrogant, the very question "What do you think of us?" I deemed it all a failed exercise, which had only served to put me further behind schedule.

The long line wasn't helping my mood, but mostly it was the reason behind it—the misguided ideology that promoted mass violence.

"What were you doing in Canada?" asked the security guard, when I finally arrived at the front of the line. It was a good question. I wished I had a good answer.

"Just traveling," I said, nodding at my bicycle. He looked at my driver's license and then my birth certificate. He determined I was who I said I was and let me through the security zone.

I pushed the bike onto the ferry, careful to lock it tight so it wouldn't fall again. Though the rack was long enough for twenty or thirty bikes, mine was the only one on board.

On the ferry, as we crossed the strait, I watched the people. Families and couples mostly—very few other solitary travelers. The smooth water, the slow drone of the engine, the thin gray altostratus clouds. All of it served to create a sense of pall over the crossing. Suddenly, from both sides of the ferry, two coast guard patrol boats appeared. The boats, each armed with machine guns, escorted us through the water. A palpable sadness filled the boat. The horror of the attack in London seemed not so far away, and watching the guards, their guns pointing out ahead from stabilizing stands, we were confronted with the reality of the threat we were all constantly living under. I walked out onto the deck and held onto the rail.

"Look," said a man standing next me, pointing toward the water, and I saw them, two Dall's porpoises. They jumped and darted beneath the water and then jumped again. Watching them, our hearts lifted. The mood change was palpable. In her book *Swimming to Antarctica*, the long-distance swimmer Lynne Cox writes about an episode in which dolphins once surrounded her as she swam in shark-infested water. I thought about the week before, when we'd been kayaking, frustrated trying to make our way against the waves, when suddenly those orcas had appeared, and we'd all moved from frustration to delight. It was as if they knew, as if they could sense somber moods and sought to provide solace.

# Port Angeles to Shoalwater Bay

HORST AND JEANNY THANHEISER had been serving food in Port Angeles for nearly twenty-five years. Now they were in their final week as owners of the Tannhauser, a small German restaurant. They had arrived in America from Germany in 1964 and had moved to Port Angeles in 1981. Now, in their mid-sixties, they were heading off in their RV to see the country. This they told me as I dined on a plate of schnitzel. It was after the dinner rush, and I was the only patron.

"I never get tired of seeing this country," said Thor.

"Won't you miss the restaurant?" I asked.

"No," said Jeanny.

"Yes," said Horst.

And they both laughed.

I had planned to ride all the way to Hurricane Ridge, where on a clear day you could see the Olympic Mountain range, their snow-capped peaks just across a short valley. Twenty years earlier deer had posed for my camera in front of those peaks. Now, though, it was cloudy, and it was just starting to rain. At the Olympic National Park Visitor Center I was told that the last few miles of the road already were shrouded in fog—too dangerous for a bicycle. Disappointed, I headed back into Port Angeles and checked into a run-down hostel. I was given a bed in a room that slept four.

San Francisco was roughly one thousand miles away, and I had sixteen days to get there in order to meet Joan's flight. I calculated: roughly sixty-three miles per day. I had no reason to believe I couldn't make it that far.

"What follows two days of rain here?" asked the breakfast waitress at the café on the outskirts of town.

"I don't know," I said.

"Ninety more," she said. "What follows five days of sunshine?"

"I don't know."

"The weekend," she said. It was a humor specific to the Pacific Northwest, and on cue the rain outside began to fall harder, a flurry of drops plunking against the windowpane. I sipped my coffee slowly, trying to wait it out. But the rain never stopped, and I shouldn't have worried. This was Washington, where even the rain was pleasant. It fell slow and gentle, and I rode easily into Olympic National Park, stopping at Crescent Lake for a short hike among the western hemlock, Sitka spruce, elderberry bushes.

At a small store construction workers were working on a slanted roof, which, given the rainy conditions, seemed to me a little dangerous.

"Isn't it slippery up there?" I asked one of the men.

"Yep," he said, "But it's not a bad fall at all, once you get used to it."

I rode on, all the way to Mora, through thick forest. Olympic National Park was a singular place, with animal species that were found nowhere else in the world, including the Olympic marmot, torrent salamanders, and snow moles.

In the morning, along the shore at Rialto Beach, I walked a solitary coastline of sand and rugged waves, the beach lined with tree trunks worn smooth by water. I looked out over the ocean. The natural world was in constant flux, and nowhere could this be seen more readily than at this shore, where beaches shifted with changing climates and seasons. What once was coastline, I could now see as distant islands or rock formations. With climates warming the sea would continue to rise.

This Olympic coast was an important habitat for a whole range of marine life, from seagulls to sea lions to whales. The food chain here began with nutrients carried to the surface by upwelling currents feeding the plankton, which in turn fed the species that provided food for others, and up the chain they climbed.

I spent the morning walking on the beach, waves crashing against the rock formations in the water and then rolling onto the sand. A Colorado landlubber, twenty years earlier I had learned about high and low tides the hard way, on this very stretch of beach.

I had walked in the sand, shooting photographs in the tide pools—a purple starfish, shells, crabs. I hiked far along the shore, past the steep cliffs. It was the first time I had ever seen the ocean enough to sense its expanse, without islands or land on the horizon. Two bald eagles circled overhead, moving closer and closer until they were low in the sky, seemingly just out of my reach. I walked and walked, entranced by this ocean, where even on a Saturday in the summer, there were no crowds.

But when I returned, later, I found those cliffs I'd walked around were now standing deep in water. I had to claw my way up the back of the steep cliffs, careful not to slip. I made it but not without effort. It was a good lesson to learn.

Now I was careful, watching the water as it rolled on the sand, gauging how far it rose. I didn't walk nearly so far, though I wanted to, wanted to see this whole coast. I vowed again that I would hike it someday. I closed my eyes, listened to the water, the calls of the seabirds, sounds soothing and meditative such that, once again, I had to force myself to return to the road and the campground.

Saturday, the sun low in the evening sky, and I was worried the next campground, Kalaloch, would be full. But when I arrived, there were a handful of open sites, and I found one, pitched my tent amid the trees. The light shone through the hemlock trees, creating a canopy of soft green light.

On the beach groups of campers sat on driftwood logs around campfires in the sand. I could hear their voices, their laughter. A group of young men played touch football. But the park-like presence of people did nothing to distract from the lure of the natural scene. Small flocks of birds flew low over the water. The wet beach reflected pink clouds, and the waves tumbled high on the shore, once causing me a quick retreat to keep my shoes from becoming submerged. In all directions large logs lay strewn on the beach, the "bones" of the forest. They'd been carried by river water to the sea, smoothed by currents, and then tossed back to this shore.

I walked away from the fires, from the football game, felt the draw of this coast, understood why so many chose to live near it. I was grateful for its preservation, that it had never been lined with hotels or cities.

Peaceful. If a cure exists for whatever it is that is ailing the twenty-first century so far—this time of terror and war unlike any we've ever known; of internal and external strife; of a raging divide over how we define who and what we are; of paradoxical waves of proud patriotism and mistrustful cynicism; of a coming to terms with a history that is by turns both proud and heartbreaking in its sadness and brutality; of an alienation from families, other countries, communities, ourselves—then that cure must reside in places like the Olympic Peninsula coastline. Ocean waves rolling onto shore, water dripping from rain forest leaves, squawks of the blue heron, the glide of the seagull, scent of pine and cedar, wildflowers swaying gently in the breeze, and rain falling gently on our roofs as we sleep at night.

We need these places for replenishment, our bodies but vessels left unfulfilled by the consumptive material goods we try to cram inside, which, rather than satisfy, send us on endless cycles of desire that can never be satisfied but must be re-created over and over again by those who would have us believe that we are only what we own, when in truth we are everything but.

When nearly all the other campers were sleeping, I returned to the shore and watched the sliver of moon over the ocean, the Big Dipper overhead, a soft mist in the distance, a young couple huddled near the last remaining fire on the beach.

It was Sunday morning. The man was sitting alone at the Kalaloch Lodge bar. The other guests were enjoying their brunch in the dining area, looking out at the ocean view through plate glass windows. He looked to be about fifty and at first glance seemed distinguished—clean-cut, with gray hair and a well-groomed beard. His clothes were clean and perfectly pressed. He seemed happy, from the short distance I first saw him, and when our eyes met, he raised his glass to me in salute. He nodded toward the seat next to him, an invitation. It was not yet eleven o'clock. Too early to drink, but I justified it, at his insistence, on the grounds that I was a resident of Nebraska, where already it was afternoon. I was in the mood for conversation. But ours was a conversation that would be entirely one-sided.

"Yes, it is the Sabbath, and the Lord said, today is the day to purify your minds, to go forth and do as you pleaseth. Do you see that shelf?" he asked pointing above the bar. "The liquor cabinet is full and beckoning, it's a good day to be alive and away from that horrid television—all it shows are my old movies, none of which I've ever received royalties for, might I add, great ideas I've had and shared, only to see others take the credit. *Animal House*? That's one of mine—executive producer, my ass—all I did was sit in my New York office, tell them do as you please—they were just going to take the credit anyway."

I was still looking at the liquor cabinet and realized I was behind. The train had roared out of the station without me. Try to keep up, I scolded myself. And before I could raise a single one of the questions that came to me, he was off again.

"Nebraska, yes," he said. "The Midwest. I went to school not far from there—Wisconsin—the Badger Republic of the State of Wisconsin, where frat living was an art form, most of which we had to leave out of that movie. I am the one who told Woody Allen that the benefit of bisexuality is better odds in getting a date—men just don't do it for me, though." He'd taken a turn I wasn't prepared for, but I managed to adjust.

"And Eastwood? Clint Eastwood, that no good SOB, cretin, worthless swine! Took my idea, never returned my calls. Bastard. Ruined Carmel. Have you seen Carmel?" There was no pause for my answer. "Most beautiful beaches in the world. The only good he ever did was make a law that people had to clean up after their dogs. Dogs can't clean up after themselves. They're like people that way. Well, people can clean up after themselves; they just don't. They're sub-dogs. Wisconsin, you know," and I shifted, as we circled back, "was the birthplace of the Republican Party—there's your argument for abortions, right there: Republicans. They should have shipped the first ones up to the Arctic Circle. And the Democrats to the Antarctic. Then the rest of us could actually read and abide by the U.S. Constitution." He ordered another beer. I had yet to so much as sip from mine, and before I'd finished half, he would be on his fourth. With each drink his anger grew, and he dwelled deeper into every injustice he'd ever known. "I have Indian friends who have read the Constitution, and they all agree: it is the only true sacred document. And daily now we must watch it be defiled!"

I was exhausted, took a deep breath. I turned around and realized that the whole restaurant was listening. Two women at the table nearest us were giggling. I was embarrassed. I tried to think of a way to extricate myself. When I turned back, I once again was lost and tried to reorient myself, in case a reply to his diatribe should ever be expected.

"—Ouray, Colorado, in the canyon. My canyon. Taking a bath in the river there, when a golden retriever with a stick shows up and a woman behind. I knew the woman because I used to date her, and I said to the dog, I'd throw that stick to you, but I'm not wearing any clothes, and she called the police on me. I explained to them that she was schizophrenic, unstable. I'd had to screw her once just to get her to shut up! Do you know what most disappointed them?"

"What?" I asked quickly, pleased to finally get a word in.

"That they couldn't find any contraband in my car. Searched every inch of it. When the city clerk, a good friend, might I add, heard about that, he gave me a joint of the best stuff I ever had."

I sensed a shift coming on, and this time I was ready.

"I think that medical marijuana should all be homegrown. The judiciary!" He snarled. "Not at all judicious. I think they should all be stoned! Take that whichever way you choose." He laughed manically, and I let out a puff of air, glad for the temporary relief.

"I should be recording all this," I said, mostly to myself. But he surprised me by responding.

"Makes no difference, recording. They recorded me, and still I was misquoted. They said that I had a glow-in-the-dark sponge bath, when what I *told* them was that I had a glow-in-the-dark Sponge Bob." Again, he snarled, a noise that gave me a chill. He was entertaining, but it was train wreck entertainment, and I felt dangerously close to the collision.

"Look at that," he said. "Still raining out there. Seven feet of rain so far since January. I presume seven feet of water falling from the sky is a lot." He sighed. "It's just as well. It gets sunny for two days, and everyone gets happy, starts scalping people."

He laughed at his joke. I looked around nervously. Technically, we were on reservation land. Not a good place for scalping humor. But no one seemed to notice. Or perhaps they were looking away as a means of avoiding eye contact, lest they too be drawn into his lair. The mood in the room had changed. No one was giggling now. I could sense his rage was moving, like volcanic magma, toward the surface, climbing to a climax I neither wanted to be associated with nor even witness. A better writer might have stuck around, seen through to its conclusion the boiling point that now seemed inevitable. If such a story is of interest, it is a common one, easy enough to find—the American male on a bender, life-beaten, angry, ready to self-destruct. Were this fiction, it would be interesting. In reality it was ugly and heartbreaking. When he excused himself to the restroom, I rose quickly to leave. The women sitting behind me smiled, sympathetically. Outside I quickly mounted my bicycle and pedaled away into a fine misty rain. It was an easy ride south, worth getting wet not only for the escape but also for the names I saw along the way: Quinalt, Queets, Humptulips, Hoquiam, and Aberdeen, a town colored by the cumulative effects of rain and clouds, its streets lined with weather-beaten homes and quickly fading storefronts.

If I slept on a picnic table in a city park, I would rise with the sun, get an early start. But a motel inspired laziness. Checkout was noon. I left at 11:59. Groceries, library, lunch. It was already 4:00 P.M. by the time I rode over the bridge that led out of town and turned onto Highway 105 for an easy twenty-five miles to Grayland State Park, by the sea.

That evening I sat in a Grayland grill. The jukebox was playing oldies, and I realized that I had been hearing a lot of that music on the trip. That longing again—a longing, I thought, for any time before September 11, 2001. Natural to rely on nostalgia for comfort, an antidote to the hatred, to the unnerving knowledge that there were people out there who would have us all dead, even at the expense of their own lives.

I looked around the room. There were no movie stars or models or any presumption that there ever might be. Instead, the people had what seemed to me an inordinate number of missing teeth and crooked eyeglasses. The place was entirely lacking in glamour; what it had instead was old-fashioned friendliness.

The song on the jukebox sounded familiar, but I couldn't place it. I walked over, saw the playing number, and matched it with the CD. Alanis Morissette, "Mary Jane." I must have nodded in recognition.

"Did you find something out?" asked a man sitting nearby. He was elderly, had crooked teeth, thick black glasses. Sitting across from him at the small table was another man who looked just like him. Twins.

"I wanted to know the name of that song," I said. "Turns out, I have the CD."

"That's what we call having a blond moment," he said.

"I have a lot of those—probably have a lot more before the night's over," I said.

"Pace yourself," said the other man. "It's only Monday."

On the TV news above the bar CNN was still reporting on the terrorist attacks in London. A security expert was discussing what Americans must do to guard against an attack here. But the sound was turned off. People were laughing, and loud, boisterous conversation filled the room.

The country had changed since 9/11, but people were still living, embracing the world, defiant in their passion for life, drinking and dancing and worshiping and lusting and loving. You listened to the music and laughter in a place like this, and yes, there was scandal and division, corruption, excess, and waste, but there was also Johnny Cash and karaoke and rain forests and mountains and oceans and art and Fat Tire beer. There were old men sporting suspenders and gray chest hair and gaudy nautical knickknacks, and anywhere in America you could talk to people, and they would speak their mind and listen to you speak yours. What we all had in common was that we wanted to be good, and what we believed in, all of us—right, left, red, blue—was freedom and living well and doing the right thing by others.

I wish you were there in that Grayland bar, you so filled with hate. I wish you'd been sitting on the barstool beside me on that cloudy night in Washington, with Elvis singing "we're caught in a trap," the baseball homerun derby on a separate TV mounted on a nearby wall, grown men seeing how far they could hit a ball with a stick. I would have shared with you a pizza made with Italian sausage and Canadian bacon. You would see that we are good, flawed, decent people. If fear was the goal, you have failed, I think. Instead, we feel disappointment, heartbreak, shame. Sadness too, in the realization that the world we all share has come to this.

On the TV a replay of that morning in London, the sirens, the stunned look on the face of a man being interviewed, a deep gash and blood streaming like tears down a human face. And then the U.S. president, his response. The sound was still down, and I watched him. I knew we were supposed to be strong, "resolute," but just once I wouldn't have minded a tear in his eye, some palpable acknowledgment of the pain we were feeling.

The woman sitting beside me hollered in celebration. She was not watching Bush. She had been playing a game of chance and had finally won a clock that was designed to look like a life preserver. It was gaudy and silly. I congratulated her.

"I've never won anything before in my life," she said. And then she laughed, admitted that she'd been coming there for three straight nights and had spent much more than the clock was worth.

I walked back to the jukebox, put in a dollar's worth of quarters, played "Homeward Bound" (*I wish I was . . .*), Jimmy Buffet's "He Went to Paris," Gretchen Wilson's "Red Neck Woman," Dr. Hook's "When You're in Love with a Beautiful Woman," Bad Company's "Feel like Making Love," Jim Croce's "New York's Not My Home."

We Americans were, despite it all, virtually unhateable, given the chance to know us. The Big Gulp. Lou Pinella. Jazz. Yosemite Sam. The "Cotton-Eyed Joe." Stupid Pet Tricks. Mascots who shoot hot dogs into stadium crowds. Brides in wedding gowns doing the chicken dance.

Unhateable.

Earlier, as I'd walked through the campground, I had watched the families, small children riding bicycles, their father's nodding hello to me as I passed. A group of boys were playing, hiding among the trees. I watched those children, saw hope in their eyes, understood for maybe the first time how they represented the best of all we could be.

Now I finished my meal and walked to my tent in the dark. I could hear the ocean waves. The shore was shifting. Time wasn't standing still.

Morning. July 10. I had simply wanted coffee. I parked my bike in front of a building that looked like some kind of resort. A small man in a maroon sports jacket and bow tie greeted me at the door. Then he asked to see my membership card.

"I just want coffee," I said.

"Only members are allowed inside."

"How much is a membership?" I asked.

"It's free," he said.

And so it was that I became a card-carrying member of the Shoal-water Bay Casino Players Club. Inside I wandered through the rooms, disoriented by the flashing lights and noise. The whimsical, electronic chimes and musical riffs reminded me of a Hanna-Barbera cartoon soundtrack, incongruent with the elderly patrons, who sat sluggishly in front of the spinning rows of symbols, rhythmically dropping coins into slots. Or they sat in small groups at long cafeteria tables, eating off of paper plates.

At the deli the coffee was free, and I helped myself to a cup. I was looking over the menu posted on the wall behind the counter, deciding what to order, when an elderly man with drooping jowls and pale skin walked toward me, eyeing me as if he expected something.

"You are standing right where I'm headed," he said.

"What?" I asked.

"Did you ever hear of the Quaker—you know the Quakers, right?" he asked. I wondered if I had missed something. I still felt disoriented from the noise and the blinking lights. I could hear coins dropping against metal in the background. I nodded at the man. Sure, I'd heard of Quakers.

"This Quaker wakes up, hears a burglar downstairs, rattling through the house. The Quaker takes a pistol from his nightstand, walks down the stairs, turns on the light, says, 'My friend, I would never seek to harm thee nor ruffle a hair on thine head. But I must warn thee, you standeth right where I aim soon to start shooting.'"

He pointed behind me, and I realized I was standing in front of a salad bar. The man before me carried no pistol, but the moral of his story was clear. "You want me to move, then?" I said.

"If it's not too much trouble," he said.

So I moved and left the man to his vinaigrette. Just then, I heard my name over the intercom, calling me to the main desk. At first I wondered what I'd done. But when I got there, I was given an identification card and a free deck of cards. All told, the coffee, lunch, and membership cost me a total of $3.99. I lost nothing to the machines, as I didn't tempt them. If ever I return on my birthday, my drinks will be free.

It was time to visit a woman named Winnefred.

# Winnefred

ON A WHIM, at the Grayland campground, I had entered a phone booth and opened a thin phone book hanging from a chain, the pages warped and crinkled from the weather. I was sure that Winnefred would no longer be listed, but I looked anyway. The number was still listed under Dick Revenaugh, even though he'd been dead for nearly twenty years. I called.

"Winnefred?" I said. "It's Daryl." And it was as if she'd been expecting me all along.

"You're coming to visit," she said. It wasn't a question.

Twenty years earlier I'd been riding just past Grayland, the stone wall lining the shoulder, the high grasses that led to the mudflats and then the sea, an easy ride, late afternoon, and I'd been unconcerned about where I might sleep. A car passed, a long black car driving slowly. A short time later the car came back in the opposite lane. It stopped on the road beside me. A woman stuck her head out the window.

"You're coming home with us," she said. I looked at her. She was elderly, spoke slowly, monotone. I would learn later that she'd had an aneurysm many years before. The driver of the car was a small, thin man with a narrow face and gray beard. He had yellow, tobacco-stained teeth.

I explained that I didn't need a ride, that I was fine. But they insisted. Finally, I relented. I loaded my bike in their trunk and sat in the backseat. The floor was covered with empty beer cans, and I noticed they each held an open can. This was 1985, when drinking and driving was more hobby than crime. Don't get me wrong. It's better now. I'm just saying that's the way it was. The man drove so slowly, I'm not sure it mattered.

"I'm Dick," said the man. "This is Winnefred." And then he pulled a beer from the six-pack sitting on the seat between them and offered it to me.

"No, thanks," I said. "I don't drink." Because for a brief period between Montana and California, I didn't.

"Cigarette?" he said, offering me one.

"No thanks," I said. "I don't smoke."

He turned back. The car was skirting the center line, and I was relieved when he steered it back into his lane. I could see him looking at me in the rearview mirror.

"Well," he said, "we smoke, and we drink. And we like to make a lot of love. You don't have anything against that, do you?"

I assured him I didn't.

We had driven to their house, and Dick, who had once been a newspaper reporter, asked me thoughtful questions about my trip. Once in a while, he'd ask the same question he'd asked before, and then he'd laugh and say, "I'm so excited about having you here that I keep forgetting what I've already asked. It's just the greatest thing what you're doing. In a car you miss so much. But you, you see a man sitting on his porch, you can talk to that man."

He asked to see my wallet and with my permission looked through its contents. Then he asked to see my journal. He skimmed through it, handed it back to me.

"Write down everything," he said. "What you see, who you meet, what they say. Then when you get back home, keep up with it. Write down everything."

I have been keeping journals ever since.

Winnefred made a dinner of fresh clams and oysters and corn and peas and cheese and salad and bread. My appetite was her personal challenge.

"Careful," said Dick. "Those oysters'll make you horny."

He told me stories about his life, growing up in Michigan, working in San Francisco. They put me up for the night, and in the morning Winnefred packed me a lunch—four ham and cheese sandwiches and plastic baggies full of fresh vegetables and fruit. I could barely fit it all on my bike.

The following January I received a letter from Winnefred. Just weeks after I'd met them, doctors had found three tumors in Dick's intestines. Cancer. He had died in October.

Would I agree to get in a car with two strangers now, being twenty years older and less trusting? It's difficult to say. Despite the beer cans, there had been no sense of danger, only a genuine curiosity.

Now I rode beneath gray, layered clouds, which hung over the ocean. The nearby cliffs were covered in pine. The traffic was light, and the shoulder was wide. The wind was behind me.

By the time I called Winnefred from Raymond, she had already sent her neighbor John out to find me.

"He's five-foot-eight. He's in a yellow truck. He said he'd find you," she said.

I waited in town. When John pulled up, I was sitting on a downtown bench.

"Drove all the way to Tokeland looking for you," he said. He said this with a friendly chuckle, and he seemed not at all inconvenienced.

"How did you expect to find me?" I asked. We had never met.

He looked at me. "You were riding a bicycle, right?"

Indeed I was. He drove me to Winnefred's home.

Twenty years later, and this is what she wants to know first: "Were those sandwiches okay? I was afraid they'd be soggy."

I assured her the sandwiches had been fine. And then she hugged me, like an old friend, which I was, even though I had stayed with them for just one night and hadn't seen her since.

She was eighty-five now and lived alone in the same house, where she tended her blueberry bushes. She walked slowly, bent, her back hunched. She used a serving tray as a walker. Her gray hair was cut short.

"Is soup okay for dinner?" she asked.

I told her I couldn't stay long, maybe an hour was all.

She seemed crestfallen by this, or maybe I just imagined it because deep down I was hoping she'd say what she said next.

"What? You're staying the night, aren't you?"

"I don't want to put you out," I said.

"You're staying," she said. "The room upstairs is already made up."

She talked with a slight slur, the result of her aneurysm. I remembered her as frail, quiet. But she seemed different now. There was something regal about her slow and deliberate movement, as if she had grown into it after all of these years. She was perfectly at home in her age, her malady. We sat at the table and drank coffee, the three of us.

John helped Winnefred, he said, in between his care for the goats, chickens, cats, dogs, geese, ducks, and rabbits, all of which he and his wife kept in the backyard next door. In the meantime he volunteered at the VFW and American Legion. He watched me as he talked, let me know that he was just next door, that he had military training. When he determined I was no serious threat, he left.

"Tell me about your wife," said Winnefred, and I showed her the picture in my wallet.

"She is nice," said Winnefred. Could she tell from the photograph? Had she learned to read character through a person's face? It wouldn't surprise me.

"How long have you been married?" she asked.

"Thirteen years in November," I said. "How long were you and Dick married?"

"Five years," she said. This surprised me. I had always assumed it was longer.

"I was married once before, for just a year and a half," she said. "I didn't like it. We divorced. I never thought I'd marry again."

"Did you have kids?" I asked.

"Never did. Do you and Joan have children?"

"No," I said.

Winnefred rose slowly, used the tray to move to the coffeepot. She didn't ask me if I wanted more until she was ready to pour it. If she'd asked me, I would've said no because I wouldn't have wanted her to get up. She must have realized this. When I first met her, I'd assumed she'd had a recent stroke. But I learned this wasn't the case.

"I graduated from high school when I was sixteen," she said. "I went to the Carnegie School of Music in Seattle. I studied piano and violin."

Later she played for churches, for choral groups. She was playing every night.

"In 1965 I had the aneurysm. I was just doing too much.

"When I met Dick," she said, "and he asked me to marry him, I said, 'Oh, Dick, I'm handicapped.' He said, 'Winnefred, it doesn't matter.' I said I was too slow, I'd slow him down, and he said, 'It doesn't matter.' He was so good to me, always patient. He loved women—all women, didn't care what they looked like, just treated everyone with respect."

She talked slowly, her speech slurred. Often she paused, trying to retrieve the word that she needed. But she was sharp, remembered the exact spot where they'd picked me up, and she described it to me.

"You were so stubborn," she teased. "You wouldn't get in the car, kept saying you had to ride, had to make it all the way. You made us promise not to tell anyone, didn't want anyone to know you hadn't pedaled the whole way." She rolled her eyes at me. I laughed. I didn't remember, but I'm sure it was true.

"I wish I could drive," she sighed. "The one thing I miss the most."

That evening we ate a dinner of soup and then a dessert of berries with whipped cream and yogurt. In the evening, as she smoked a cigarette, we sat at the table and talked. She asked me about my teaching, and I told her I was still trying to decide what books to use for the coming semester. She wanted to know what I was thinking, and I told her either Dante or Chaucer.

"Oh, not Dante," she said. "He's too dark."

And so it was decided. I would be teaching *Canterbury Tales*.

I watched her as she set her smoke on the plate she used as an ashtray. She had macular degeneration, which made it hard for her to read. She was arthritic, her hands crooked and bent, twisted at the joints. Earlier she had refused help with the preparation of the meal, with the dishes. She didn't need help—only patience. I looked around the small dining room and kitchen. Something looked different.

"This table was turned the other direction," she said, "when you were here last."

"Did you and Dick buy this house together?" I asked.

"No. I grew up in this house—it was my parents' house. We moved here in 1936. My mother came here from Sweden. Her family was in Ontario and then Minnesota and then Portland. She met my father there. I had a brother. He was an engineer. He passed away. I never had kids. I'm alone, no family anywhere. So? Who cares? Do you care? I don't care." She took a puff of her cigarette.

The house, too, showed its age—cracks in the ceiling, worn carpets. But it was clean, perfectly organized. Together we moved to the living room, where we watched the National Geographic channel and then the news, her nightly routine.

I walked up the stairs to the guest room, that room full of books where I had slept once before. On the wall hung a photo: Dick, his arm around Winnefred, the two of them smiling, happy. The picture was faded. I looked at it for a long time. Never since have I met a man so curious, so interested. I understood what he had seen in Winnefred, what he had meant when he told her "it doesn't matter." It wasn't that he was willing to overlook her handicap. It was that he recognized how she had transcended it. She had once had a gift for music, and then the gift had been taken away. Her life had been a daily struggle since, but she had made that struggle her gift, without ever giving in to bitterness. Her life was a courageous act of grace, and she was no less an artist for it.

Our teachers are everywhere.

In the morning, after a breakfast of bacon, eggs, and toast and fruit with yogurt, I loaded the bike, said good-bye.

"I want to meet your wife," she said. "You don't have to wait twenty years."

I wanted them to meet also, and I hoped that they would.

I hugged Winnefred good-bye and then rode down the driveway. Not long out of Raymond, it started to rain, a slow drizzle, and I moved through tunnels of cedar and birch.

# Oregon

# Astoria to Newport

A CYCLIST I'D MET had warned me about the Astoria Bridge, said it had been the worst three miles of his journey.

"Traffic was heavy," he said, "there was a cross-wind so strong it kept forcing me onto the road. The ride wasn't steep really, but at its top, you look down, and the water seems a long way away. If you're afraid of heights—like me—it can be harrowing. I white-knuckled it all the way across."

"The water" was the wide mouth of the Columbia River just before it opened into the Pacific.

The continuous truss bridge had been built in 1966 and was engineered to withstand 150 mile per hour winds. Fortunately, the wind was calm and traffic was light as I crossed over the bridge. Even so, I could feel it sway as cars passed. The narrow shoulder was full of debris, and there were grates I could avoid only by swerving onto the road to get around them. It was frightening and exhilarating.

The bridge ended in Astoria, a town that had been a happy landing for many a journey. Lewis and Clark spent the winter of 1805–6 at nearby Fort Clatsop, eighteen months after leaving Missouri on their expedition. Astoria was named after German immigrant and millionaire John Jacob Astor, who in 1811 sent a ship with instructions to build a fur trading post. His vision, as Washington Irving wrote in his book *Astoria*, was an "emporium to an immense commerce . . . a colony that would form the germ of a wide civilization." The War of 1812 put an end to his plans, however, and Astor sold the post to a Canadian company.

By 1840 word of Oregon's rich opportunity spread, and the great emigration westward along the Oregon Trail had begun.

As I pedaled southward on Highway 101, it was easy to see what had drawn all those people here. It was sunny and warm, with soft ocean breezes. If ever a stretch of roadway was created for bicycle touring it was the Oregon coastal highway, and for its part, the state had gone far to encourage it. The Oregon Department of Transportation first started developing bike routes in 1971 and for years had been publishing and distributing free maps of the Coast Bike Route, complete with information on road grades, campgrounds, and bike shops. Tunnels through the coastal cliffs had buttons that, when pushed, alerted cars to the bicycle's presence, and campgrounds had set aside sites for cyclists at minimal rates.

At Arcadia Beach I stopped to look out over the blue water, the cliffs, the spotted towns along the coast. Then I rode past Wheeler and through Rockaway Beach, resisting the temptation to stop at every gallery and café along the way. In all I pedaled 111 miles. It was already dark when I pulled into Bar View County Park.

So focused was I on my ride that I hadn't stopped for food, so my dinner consisted of spoonfuls of what remained from a small jar of peanut butter. That night I walked on a trail through high grasses and then onto a beach of fine granules of sand, soft beneath my feet. A crescent moon hung over the water, and the star Spica glistened in the northwestern sky. It was warm, with no threat of rain. I listened to the waves on the beach, waves that lulled me easily to sleep. And in the morning I woke to two startling matters of significance: (1) the sun was shining, and (2) the wind was blowing from the north. Since I'd left, over two months earlier, I'd scarcely seen a day over seventy degrees, had faced headwinds and rain. Now, at last, it felt like summer.

It was a kind of ecstasy, that rhythm of physical movement, the perpetual turn of the pedals so natural to me at that point it felt effortless, as if I were gliding, the physical exertion entirely disassociated from my mind such that while my body worked, my mind was free to feel the breeze, the sun.

At Pirate's Cove, out the plate glass window looking toward the sea, a seagull, hovering lazily, peered inside the café, as if to see what the humans were having for breakfast, and then skillfully it turned its wing and let the wind carry it away. The waitress was young and cheerful. She had blonde hair and a silver stud in her pierced nose. I had the option of ordering a fruit plate instead of hash browns with my crab Benedict, and I expected a small portion, but what was delivered instead was a platter, piled high with bananas, strawberries, oranges, honeydew, and watermelon. I sat, staring at the plate.

"Is everything okay?" asked the waitress.

I smiled. "Everything is very okay." I ate the fruit, savoring each bite. Jack Johnson's soft music played from the restaurant speakers. I felt healthy, the healthiest I'd felt in a long, long time.

After my century ride the day before, I was taking it slow but still managed nearly seventy miles, despite a long rest on a sidewalk bench, where I savored a cone filled with vanilla Tillamook ice cream.

My bike map showed a detour away from Highway 101, a small back road that wove through the towns of Sandlake and Pacific City. I came upon a road construction crew and was delayed. A woman holding a STOP sign waved me to the front of the line. When the pilot car arrived, she said to follow it closely. It was about a mile over a very rough road. Just a couple of miles beyond, there was more construction, and I repeated the drill, breathing in the exhaust and the gravel dust of the pilot car. But after the cars had all passed, I knew that a new line of traffic had been stopped back at the site, which meant that I had the road all to myself for long stretches at a time. The back road was mostly flat and wove through green fields, the hills to the east covered in brush and everything green beneath that soft pastel blue of the Oregon sky.

In Pacific City I walked along the street, browsed a small gallery full of color photographs, sand paintings, and handblown glass. Then I walked across the beach. A man and his son were flying kites, which were hovering gently in the sky. Two surfers wearing dry suits and carrying surfboards walked to the water's edge, and against the horizon I could see other surfboarders on the water. There were old graybeard beach bums, women in bikinis, and middle-aged couples holding hands as they walked barefoot on the sand. Seagulls scavenged for bread, a kind of dance, with head bobbing approaches and swift getaways. A man in a Harley-Davidson jacket and black leather chaps and a heavy-set blonde were making out at the edge of the parking lot. An elderly man in a sun hat and light-blue windbreaker stood with his hands in his pockets, the silver light of the water inducing him to close his eyes and sigh in the sun. Nearby a woman was bending, her head low to the viewfinder of a Hasselblad 8x10 camera.

Trees on the cliffs stood skeletal, leaning and bent from years standing in the wind and water spray.

All of this I observed from my perch at the Pelican Brew Pub. At first I'd lamented the sight of the pub so close to the beach, but once I was situated at one of its tables, sipping from a frosty mug, I made my peace with it. I wanted to make it to Lincoln City, wanted to maintain a pace to assure myself I'd be in San Francisco in time to meet Joan. But when the waitress returned, saw my empty mug before me, and asked if I wanted another, I didn't answer. I knew I should leave. But it's hard to leave a brew pub on a Thursday afternoon on a sunny July day on the Oregon Coast. I tried to will myself to go. The waitress stood, waiting patiently, as I made up my mind.

"Sure," I said, finally. "One more." And I settled back in my chair.

The map showed an alternative route, up a steep hill, through cool, moss-filled forests of shade. I rode and rode, and it was starting to get dark, and the hill wound around, switchback after switchback. I didn't know where I'd camp. I could hear an incessant squeak coming from the drivetrain of my bike and knew it was time for a good cleaning.

But the road was beautiful, the forest thick with ferns and cedar trees and a flowing stream. The climb was five miles long, followed by a long descent, the air cool against my sweat, and a rush into Lincoln City and Devil's Lake State Park. I set up camp in the dark. The nearby sites were occupied by two cyclists from Connecticut, who were biking the whole coast, and John, a cyclist from England, who had ridden clear from Calgary. That evening we sat around a warm fire and swapped stories of our trips so far. The two New Englanders were young and had been riding for just over a week. This was their big journey before they began graduate school in the fall. John had toured all over the world. He was small and thin, with wire-framed glasses and an infectious smile that never went away, even when he described riding through blizzards in Alberta.

I had nine days to get to San Francisco, which was roughly 650 miles, or 72 miles per day. I would need to hurry, I knew, but how was one to hurry through Oregon, where the soft sand beckoned, along with the coffee shops and galleries, the friendly people, the ocean views, the hypnotic rush of water rolling onto shore?

In Newport I leaned my bike against a streetlight pole and followed a sign pointing to the Newport Visual Arts Center, where I walked down a short flight of stairs into a brick building. On display was an exhibit by a Japanese photographer named Takashi Morizumi titled "Children of the Gulf War."

The photographs were heartbreaking: a baby, deformed and bloated, the result of anencephaly; a seven-year-old girl named Fadel, screaming in her hospital bed, her kidneys and liver damaged from metal poison and radiation; a mother clasping her child's hand as the child suffered.

The photo that most struck me, though, was not of a child but of a middle-aged man. Fadel's father. He stood in a hospital corridor looking at the camera through weary, deep-brown eyes, his head resting against his arm. From the caption of the photo I learned that he had retreated to the hallway as a respite from Fadel's screams, screams resulting from an injection to draw out abdominal dropsy.

After the Gulf War Iraqi hospitals had been overwhelmed with children diagnosed with leukemia, cancer, and physical deformities. According to the exhibit flyer, the cause of these maladies could be attributed to the use of depleted uranium weapons used by U.S. and British military forces. Depleted uranium is a form of nuclear waste, which, when made into shells and fired at high speeds, causes severe burning. It also leaves behind toxic particles in the air and water. It can lead to cancer, leukemia, liver and kidney disorders, tumors, and physical deformities.

There was another woman in the gallery, and then a young couple entered. I watched them out of the corner of my eye, saw the stunned looks on their faces as they read the captions. I briefly made eye contact with the woman. She smiled, seemed embarrassed. And then I realized she'd been crying, and I looked away. There was a book you could sign and respond to the exhibit, and before she left, I saw the woman write in it. I walked over to see what she had written.

"May God forgive us," it said.

# On a Sunday Morning

THE MAN SAT SO STILL AND QUIET, I didn't notice him at first, sitting on the picnic table bench. The sun was almost down, and in the shadows of the trees it was dark, difficult to see. The Carl G. Washburne Memorial State Park hiker/biker site had been empty when I checked in, and I'd been hoping to have it all to myself. Now, as I returned from a much needed shower, he was there. I thought I recognized him as one of the Connecticut cyclists from the previous night, but as I walked closer, I realized I'd never seen him before. He was scrawny, unshaven. I noticed a frame pack resting against the table. He was watching me intently. I greeted him, and he looked at me warily, and I thought of the alert eyes of a deer just before it runs away.

He glanced at my bike leaning against the table. "How did you like that tailwind?" he asked. There was something of an apparition about him, a ghostlike stillness. It was as if he'd emerged from the woods, and in fact he had. He told me he'd backpacked through the forested hillside, had left Florence two days earlier.

I introduced myself. He said he was happy to meet me, but he was careful not to give his name. He asked me how much was the camping fee, and I told him four dollars. He nodded.

"I don't really like to pay to camp," he confessed.

I left him and walked down to the beach, hoping to see the sunset. But low clouds filled the horizon, and the sun disappeared without drama. By the time I returned, it was entirely dark, save for a small fire. I found my way back to the picnic table and lit my stove to boil water for hot chocolate. While I waited, the hiker appeared at my camp, startling me. I never heard him approach.

"Stop by if you want to share my fire," he said. I told him I would.

After I poured the hot water in my cup and stirred the cocoa, I walked over. He moved with quick, flighty motions, his shadow a dance that mirrored the flames as he took a log and placed it on the fire. The flames grew. I could see his thin, brown beard, and I guessed him to be roughly my own age.

213

I inquired as to his employment.

"I windsurf," he said. He was kneeling by the fire, adjusting the logs with a stick. "Part-time, actually. I work two months in Sacramento, and then I live half the year in Baja California, where I windsurf. The rest of the time I stay with my parents in Florence.

"I used to bike tour," he said. "But now I prefer to kayak. I've paddled up the coast many times. I usually leave from Seattle. I paddled all the way to Haines, Alaska, once. I saw a lot of bears, but bears don't bother me so much. It's raccoons I hate. I had a raccoon rip right through my tent once. Another time I was camping on the coast, way up in British Columbia. It was just at dusk, right before it got dark. I had an eerie sense that someone was watching me. I turned around. It was a mountain lion."

I was skeptical. Mountain lions have a reputation for steering clear of humans. To have one approach would be rare. He must have read my eyes.

"I couldn't believe it either," he said. "I'd been paddling alone for several days, and I thought my brain might be playing tricks. I blinked a few times, but it was still there. My heart was pounding. I stood up, waved my arms, tried to make myself look big, as they say to do. Not easy for a skinny guy like me. The lion didn't move. It didn't seem scared, and it didn't seem aggressive or mean. Usually, supposedly, when there's an encounter like that, it's because the animal is rabid. But the cat had an odd sense of calm, like it was just curious, was watching me. I picked up a branch and threw it toward him. Nothing. I threw rocks. Nothing made it run. It was getting darker. Finally, the lion left on its own accord, just turned and disappeared in the dark."

The fire had burned down, and there was only the glow of the embers. He spoke with the loopy stream of consciousness of one who spends time alone in the woods. I have heard myself talk that way. No, *loopy* is the wrong word. It was something else entirely, an intellect gained from solitude, an archaic form of wisdom, no longer valued. It was something I understood and envied. For what was this very trip to me but an attempt to reacquaint with what I had felt those years before? Such opportunities were fading, diminishing, so slowly and discreetly that even before our very eyes we did not see it happening, did not entirely feel its loss, though evidence of its effects were everywhere.

"I've bicycled this coast too," he said. "A couple times. You've seen the best of it. It gets different once you get to California."

"What do you mean?" I asked.

"Just relentless traffic, and the people are different."

"Different, how?"

"There are people," he said, "strange people who live on the coast. And by 'live on the coast,' I mean that literally. They move up and down the coast, sleeping covertly in the woods. The farther south you go, the more of these people there are, and the stranger they get. Be careful. Best to stick to organized campgrounds or motels."

The fire was nearly out, and I grew cold, realized I was tired. I excused myself and stood to leave. I looked at him but couldn't make out his face in the dark. There remained a slightly haunting quality to him. Had I not just conversed with him, I would have believed I was alone.

That night I had dreams, bizarre dreams. I was watching the stars through binoculars, and I could see them in detail, and then I was with Joan, and we were standing on a pier, looking out at the sky, and we could see Earth spinning slowly, glowing against the black darkness. I was back in Alaska, and I saw one of my former students, who, upon seeing me, immediately hunkered down to a wrestling stance, ready to grapple.

When I woke the next morning, the hiker was gone, his site sitting untouched in the early-morning air.

In Florence I ate a late breakfast and then walked across the street to a Safeway, where I overstocked on food such that I couldn't fit it all on my bike. Enough food, I thought, to get me to San Francisco—Bing cherries, Power Bars, peanut butter, Wasa crackers, instant mashed potatoes, pasta mixes, canned soup, stewed tomatoes, oatmeal mixes. My panniers were stretched to their limits, and I had to resort to putting the cherries and Power Bars in my handlebar bag, which was already heavy with my camera, lenses, film, my journal, a book, binoculars, a stack of fliers, business cards and newspaper articles I'd collected along the way.

Past Florence dunes of sand lined the road, miles and miles of sand. Twenty years earlier an entrepreneur who called himself Lawrence of Florence had led camel rides through the dunes, but Lawrence was gone now, had given way to a bundle of new dune buggy rental companies. Earlier, as I sat at the café, a cacophony of sirens rose and went speeding by. The waitress said it was about a daily occurrence: dune buggy accidents.

"People don't know that even a dune buggy flips when you try to ride it sideways," she had said.

I rode on. A Ford Explorer passed and, not far ahead, stopped on the shoulder. A boy, maybe eight, jumped out, and without even bothering to move to the curb side of the vehicle, pulled down his pants and vigorously brushed sand away. That I was riding toward him seemed not to bother him in the least. I heard laughter from inside the vehicle, and then the boy pulled up his pants and jumped back in, and the suv zoomed away.

With the sun bright in a late-afternoon sky I rode over the bridge into North Bend. On the other side of the bridge stood a pair of shabby motels. I stopped at one of them. A short man with crooked teeth met me at the office door and told me there was only one room left. The parking lot was empty. Then he quoted me a price of seventy-five dollars.

North Bend, from the north, seemed a run-down railroad town, with old, weather-beaten buildings, less than ritzy. Seventy-five seemed extreme. I rode on. It was warm, the wind still from the north, the pedaling easy. I was feeling cocky, unconcerned about sleeping. The road would take care of me. I had learned to trust it.

An old Arab proverb: have faith in Allah, but tie your camel at night.

Farther into town I saw a Comfort Inn, and I pulled into a convenience store pay phone, where I called for a price.

"One hundred thirty-five dollars," said the female voice on the other end. For a single room. It seemed odd. North Bend wasn't exactly a resort town from what I could see. All I needed was what amounted to an eight-hour nap. I would figure something out. In the meantime I needed to call Joan and then to eat. I found a pay phone at a convenience store, pulled a calling card from my wallet, and set the wallet on top of the phone.

Then, nonchalantly, I walked the bike to a pizza place. But I realized I didn't have my wallet. I left the bike parked against the restaurant wall and sprinted back to the convenience store. The wallet was still there, where I'd left it on top of the phone. Stupid, I thought. I was getting careless. I remembered the man's word's from the night before: be careful. I looked inside my wallet. Then I remembered—I still had the number for Randy and Carolyn Randall placed neatly inside the wallet, from when we'd met in Montana. They lived in Coos Bay, which was adjacent to North Bend—the same town, really. Was it rude to call so last-minute? I couldn't decide. I could just call, tell them where I was, see what they'd say. I called the number. A teenage girl answered. No, she said, Randy and Carolyn were out for the evening. I thanked her and hung up. Part of me was relieved. It was awkward calling people you didn't really know, hinting for a place to stay. I needed to eat. Then I'd figure out where to sleep. It wasn't a problem. I had a plan.

I walked into the restaurant, and a cell phone rang. About twenty people immediately reached for their hip, as if for a holstered gun. Twenty years earlier people had told me I should carry a gun. This time everyone had told me to get a cell phone. This was the new West, I thought—a room full of people reaching for their hips at the sound of a ring.

I ordered a small pizza and sat at a booth by a window so I could keep an eye on my bicycle. I felt restless, spooked. I shrugged it off as the result of getting into better shape. More energy. I wasn't so tired at the end of the day. When I'd weighed myself last, I'd lost over thirty pounds. I sat back and enjoyed my meal, listened to jukebox songs: Lynyrd Skynyrd, Sarah McLachlan, George Strait, Matchbox 20, Sheryl Crow.

Twenty years earlier I'd ridden into Sumas, Washington, just south of British Columbia. I was nearly out of cash. This was before ATM machines, before twenty-four-hour access to money accounts in faraway states. I went to a local bank to have money wired. But the money hadn't arrived before the bank closed, and I found myself suddenly stranded without cash. I rode to the edge of town. Behind the local high school there was a football field with a track running around it and covered bleachers. Because it was summer, I realized, no one would be around the school. I leaned my bike against the wall at the bottom of the bleachers and slept comfortably between two rows of seats. I remembered that now, and I looked up the address for the local high school in a phone book. It would be easy to slip into the field after dark, get a good night's sleep. I needed to do laundry, first. I rode to a small Laundromat, where a short heavy-set woman was doing what seemed to me an exorbitant amount of laundry. The only other patron was a man with arms full of tattoos and a black Budweiser T-shirt.

After a short time a car pulled up, and a man got out, walked inside, and started helping the woman fold the clothes. He carried a load to his car. He came back in, said something to the woman, and then went back outside. I could see him standing there, looking up at the sky. I wondered what he was looking at.

I finished my clothes and then walked outside. The man nodded at me and then proceeded with his upward gaze. I looked up. The sky had grown hazy, and through the fog I could just make out the lights of a plane, flying low, circling. The man in the parking lot seemed very intrigued by this.

"How long's he been circling?" I asked.

"I don't know," said the man. "He can't land because of the wind and the fog."

As we watched the lights circling in the sky, the man told me that he was from Fairbanks. "Three years ago," he said, "my wife and I decided enough of the snow and cold. We packed up all our stuff and started driving, headed to Florida. It was more expensive than we thought it would be, especially through Canada. We were running out of money. We were here on the coast because my wife had a sister up in Washington. We came through Coos Bay, and while here, I picked up a paper. There was an ad for a three-bedroom apartment, $250. I called. We've been here ever since."

He gestured toward my bike and asked me about my trip. I told him how far I'd come.

"Where are you staying?" he asked.

"A motel," I lied.

"Do you have a room yet?" he asked. I admitted that I didn't. He told me about a cheap place just south of town. I thanked him, and then I lifted my bike off the curb to leave.

He wished me luck. And then he said: "Listen. Keep your bicycle close around here. And do get a room. It's a good idea to put your bicycle inside tonight."

But my mind was already made up.

I rode for several blocks and then walked my bike. It was a hot night, muggy, a haze muted the streetlamps, and I pedaled, moving in and out of their circles of light. I headed to where I thought the school might be, up a steep hill. It was late, nearly midnight, and I was tired.

But the school wasn't at the top of the hill. There was a large grassy field with soccer goals at each end and a single, small set of bleachers. I considered camping right there, at the edge of some trees. The park was surrounded on three sides by residential areas. There was a well-lit parking lot adjacent to the field. On the other side of the parking lot there was a large chapel. No, I thought, better to find the high school football field. It wouldn't be so wide-open, would feel more enclosed, more secure.

Safer, I thought.

I walked back down the hill, crossed the thoroughfare that led through town, and then rode through more residential neighborhoods. Finally, I found the high school. The football stadium was bigger than I imagined it would be.

Interesting, this need for familiarity. A former high school teacher and coach, it made sense that I would seek out an athletic field. Even in travel, you seek recognizable patterns; cling to the familiar, where you make your temporary homes.

I leaned the bike against a small brick building, which looked like it was in the process of being rebuilt. There was no door but a large opening in front. Storage maybe, or a concession stand. I walked inside, even considered placing my sleeping bag on the concrete floor. But the floor was covered in debris—sawdust, nails, splinters of wood. I decided to stick to my original plan.

I took my sleeping bag from the rear rack and walked up into the bleachers, beneath the overhanging roof. The bleachers, which were made from aluminum steel, creaked in the wind, and occasionally, I could hear water, which must have been caught in the beams. It was a restless sleep.

When I woke, it was nearly 5:30, light but the sun not yet up, a Sunday morning, the air already starting to warm. I rose, stuffed my sleeping bag in its sack. I wanted to leave before some early-morning jogger saw me and reported me to the police. An early start would be good, I thought. It was 530 miles to San Francisco, and I had exactly a week to get there. A hundred-mile day—which seemed feasible, given the terrain ahead—and I'd be ahead of schedule. Could even be in California by the next day. I walked down the steps, bleary-eyed.

At the foot of the bleachers, turned top side up, lay my helmet. I stood, looking down at it. Weird. Had it been that windy in the night?

And then I looked over at the shed where I'd parked my bike. I stood staring. I closed my eyes tight, tried to shake off the sleep. I opened them, not wanting to accept the obvious truth.

My bicycle was gone.

# A Coming to Peace

FOR FORTY-TWO DAYS you ride through the rural West, and you reach a point where your body is fit and you have become attuned to the rhythms of nature. One day you take the ferry to Vancouver, British Columbia, through rush hour traffic, honking horns, sirens, and crowded streets, and the beauty of the harbor, the high-rise buildings beyond. That night, invigorated by the city's energy and unable to sleep, you wander aimlessly through Stanley Park, which is crowded with vendors, jugglers, tourists, young lovers, and more diverse cultures—East Indians, Asians, Pacific Islanders—than you have ever be-

went inside. When she returned, she handed me a bag of fruit—apples, bananas, an orange—and waved off my gratitude, as if buying food for strangers was nothing at all.

When they dropped me off at Wal-Mart, I assured them I'd be fine. Inside I wandered the aisles, contemplating my next move. I would wait around a day or two, hope the bike was found. But I didn't believe it would be. I thought about my journal and felt my heart sink. All of those words I'd written down, memories preserved, now lost forever. I just wanted to fly home. I believed my journey was over. I was scheduled to meet Joan in San Francisco in less than a week, anyway. Maybe I'd just fly there and then fly home with her. Or I could rent a car, still see the coast. I didn't really have the money for a new touring bike, but maybe I could replace mine with a less expensive model. Or look for a used bike? Would a bike store sell at a wholesale price, just for me to finish? Did I want to finish?

I was heartsick. But also something else, a peculiar, perverse feeling that had surprised me when I first saw the bicycle gone that morning. Alongside the panic, the anger, the sense of loss, all of which was real, there was a paradoxical giddiness, not joy exactly but a burden unloaded. The point of the bicycle was to live more simply, to be—if only temporarily—free of material burdens, to sleep beneath stars, to live on the cheap. To be stripped down with nothing but the clothes on my back, a reliance on strangers, the love of my wife miles away encouraging me forward. Maybe this was a new opportunity, a chance to get even closer to the people, to the earth. Maybe I could hitchhike? I remembered the words of the man I'd met at the campground in Washington, how things get more dangerous the farther south you go.

What was this desire to strip away all that was material? Was it a search for self, for soul? Or was it a response to my own failings—I have never been particularly good at the capitalism game, have often lived month to month, have dealt with mounds of debt, which never seemed fully to go away. I thought about Richard in Yellowstone and Richard in the San Juans and the windsurfer and others I'd met on both of my journeys, pursuing Thoreau-like lives. Was it a brave life of minimalism or a giving up? How does one live simply in a culture where success is measured in excess?

And as for the person who stole the bike, what of them? Where was the rage I knew I should feel? Was my lack of anger a Zen-like acceptance or a cowardly meekness? Was it not the American way to want to hunt down an adversary and seek revenge?

I wanted nothing more than to be with Joan, and yet I felt this notion that I could disappear now, could be anyone, could go anywhere. I thought about men I'd read about who had walked away from their lives, never to return. Christopher McCandless, determined to live a life of autonomy, only to be found dead in the wilds of Alaska, or Everett Ruess, an aesthete, so entranced by the desert beauty that he had walked into Utah's Escalante Desert one day, never to be heard from again. It was not an impetus I intended, only one I understood. I could give it all up, my ego, even my physical body, all of my material possessions, and what would be left but a wisp of spirit, to be carried forever in the hearts of those who knew me.

And my journal, what if it was indeed gone forever? For years I had struggled in my attempts to become a writer, and now, finally, a book contract in hand, and all my words were gone. Could I let it go? Who was I if not my words? What else would be left behind?

All these thoughts of disappearing into a life of antimaterialism, and yet where was I? Wal-Mart. I purchased two shirts, some toiletries. Then I dialed the number given to me by a man and his wife on a rainy evening in a campground outside Anaconda, Montana, just over a month before.

I wasn't even sure I would recognize him, but as soon as he walked into the store, I knew him immediately, and he walked over, embraced me.

"I knew when I first met you I'd see you again," he said. "I'm so glad you called."

Then I told him about the bicycle. His face dropped, as if the bike had been his own.

"Don't worry. We're going to take care of you," he said, and he drove me to his home, where I showered, and he saw to it that I was comfortable, well fed. Immediately, he was on the phone, telling my story to the prayer group at his church, Calvary Chapel. He and his wife, Carolyn, and Hannah, Carolyn's daughter, were packing, planning a move to Cody, Wyoming, trying to sell their house. For them it was a stressful time, I knew, and I didn't want to contribute to it. I offered to stay at a motel, to which Randy replied a saying he'd repeat often, every time I would try courteously to decline his help: "Don't deny me this blessing."

That night, after dinner, Randy and Carolyn and Hannah went to a prayer meeting at their church, and I stayed behind, left alone in a house belonging to people who barely knew me.

"You're pretty trusting of a stranger, aren't you?" I said as they left.

"You're no stranger here," said Randy.

That night I called Joan. Earlier that day she had told a friend about the bike. The friend later wrote her a check for two hundred dollars, to be used toward a new bicycle. On my first bicycle trip I had developed a faith in the inherent goodness of people.

Now, ironically, because of the theft, that faith was being restored.

Randy was in his mid-fifties, with broad shoulders, and, though not exactly what one would describe as fat, he had the gut of a man who knew the joy of a heaping full plate. He had red hair and a mustache, a sly wit.

"God is teaching me patience," he said, "but I'm a very poor student."

He claimed to be a flawed individual, and perhaps he was. I never saw any evidence of it. He was pure of heart and filled with a kindness that defied the story of his past. In his own words, he was "a work in progress," but it was a work in which the edges had been smoothed, and the jagged, gnarled anger and hatred that had nearly resulted in a tragic, explosive end had been calmed. He was the sea, the morning after a storm, rolling peacefully onto the shore, his life now washing over all he encountered.

On my second evening with the Randalls, Randy and I took a drive along the coast. We were standing on an ocean overlook, gazing through his binoculars at a rocky island cove, listening to the raucous barks of a large group of California seals. Randy had in the past led tours about the coastal wildlife, and his knowledge was extensive. We had spent the previous two days driving through Coos Bay and North Bend, Randy graciously taking me to each of the local bicycle shops, all to no avail. I had called shops in Ashland, Medford, Roseburg, Eugene. But none had touring bikes my size. I had placed an ad in the local paper offering a reward for the journal. But I didn't believe it would ever be returned.

Fortunately, there was an airport in North Bend, with reasonably priced flights to San Francisco. I'd been sleeping on the Randalls' couch for two nights, and I knew they'd let me stay indefinitely. But my mother had a saying: "Guests, like fish, start to stink after three days." I had booked a flight for the following evening.

We watched the seals on the rocks. Randy was a skilled photographer, and displayed in his home were several of his photographs, images of boats and the sea as well as mountains and forests. He talked about his love for the natural world. I asked him about this, about how it fit with his faith. I reminded him how some passages of the Bible were used to validate practices that were destructive to the environment.

"The Bible says we're supposed to be stewards of the land," he said.

It's what I believed too.

That afternoon Randy and I drove to a small coffee shop in the mall. In less than two hours I would be boarding a plane to San Francisco. Early in my stay with the Randalls, Randy had spoken about how he believed God had saved him from the post-traumatic stress disorder he'd experienced after Vietnam. I asked him about this now.

"When I was seventeen," he began "I hitchhiked to San Diego to join the army. My mom signed the papers so I could go in. I started in Fallbrook, California. I went from there to Ft. Polk, Louisiana, of all places, where I started finding out about segregation—what a shock that was—and what humidity was all about. By the time they got through with me I had grown up physically and emotionally. I grew almost two inches in basic training."

"Just in Louisiana?" I asked.

"Just from having exercise and food and just at that time of my life."

228

"What made you decide to sign up for the service?"

"I wanted to get away from everything. I was living in an alcoholic family, so home was bad, and I have a learning disability, so school was bad. I was just miserable. I wanted to get away, and joining the army was the only way I could see. I was an angry young man, and the army helped me to focus that anger. And then they sent me to a war where I could use it and perfect it, to do the things that aren't natural for you to do. And then they sent me home. In forty-eight hours I went from Vietnam to walking the streets.

"I had started drinking and doing drugs in Vietnam, to just cope, and then I came home and was very angry, very dangerous, extremely depressed. Very suicidal. You just can't imagine the depth of the emotional pain and depression caused by being in the events that you see and participate in. Even then, God had his hand on me. But I didn't see it. Even when He saved me from myself one night."

"What happened?" I asked.

"I had gotten very angry at God in Vietnam and said, 'Well, you'll let something like this happen, I don't want anything to do with you.' I went through probably two real serious suicide attempts where I took medication, stole drugs, bought drugs, stole medications and took them because I didn't want anybody to see me like that, to see the gore that I had seen. I didn't want to hurt anybody else; I just wanted my pain—my deep pain—to quit. In Vietnam we learned not to have relationships with anybody because either they'd get killed or they'd get wounded and go home or they'd rotate back out because we were on a twelve-month cycle. Vietnam was an emotional, physical survival. You didn't want to get close to anybody because you were gonna lose them."

"Wasn't camaraderie important?" I asked. "If you couldn't get close, but you had to work together—how did you balance that?"

"We didn't have that, not in Vietnam. That was why we suffered so much over there. Everyone in wars suffers just because of the nature of being in war. But in World War II the men went to war as a unit. They trained as a unit. They got together as a unit. They got on a boat. They went on the beach and fought the war together, they stayed for the duration and they came home together on a slow boat, and they had a month or two to decompress together, and then they went back into society. Now the war part still bothered them, but they were bonded. When the guys came home from World War II, they got a big parade, and they were heroes, and when we came home, we got called "Baby Killer" and had things thrown at us and terrible things said to us. Friends wouldn't even have anything to do with us, you know. We were still in combat mode, walking the streets. Also, in World War II they had a purpose."

"Do you think we went in to Vietnam with a sense of purpose and then it was lost, or did we never have a sense of purpose at all?" I asked.

"I don't think we ever had a plan. We looked at it as a research and development war, and it was a war to prove tactics, although the generals never got to do much because Johnson and McNamara ran the war from the White House—and they didn't have a clue as to how to fight a war or even what the terrain was like," he said.

"So I went for quite a few years in and out of the VA system. Their system was to keep you drugged up so that you're not a problem, which is a terrible system. They kept me drugged up pretty heavy for many years.

"I went through misery, through many relationships. I finally got a trade, and I moved to Oregon, where I thought I could find some peace. It was okay for a while, but then the PTSD came back, and the depression came back real hard, and I was renting a little house in town. The person I rented from was a little German lady name Gisela Bear, and she lived up on the mountain with her husband—real neat people. Gisela would come down to my house—I was in severe depression at this time—and she'd pull up out in front of my house in her Volkswagen, and I'd see her out there, and I'd go, 'Oh, no, not her again.' Of course, I was pretty stoned from smoking pot, and I'd go hide in the closet. I'd hear her come up, hear this knock, and I'd be thinking, *Go away, go away.* But she'd keep knocking until finally the door would open up, and she'd say, 'Hello honey, I know you're home and want you to know I love you and Jesus loves you,' and the door would close, and she'd leave. I'd be like, 'Oh man, she's out there praying for me.' She was relentless. She'd come by a couple of times a week. One time they invited me up to this beautiful homestead on the mountain for Thanksgiving. Her husband, Gary, shared the Gospel with me. You know, that I needed to be born again, that Christ promised me peace, and that if I would ask Him into my life as my savior, He would kind of take care of my pain. I thought he was crazy. But something in my heart couldn't deny it.

"For the next month or two I got worse, worse than ever, and I decided again that I was going to stop this pain for good. I stole some drugs, got a big bottle of Vodka to wash it all down, and took what little money I had—I had lost my job—and went out drinking. That night I came home and sat down at the edge of the bed, getting ready to take all those drugs. And this thing came over me. I said, 'You know, if what Gary told me is true and You're really who he said You are and You're real, then I need You to come into my heart and take care of it right now.' I passed out. The next day I felt like some big trunk had rolled off of my shoulder.

"But there were still things that lingered. I did start going to a little church in Ashland, called Ashland Christian Fellowship. Pastor Andy Green. He taught the Word verse by verse, and I started hearing things that I'd never heard before, and it did start to change me and affect me, and I started to realize that God does love me and cares about me. I'd like to say that I woke up and everything was beautiful and sunshiny and that it was a whole lot better, but this thing still was hanging over me. I didn't trust people, and I still didn't like people too much.

"One time I asked Andy, 'How am I supposed to love people if I don't even like people?' He said, 'Don't worry about it. In time God will take care of everything.'

"So, then I met someone, and we got married, but it turned out the lady I got married to was an alcoholic, and I was stubborn. I don't believe in divorce. I kept hoping it would get better. Eventually it dragged me down. I started drinking again and started smoking pot again and wandered away from the Lord and from the fellowship. The minute I got away from it I was fair game. It's like being that young or wounded animal at the end of the pack—you're gonna get picked off. That's what I did. I got picked off, and I got back into it, and then I got back in the VA system. I was actually the second in the state to get disability for PTSD, once they finally figured out what was really wrong with us."

"Do you have concerns with that about Iraq, or is our understanding of it better, where they're taking better care of the soldiers?" I asked.

"They are taking better care of them. Coming home is a very important thing. When our guys came home here in Coos Bay, it was all over town when they'd be coming in. The town turned out and was lining the streets to welcome them. From the big bridge it was shoulder length all the way down there, all the way up this street, all the way down Newmark and all the way to the Armory. My concern is that there's a lot of wounded young men and women that are in the VA hospital suffering from severe wounds, and they need support too."

"You mean, because they're not riding the bus and coming home as a group?"

"Right. We can't forget them."

"So then, what happened in Ashland?"

"I went downhill. I became a very dangerous antigovernment separatist. I was in the gun business, and I was not a nice man. The VA started putting me on medication, and then they'd give me medication for the side effects of that medication. The VA had me on fourteen different medications—personality changing, mood altering—and I was in severe pain with my back, so I took a lot of painkillers and drank whiskey just to get rid of the pain. I smoked pot and just did everything I could to deal with the pain and trauma.

"It came to the point where I was extremely dangerous. I had weapons everywhere. I lived on a farm outside of Medford. My wife and I never fought a lot, but we got in a big fight that day—maybe because she was drunk and I was on all these drugs—and I wigged out completely. She wanted to get rid of me because I scared her, so she called the police.

"The sheriff came out to the farm and asked me by phone to come out. I told them, 'That's not going to happen, and you probably should not even attempt to make me,' and I decided, here was a good way out. They call it suicide by cop. I got all camied up and grabbed my best AK47, went out through the woods in the back and outflanked them. In other words, I got behind them. I was getting ready to drop these four sheriffs, and it would have been no problem. I had been a competition shooter, and I had good equipment.

"But then my life changed forever. While I was in that ditch, I felt a hand on my shoulder, and I literally heard the voice that said, 'This is finished, this is over with.' I had a vision of children and women crying over these sheriffs. I started to weep. I backed off, went back into my place. I had the place all booby-trapped up. I had more explosives than you even want to know about. I got rid of everything, and I said 'Okay God, you're in charge.'

"But I was still agitated because of the drugs in my system. Then all of a sudden my friend Don Shevcheck comes driving up to my front gate, right past the police, and he gets out of his van, and they're yelling, 'Stop! Stop!' But he opens the gate, gets back in his van, drives through, gets out. They're still hollering, 'Stop! Stop!' He closes the gate, drives up to my place, checks on me and sees that I'm okay.

"Then he went back out to the police. He talked to them and said, 'You know he's really agitated. He's on a lot of medication, and something bad is going to happen here if you keep pressing this. The very best thing that could happen is if you left. That will defuse the situation. I know you can deal with it, but otherwise this is going to be bad.' The sheriffs agreed to that. They packed up and left.

"Later I asked Don, 'Why didn't you stop when they said stop?'

"And he said, 'Well, they didn't say stop what. I thought it was multiple choice. So I just stopped listening.'

"So you know, the Lord sent my friend Don to come in. He moved immovable things. Like sheriffs.

"The last bit of anger I had in me was focused on her. It was funny because we were sitting at the court date one day—me and my attorney, Bruce Smith. She walked by, and I heard myself kind of growl. But then I remembered: pray for those who spitefully use you and wrongfully accuse you.

"So, being the obedient Christian that I am, I said, 'Well okay Lord, but I won't mean it.' So the Lord, He said, 'Well, okay then, let's just make you wait in here, so you have plenty of time not to mean it.' I had to sit there for an hour and a half thinking about it, and by the time it was over, I almost meant it.

"After that court date I went down in the parking lot and got in my van, and the spirit of God came upon me. I had this overwhelming compassion for her, and I started to pray blessings on her, and since that moment I haven't found too many people I don't love. That was the final deal, starting to pray for her. That was a big turning point. I seem to love everybody and get along with everybody anymore.

"I've had a lot of lessons to learn—had to learn some of them more than once because I'm so hard-headed. But I'm so grateful for every one of them. God moved me to the coast here where I had time to heal physically and spiritually. I got involved in our family Christian fellowship, and I started to hear the Word of God and grew able to serve in capacities that I'd never been able to serve before. God answered my prayers above and beyond anything I could have ever asked for.

"I'd been praying, telling the Lord I didn't like being single, so He brought the most wonderful gift ever—except for His salvation—into my life. Carolyn. I am totally convinced He made that woman just for me, and it is the most wonderful thing. I had no clue what love in a relationship was about before I met her."

He looked at his watch. "You've got a plane to catch," he said.

I tried to reconcile in my mind the man before me with the man who had outflanked those sheriffs. I looked at him and thought about when we'd first met, how he'd brought food to my Montana campsite in the rain. His was a story I'm sure wasn't easy to tell, and he had told it in a voice so calm and full of peace, with no hint of resonance of anger from the past.

At the airport he asked if he could pray a blessing over me. I thought that would be all right.

"I have a feeling the bike'll turn up," he said.

I nodded. I was starting to believe it, or at least to believe that whatever happened would be okay.

# At the North Bend Airport

THE AIRPORT SECURITY GUARD was tall and muscular, with blond hair and perfect teeth. Sympathy wasn't the man's strong suit. I told him about my bicycle being stolen, and he laughed.

"That's hilarious," he said. "You rode all the way from Colorado?"

I nodded.

He thought this was a hoot. He repeated the story to two other security guards standing nearby as he frisked me with a security wand. To add insult, the security wand beeped. Inside my wallet I carried a cheap, credit card–sized "multipurpose" tool. I took it out and showed it to the security guard

"We'll have to confiscate this," he said cheerily. "Do you have anyone who could come pick it up?"

"I'm not worried about it," I said. It was just one more thing to live without.

From my airplane window seat the city appeared like a computer motherboard, a chaotic network of lights and wires, all organized on a grid. The plane descended, and the motherboard slowly transformed—high-rise hotels, the lights of moving traffic, billboards, and lit green highway signs. The mechanical shifting noise of landing gear, that rush of approaching ground a jolting reminder of the speed with which we had just traveled, and then the touchdown of tires. What I had planned as a week's worth of travel had just been reduced to hours.

# Intermission
*San Francisco*

# Like a Haggard Ghost

THROUGH A PLATE GLASS WINDOW I watched a mangy, disheveled pigeon stagger across a grate on the sidewalk. I was sitting at a Starbucks on 4th Street and Mission on a Friday, taking in the scent of coffee and biscotti. The Van Morrison song drifting from the ceiling speakers masked the rumbling of the traffic outside. *Feels like I'm stranded / I'm stranded between that 'ol devil and the deep blue sea.*

San Francisco is a city that engages the American imagination; even for those who've never been there, it represents a bohemian Mecca, a reputation informed by the observations recorded by those who've come before. Just a few blocks from where I sat, Jack Kerouac's Sal Paradise once stepped off a bus and as Kerouac wrote in *On the Road*, "wandered out like a haggard ghost" into these same Frisco streets, where "long bleak streets with trolley wires were shrouded in fog and whiteness" and "weird bums asked for dimes in the dawn." John Steinbeck, in *Travels with Charley*, described the city as a "rose on her hills like a noble city in a happy dream." Mark Twain, in *Roughing It*, observed "decaying, smoke-grimed, wooden houses," "barren sand hills," and a climate that was "sometimes pleasanter when read about than personally experienced." Like the fogs that rolled into the bay, the city has been invented, and reinvented, daily by millions of eyes. Steinbeck saw happy dreams. I saw desperate pigeons.

My own memory held a different city than that I saw out the coffee shop window. Twenty years earlier, I'd been met by my brother-in-law John on the Golden Gate Bridge. He jogged along beside me as I pedaled across. I had stayed with him and my sister Debbie in their small but clean apartment in nearby Mountain View, a complex with a swimming pool. On a Saturday we drove to the city and walked around Fisherman's Wharf, with its street musicians, artists, mimes, a man juggling sticks of fire while riding a unicycle. The city seemed jester-like then, in full makeup, smiling and telling boisterous jokes, making balloon animals for children. John and Debbie had been married just under a year, and they were still mired in the throes of newly-wed love. We had zigged and zagged our way down Lombard Street, shopped Chinatown, drove up Polk Street, where a six-foot, four-inch woman with an Adam's apple wearing high heels and a blue dress walked haughtily across the street in front of us. It seemed to me then the city was full of music and art and life, rich with possibility and romance. Less than a year later, on a spring break road trip with friends, we had stayed with a neurosurgeon in a large house overlooking the bay. At night, from a stone porch, we'd looked out at the city lights before us. So easy to fall for something that glimmered in the distance, to be steered as a tourist to the comfortable edges on the front side of polished veneer.

Now, though, staying in a cheap downtown motel, the city revealed to me a different side. It was as if the jester was now slumped in a tenement chair, wearing boxers and a white T-shirt, his face paint fading and peeling, a cigarette hanging from his bottom lip.

I sipped the last of my coffee, down to the bitter grounds at the bottom of the cup. Outside the pigeon stopped, as if to rest. It had bloodshot eyes and dingy ruffled feathers, like a poor man's tattered jacket. It turned and glared back at me, and caught staring, I averted my eyes. Behind and above the pigeon, the theater across the street advertised a movie called *The Devil's Rejects*, the words moving like a prowling shark on a scrolling marquee.

What determines our perceptions, the details our minds take in? At the age of twenty I was all hope and optimism, looking at a city that seemed so alive with jazz musicians on the corner, boats in the bay, young women everywhere. Now I focused instead on the peeling of paint, tape on broken windows, an old man, unshaven and toothless, his gray hair unkempt, sleeping with his head against a doorway. How much of what I took in, either then or now, was accurate? For I could only see through eyes tainted with preconceptions, prejudices, expectations.

The man woke, looked at me, scowled, and then took a cup from the ground and held it out. This was where the truth became complicated, where fiction intersected with non, because each moment of perception was an engagement with the imagination, so much riding on the words I choose. I could say the man looked grumpy, looked sad, looked content, looked lazy, looked like the result of a single nation's apathy. Looked dangerous. Looked helpless. Looked psychotic. Looked a lot like you or a lot like me.

San Francisco. From North Bend it had taken only three hours by plane. By bicycle it would have taken at least eight delicious days, and I mourned all I wouldn't experience along that northern Pacific Coast—the lighthouses, the mist shrouded redwood forests, those northern California coastal towns: Fortuna, Arcata, Fort Bragg, with their art galleries and cafés and coffee houses. I wouldn't see Wright's Beach or Point Reyes, with its rocky coast and windswept oak trees. I imagined myself sipping hot tea from a perch on a cliff, gazing out onto the fog-covered ocean, or sitting in a local pub at night, listening to the stories of men whose faces had been weathered by lifetimes spent in the salty sea air. Instead, I was stranded in a room in the Mosser Hotel, alone, my money quickly running out, my bicycle gone. It was silly, I knew, a forty-year-old man crying over a stolen bicycle. And yet I had come that far. By boarding that airplane, it felt like I'd betrayed a twenty-year dream.

Two nights earlier I'd checked into a nearby motel, and I lay back on the bed and suddenly felt the exhaustion that had been slowly building for the last several days, a heavy, mental drain that was accompanied by a realization that the flight made official—I wouldn't be finishing the bicycle trip, at least not as planned. I was wallowing in this state of pity when the phone rang. I had assumed it was Joan. She was the only person who knew where I was.

"You want some companionship?" said a breathy female voice on the other end.

It wasn't Joan.

"I think you have the wrong number," I said. I hung up. Not five minutes later, the phone rang again. A different female voice.

"Hi. You're looking for some company?"

"Who are you?" I asked.

"I'm Melissa. Would you like to hear a little bit about me?" asked the voice on the other end.

I sighed. "Sure," I said.

"I'm 34B-25-32. I have blonde hair and brown eyes. I'm very open-minded. Would you like to make an appointment?"

"No thanks," I said.

"My name is Mandy," said the third caller. "Would you like me to come over?"

It was nearly midnight. "I'm here with my wife," I lied. "Stop calling me."

"I am couples friendly," she said.

"Well, I'm not," I said, and hung up.

Minutes later, the phone rang again.

"I wish you all would stop calling me," I said.

"You called us," she said.

"I didn't," I said. "Stop calling me."

But the calls didn't stop. Over the next hour and a half the phone rang a half-dozen more times or so. I tried to sleep, but after the third call, just knowing that the phone might ring kept me awake. Finally, nearly asleep, I heard the familiar jingle, and I picked up the receiver, lashed out angrily.

"Stop calling me," I said. "Just stop. Stop calling me!"

"Geez," said the voice. "You know, you could just unplug your phone."

Unplug the phone. Somehow, I hadn't even considered that. Sheepishly, I disconnected the cord from the wall and finally fell asleep. That was my first night back in San Francisco.

Now I walked outside. The pigeon waddled into an alley, turning to look back, making sure I wasn't following. I stood surrounded by the street crowd, the traffic and noise. It was disorienting, like a quantum leap. A woman nestled on concrete steps held out a cup and shook it, loose change rattling like die in a Yahtzee game. From my left a man approached. He was wearing a black tattered jacket, old worn green army pants. He was hawking a paper called the *Street News*.

"Can you help me, man? I'm trying, really trying, you know," he said.

I didn't doubt it, but I didn't give him money. Less than a block later, a man in a purple T-shirt with yellow letters so faded I couldn't make them out said, "I got a job interview, if I could just get there. Could you give me a little money for the bus?"

I put my hand in my pockets. "I got nothing," I said.

"It's cool, man," he said, and moved off. I hoped it was true, hoped he made it to the interview.

On every crowded street the panhandlers all aimed for me. Somehow it was obvious to them I was an outsider, and I couldn't figure out what marked me because I tried to strike my best San Fran cool pose, the look-straight-ahead, got-places-to-go purposeful stride of the city. But try as I might, I couldn't refrain from star-crossed gazing, at the buildings, the myriad of people in their strange clothes, the uninhibited way they strolled the streets. A woman in a cocktail dress with sunglasses and high black boots sang out loud, and a man in a red leather jacket across the street called out to her, "Sing it, now—there you go," and after weeks riding through the small towns and wilderness of the West, I was overwhelmed with the blending of crowds and traffic and noise and scents and signs, and, of course, that must be it, it must be obvious to people who knew their territory so well who was out of their element there, who might be persuaded to give a dollar or two, and so they approached me seeking cash, for food, for coffee, for beer.

In the late afternoon the sun moved lower in the sky, and the downtown was a collage of golden light and shadow. I turned onto a narrow side street that led down a steep hill. A man slept against the side of a building, his sleeping bag bundled up tightly around him, despite the seventy-degree weather. He looked young, maybe in his early twenties. His unshaven face was covered with dry blood, no doubt from the visible cut beneath his left eye. Later, on a side street, I saw from a distance a man sitting against a wall, rocking forward and back, holding up a cup in his trembling hand, and saying like a mantra, "pleasepleasepleasepleaseplease . . . ."

I checked into a motel where both the air conditioning and the elevator were out of order. I walked the narrow stairs, and by the time I reached my floor, I was covered in sweat. The room was small but clean, surprisingly stylish for the low rates. A single flower in a small glass vase rested on the tray beside the bed. It felt good to have a space all my own in this city, a roof over my head. The days since the bike was stolen had worn on me.

I had to make a decision soon: what to do next? I called bike shops until I found one with a touring bicycle my size.

I could have gone to buy the bike, but I didn't. I didn't want to deal with the travel logistics or to replace all that I would need to continue—a tent, rain gear, panniers. Mostly, I didn't want to spend the money. The smart thing would probably be to quit, to just fly home with Joan, who was scheduled to arrive the next day. I turned on the TV, flipped through the channels. I'd lived without television for the past two months, and now it made me jittery, anxious. What Tocqueville predicted about America nearly 165 years ago had proven true—that we'd ultimately develop pop culture tastes. Even he couldn't have predicted the influence of the television, how easily it would diminish the substance of art and yet how significant it would be in the shaping of culture. I turned it off. San Francisco was just outside my door. I returned to the street.

As I walked, the change in my pocket jingled, and I used my hand to silence it. I decided to give it to the next person who asked. I didn't have to wait long.

His name was Ricky, a self-proclaimed street poet. He looked down, as he softly explained he was selling homemade books of his collected poems. I read the poems and thought they weren't bad. I liked him. I didn't have money enough on me for the book, but I gave him the change. It totaled about fifty-seven cents was all, but he seemed grateful, and he gave me a photocopied page with four of his poems. I still have it. I wish now that I'd purchased his book, not out of any sense of charity but for the genuine gift of his poetry.

I walked on, making my way through the hilly and narrow streets, the stores now closing, the cable car tourist lines gone.

"Hey, man, hey man." The voice came from behind me, and when I turned, I saw him quickly gaining on me. I started to walk faster, but he caught up and then walked beside me, matching my stride.

"You want to join my martial arts school, man?" he asked. It was a good tactic—a guy like me might just be looking for ways to defend himself. I looked at him. He was wearing a New York Yankees cap and an old jean jacket. He held a can of beer in a brown paper sack, and I could smell the sour scent of the alcohol on his breath.

"Martial arts school?" I asked.

"Yeah man, and not normal like the movie stuff, either, but real martial arts. This is Ninja martial arts. You work with me, you will have all power. I can help you overcome any obstacles."

"A Ninja school?"

"Yes. This is the real deal, bro," he said. We came to an intersection, just as the lights changed, and I was stuck on the corner with him. But I didn't mind. The truth is, it was the best conversation I'd had all day—there was nowhere else I needed to be. "I can teach you to run up the sides of that wall," he said.

"Can you run up the side of that wall?" I asked.

He feigned offense. "Of course. How I'm gonna teach you if I can't do it myself?"

I pointed to a nearby building. "Let's see it," I said.

"Well, I'm not gonna do that right now," he said. "You want to help me out, man? I just need some money, so I can start my school right here."

"Look," I said. "I have no change at all."

"Change. Change? Do I look like a change kind o' guy to you? Bills, man. No change. Change," he said with disgust. "I had no idea—I thought I looked better than that. Change," he repeated, shaking his head. "Things must be worse than I thought." The light turned, and I walked across the street. He didn't follow, and as the distance between us grew, I could still hear the word *change* echoing through the city.

I decided then—I would not buy a new bicycle. I would fly back to Lincoln with Joan, wouldn't finish the trip. It would be okay. A stolen bicycle, after all, was not a tragedy. It was a Pee-wee Herman movie.

Later that night, in the dark, I walked by a group of college kids. One of them had a large camcorder on a tripod with a bright light. The rest had push brooms. The camcorder pointed toward a man with a clapboard sign that said, MARKET STREET NEEDS CLEANING. Less than a block away, I noticed a sign on a Bank of America window that said, NO CAMPING. Over the last two months I'd slept in organized campgrounds and motels and had snuck into city parks, school grounds, hidden in forests on the outskirts of towns. There were a lot of places in America where it was illegal for a person to sleep.

If I dwelled on the beggars in the street, it was perhaps because they were the only ones who interacted with me at all. Most people stared straight ahead, made no eye contact. The homeless problem in San Francisco was perhaps the worst in all of America's cities—between four thousand and six thousand that summer. If those who stayed in shelters and clinics were taken into account, the number rose to nearly fourteen thousand, all in a city where the average apartment rented for eighteen hundred dollars a month, with a roughly 1 percent availability.

It was better, perhaps, that the problem was visible and not swept under the carpet, as it was in some places. I thought about the homeless sweeps in New York, Denver, Atlanta, and Gallup, New Mexico, where the downtrodden were moved away from public view, lest they offend sensibilities. San Francisco was a city of tolerance—one of its great strengths. Of course, tolerance can be indifference in disguise.

I thought, too, of the last presidential debates, all the talk of the wealthy, the middle class, but no real discussion of the burgeoning poverty. When did the plight of the poor stop being part of the political discussion? Was it a shortening of our attention span, the idea that old issues didn't sell, weren't fresh? So, we obsessed on a runaway bride or a missing debutante on a Caribbean junket. It wasn't the plight of the people living on the streets that was so disturbing as much as the pretense that the rest of us weren't affected or didn't realize our complicity.

The next morning I was standing with a crowd at the busy crosswalk on Market and 4th Street, waiting for the light to change, when a homeless man approached hawking the *Street News*. A gray-haired man standing next to me shook his head in disgust.

"Lazy," he said to me. "These people—young people—they don't want to work."

I shrugged, didn't know how to respond. I'd been in the San Francisco downtown for less than a day. What did I know about the world?

That night, back at the Mosser, I called Joan. She'd been waiting for my call.

"Guess what?!" she said.

The police had found my bicycle, lying in a ditch beneath a row of bushes, my camera and journals secure in the handlebar bag. The bicycle was now waiting in Randy and Carolyn's garage.

# City of Hills

"I BELIEVE GOD HAS VERY LOW STANDARDS," said Anne Lamott. This was, as I understood it, her way of saying that He loves us despite everything. I was sitting in the auditorium at the Books by the Bay Independent Book Festival. Lamott had just read an essay titled "Flower Girl," from her book *Plan B: Further Thoughts on Faith.* The essay was told in her usual straightforward, humorous style. Lamott was a study in contrast, a white woman with dreadlocks, a self-proclaimed left-wing Christian whose writing burned with a passion that bordered on anger, and yet everything about her sought healing. She could run from profane to reverent without ever breaking her stride. It was no exact science, this pursuit of faith, of truth, of inner peace. We all had our own paths to follow, and as Lamott spoke, I felt proud to live where we were able to do so, messy as such freedom could be. Freedom was like faith, like love: if you tried to constrain it, you lost it.

That evening I checked into the Andante Motel, which Joan and I had booked months before. I was anxious for her arrival that evening, so anxious that I took the BART to the airport at seven o'clock. She wasn't scheduled to arrive until eleven. To fill the time, I sat at an airport bar and read from Paul Theroux's *Fresh Air Fiend: Travel Writings.*

A man came and sat on the barstool next to me. He told me he was from St. Louis but had spent the last twenty years living in Cambodia.

I asked him what changes he had noticed most when he returned to the United States.

"America," he said, "doesn't make anything anymore. It's all service and everything like that. Most of which we don't really need. The whole economy's based on convincing people they need things that they don't."

"Like what?" I asked.

"You see all these people with cell phones. Of course, everyone in Asia has cell phones too. But what are they paying for really?"

"They're paying for air," I said.

"Not even air. It's more abstract than that. They're paying for the privilege of using the air, or at least the airspace. In Asia people are poor, much poorer than here. But they produce actual items."

I had often thought of working in Asia, and I told him this.

"It's a good idea," he said. "The possibilities are endless, I think. And you really get to understand the world, this country, and our place in the larger scheme and everything like that. I went there—I thought I'd stay a year or two. I've been there for twenty now."

"Do you think you'll ever come back to the States for good?" I asked.

He laughed. "I keep thinking I will. But I've been planning that move for twenty years now," he said.

It was time for Joan's plane to arrive, and I watched the people who came through the gate, looking closely for the one familiar face I longed to see. But she didn't arrive. Finally, I walked to the American Airlines ticketing counter.

"She's not scheduled to arrive until tomorrow," said the agent.

"Why?" I asked.

"I can't say," she said, without looking away from her computer screen.

I called our home number, thinking maybe she'd left a message on our answering machine. I was surprised when Joan herself answered.

"Mechanical problems," she said. "We never even left Omaha. We're scheduled to get in tomorrow by noon."

I wilted. By the time I got to the BART stop at the airport, it had stopped running for the night, and I had to take the shuttle back to the hotel alone. I found solace from Theroux, who, in an essay titled "Being a Stranger," writes about the people who inhabit the Trobriand Islands off the coast of Papua New Guinea. In their culture, he writes, "the friendship of people who come and go, for whatever length of time, is not diminished by their absence. What matters in the Trobriands is your existence in the consciousness of the village. If someone talks about you, or if you appear in their dreams, you are present—you have reality."

I was anxious to see Joan, and yet in a sense she was already there.

The next morning Joan called my hotel from Amarillo, Texas, where the plane was grounded after one of the engines broke down. She had driven fifty miles to Omaha the night before then had driven back to Lincoln. I'd called her at nearly one o'clock in the morning, and she had to get up at four to drive back to Omaha, fly to Dallas. Then they were diverted to Amarillo, where they had to board a different plane. By the time she arrived in San Francisco, it was after three o'clock. She was exhausted.

We rode the BART to the Powell exit and then walked the crowded streets to the motel, carrying her two heavy bags. Later, in a gallery, an immaculately dressed woman sized us up, asked us if we were looking to buy. The answer was no, but we shrugged a noncommittal maybe. She gave us a tour of the gallery. There was a painting we both liked, a large mixed-media abstract, painted in vibrant, dark colors and then textured with scraped designs in the wood.

"That would look great over the fireplace," I said. We didn't have a fireplace. We did have a wood-burning stove.

Joan, not prone to such pretending, graciously played along by nodding.

"How much?" I asked.

"Twenty-eight thousand," said the woman.

We stood, gazing at the painting, nodding, as if considering it.

"I'll tell you what," I said. "Why don't you give me your card, and we'll think about it."

The woman nodded. "We do ship all of our artwork."

"Wow," said Joan, when we were back out on the street.

"Probably worth it," I said.

On the sidewalk outside our hotel a woman living out of a shopping cart was sitting on a bench. The storeowner across the street swept the night's debris onto the curb.

San Francisco is a city of hills. People walk on a lean, angling to counteract the incline or descent. Living quarters are bisected by the walks in front such that one side of a building is lower than its opposite. Cars sit parked at forty-five-degree angles.

To walk those hills for the first time was to delve into a skewed reality, not a house of mirrors but a maze of angles. Moving between downtown and the wharf, through residential neighborhoods, the streets were oddly quiet, empty, devoid even of traffic. I heard the opening of a door at the top of some patio stairs, then a cat entered a narrow slit of doorway, and the door closed.

We watched sailboats in the bay, Alcatraz Island in the distance, the thin haze giving it a ghostlike appearance. I looked at the water, measured the distance, tried to gauge whether it was swimmable. Probably not. We ate lunch at an overpriced restaurant that charged an additional one-dollar "surcharge" per customer. Smart, I thought. Why not an ice water tax? A ketchup and mustard fee? The possibilities were endless. I thought of the St. Louis man now expatriated in Cambodia: *they pay for the privilege to pay.*

On the pier it was sunny and warm, with invisible wisps of cool air breezing off the water. Ferry boats lined with tourists moved slowly out toward the island. A fat seagull landed on the pier railing, eyed the tourists, squawked, and then flew away. On a floating dock sea lions lounged in the sun, two of them raising their heads to bark at each other.

We walked along the wharf, stopping to rest on concrete steps overlooking the ocean. Several people were swimming. A woman in a long cotton dress skillfully rehearsed dance steps in the sand at the water's edge.

The Russian child wore a white hat and a blue spotted dress. She was looking at us from over the shoulder of the woman who held her, and when Joan smiled, she smiled back, shyly lowering her head. We were unwitting guests at a Russian family baby shower, something we didn't realize until we'd already been seated at a corner table in the small café. The rest of the dining area was filled with carefully wrapped gifts and families dressed in their Sunday best, though it was Tuesday. Old men in dark suits and women in dresses greeted each other with embraces and pecks on the cheeks. A festive occasion, all spoken in Russian.

We were underdressed and without gifts but not at all unwelcome. Our food was brought steaming hot, cabbage rolls in tomato sauce. It was like being beamed suddenly into a Russian living room, a very mundane, universal family event and yet wholly exotic. It was our last full day together in San Francisco. The whole world is here, I thought, in this city.

In Haight-Ashbury I had hoped for art, for a bohemian atmosphere, interesting people, a creative vibe. Hippies. But mostly it was middle-aged tourists, like us, in shorts and summer clothes, licking ice cream cones, and pushing baby strollers, their children holding balloons. The only tie-dye was in the storefront windows; the shops were filled with overpriced hippie kitsch. Like everywhere else in San Francisco, there were beggars on the street. But here the beggars were young and white.

A black man, with Rasta dreads and a beard, came around a corner and started walking toward us. He had a carved wooden walking staff. An African-American Moses. He wore an old dirty brown T-shirt and a long turquoise skirt. When he saw me he smiled broadly.

"Your beard. Where's your beard, man?" he asked. Then he looked at Joan. "And where's your other wife?"

This was a new approach. I tried not to stare at the skirt, which seemed particularly incongruous with what was otherwise a very masculine dude. It wasn't a skirt, though, exactly. It was as if upon leaving his house and having nothing else to wear, he'd pulled the tablecloth from his table and wrapped it around his waist.

"My other wife?" I repeated, dumbly.

"Yeah, man. The one I saw you with last time." Before I could reply, he put his hand on my shoulder. "I gotta get. I'll see you around," he said. And then he walked away.

I was so disoriented by his questions that it didn't occur to me until later that he had simply mistaken me for someone else.

"Joan," I said. "I swear to you, there's no other wife."

"I like that skirt," she said.

It was four o'clock in the morning, and we were up, the shuttle to the airport outside waiting in the dark. The shuttle was scheduled to leave at 4:30, and we were showered, packed, and seated by 4:27. But another couple was late, and the driver patiently waited. Finally, a woman in a jean jacket, fifty-something, her long hair in a braid, came out and started talking to the driver. I could hear her through the window, a convoluted story about the hotel not giving the wake-up call, a bad excuse given that there were alarm clocks in every room. Finally, her husband arrived, his fluffed white hair blowing in the wind. The couple entered the van and sat in the seat in front of us. Their clothes reeked of pot.

At the airport Joan and I walked together to security, where we said a too-quick good-bye, and then she was in the crowded line, the people removing their shoes, placing belongings in plastic tubs that rolled slowly on a conveyer belt through the x-ray machines. I walked to the top of the escalator, where I could better see her, and she turned, smiled.

When she was through security, she looked up through the wall of glass, blew a kiss, a silly gesture, which I returned. Then she turned down the long hallway, and I watched her until she was gone.

I walked back to the BART stop and sat alone in a nearly empty car, which started to move. Outside my window a soft mist filled the morning sky. Square houses, pink in the morning light, covered the hills. In the distance a man in a three-piece suit, his jacket thrown over his shoulder, slowly dribbled a basketball across a schoolyard court.

That evening I would have my own plane to catch.

# Return to Oregon

# North Bend to Gold Beach

ABOVE NORTH BEND the plane circled in a dense fog. We'd had a long delay waiting for the fog to clear, and even after takeoff, we were warned, there was a chance we'd need to return to Portland, that the plane might not be able to land. Even so, the atmosphere on the small plane was festive. The passengers included a group of old friends who were en route to a reunion of playing golf and reliving drunken days, both through talk and deed. This I gathered from their conversations. Circling the airport in the fog did nothing to temper the men's enthusiasm, and when finally the plane touched down, all on board let out a raucous cheer.

I'd been off the bike for nearly eleven days, and I craved the exertion of riding, the slow rhythmic pace. Everything had changed now. The eleven-day delay had made a cycling return to Colorado Springs impossible. But I hadn't actually finished the first trip as planned either. Originally, my goal had been to cycle the entire coast and then head east along the Mexican border.

For now I simply wanted to finish the coast of Oregon.

The plane had landed two hours late, but there was Randy, waiting patiently. He drove me back to his house, where my Trek leaned safely against the wall in the Randall's garage. I quickly went through the bags, checking to see what, if anything, was missing. My journal rested neatly inside my handlebar bag, along with my camera and lenses and cell phone.

All that was missing: three Power Bars and the bag of Bing cherries.

In the morning Randy and Carolyn drove me to a spot just outside of town. I unloaded my bike from the back of their truck, attached each of my four panniers and the handlebar bag, bungeed my tent, sleeping bag, and ground pad. We stood on the side of the road, and I hugged them both, the Vietnam veteran who'd turned his rage into peace and his hatred into love and the woman who'd overcome her own abused

past. My own miracle was small in comparison, but it was a miracle all the same. Hope reigned in the most improbable of human lives.

I placed my feet in my toe clips and pedaled south.

A steady southwestern breeze had turned into a full-fledged wind by the time I pulled into Bandon, where boats moored at the dock bobbed in the waves. Then south again, through pine coastal forests, along beaches of sand, a slow fog drifting toward shore and rock formations standing resolute against crashing waves.

Traffic was light, and even against the resistance of the wind, it felt good to be moving again, to feel the salty air against my skin, to hear the seagulls call, to smell the ocean. I rode through the sleepy town of Port Oroford just past evening, diamonds of sunlight glistening on the water and a thin trail, enticing, leading down to the small sandy beach.

At Humbug State Park I camped in the last remaining site in the hiker/biker area. The site was on a slant at the bottom of a hill. I met a woman who was biking with her husband. They were from Washington DC, she said, and on their way to San Francisco. I told her I had just come from there.

"Which way are you headed?" she asked.

"South," I said. Her face registered puzzlement, but she didn't pursue it further.

"Those guys rode all the way from Alaska," she said, gesturing to a campsite across from mine. There was gear spread out across the site, cookware on the picnic table, clothes hanging from trees, tools on the ground. There was so much gear, it was hard to believe it could all be carried on two bikes. There was something protruding from the tent, and I stared, thinking it was some sort of vestibule, but I didn't recognize it. One of the riders, "the quieter one," she said, was from Wales, and the other was from Argentina.

Just then, the vestibule moved and morphed into a standing human being, with his back turned. I'd been staring at the hind end of an Argentinean.

"All done," he said loudly, rubbing his hands together. And then, as if giving an oration, loud enough for all to hear, he proclaimed,

"We are here in sunny Oregon, by the sea." And then he broke into boisterous song.

I set up camp quickly and walked on the road, past campers and couples in lawn chairs, children roasting marshmallows, the smell of burning wood and charcoal, car doors slamming, the soft murmurs of a television from inside a camper. At the edge of the pavement a trail led through sand and under a highway bridge and then onto a beach, where the surf crashed against rocks and a flock of birds flew low over the water in front of a setting sun. I waited until the sun was down, and then the water reflected clouds that transformed from orange to pastel pink to lavender.

Oregon thieves take a variety of forms, and in Humbug State Park they were nocturnal and wore a bandit's mask As I slept, the burglar crept from the nearby bushes, ripped a baseball-size hole through the vinyl of my front pannier, and gnawed on the edges of a bag of crackers, just enough to determine that the flavor was not to his or her liking. Left behind in the dirt was this incriminating evidence: the unmistakable prints of raccoon, a greedy little species I long ago determined was not one of God's creatures but Satan's. One should not be deceived by their apparent cuddly cuteness. Not far from here, while camping in the redwoods of northern California, I once turned my back on a full plastic tub of whipped honey, only to later find the lid with two claw-size holes in it resting neatly next to the tub, which was licked so clean you'd have thought it had been run through a Maytag dishwasher.

Disgusted, I threw the crackers away and hoped it wouldn't rain before I could somehow patch the pannier.

As I made a slow descent, I saw, coming around the curve on the opposite shoulder, a rider pedaling north. Something rode behind him, but I couldn't make it out. As he got closer, I saw that his bike was an old ten-speed, and he struggled up the hill, his thin legs churning the pedals slowly. He appeared to be in his sixties, and he wore a mud-stained gray sweatshirt with old cut-off jeans. He was pulling the largest homemade trailer I'd ever seen on a bicycle. It looked like

an old wagon the likes of which were once pulled by horses. The trailer was piled high and covered with a canvas tarp. And that wasn't all. Behind the first trailer was a second, smaller trailer of the same design. The man had an unkempt beard, and his sallow cheeks were wrinkled leather. But his eyes lit up as he passed me.

"Are we having fun?" he asked.

"Sure," I said. If he was, I must have been.

It was not but a few miles farther, as I rode through a thick canopied forest, when I was startled by another bearded man. It was not as if the dirt he wore clung to him so much as it seemed he had emerged from the soil. He stood still at the edge of the brush, his wild hair blowing in the wind, and he was holding a large stick, like a baton. It seemed to me that he held the stick not as if it were for walking but for defense.

I said hello and smiled, but the man only glared, his grip on the stick tensing as I passed. I felt a chill and pedaled harder.

In the afternoon the wind changed, blowing steady from the south, and I knew I'd experienced the last of my Oregon tailwinds. The temperature was dropping, and I rode out of the trees into an opening, the road following the coastline. Through a thin haze, rock formations rose from the water like apparitions, resolute against the crashing waves, which rolled as white foam onto the beach and then retreated, slowly erasing inscriptions in the sand.

Just before Gold Beach I passed yet another bearded man, sitting beneath a ramshackle nomadic shelter by the side of the road. His face was mostly in shadow, but I could see his eyes, and I felt them follow me as I passed. I imagined I had entered a region inhabited by a nomadic tribe. That evening I read from Twain. "We are descended from desert-lounging Arabs," he wrote, "and countless ages of growth toward perfect civilization have failed to root out of us the nomadic instinct." Three bearded men: were they madmen or wise? I would never know, but either way I sensed a spirit both distant and kindred.

By the time I left Gold Beach the low clouds had grown thick such that the ocean could be heard but not seen, and the cry of a seagull preceded its emergence from the fog as it flew just over my head.

257

The grayness of the day internalized into a cold melancholy that I recognized as the same I'd felt in Port Angeles, also in the fog, just days after a different good-bye with Joan. I stopped at a motel. Fifty dollars, said the man behind the counter. Foolish, when there was a four-dollar campground just miles away. But a splitting headache and the prospect of a warm bed and a hot bath decided it, and I filled out the registration card.

It was my last night in Oregon, and I celebrated with two aspirin and a deep, invigorating sleep.

Saturday morning began as a thin sliver of light shining between curtains. I looked at my bicycle, leaning against the corner wall—its sleek design, a perfect combination of straight lines, angles, and curves. For the first time since I'd left Randy and Carolyn, I realized how much the bike had meant to me, how heartbreaking the loss had it not been found. I had twenty years of identity wrapped up in that bike and all that it represented—my love for the West, for the country, for travel, for exercise, for encountering the natural world on its own terms. In my academic studies now, I was focusing on travel and environmental literature, interests that were rooted in that summer of 1985.

Consider the problems a bicycle solves: health, economy, environment. Peace of mind. How might one benefit from hearing the chirping of birds during a daily commute, to feel the breeze against skin? Bicycle technology, like everything else, was changing all the time, but it was still the same basic concept that Thomas Stevens used on his trek around the world in 1884, that Dervla Murphy used to ride from Ireland to India in 1965, that Barbara Savage and her husband, Larry, used to see the world in 1978. Bicycles were relatively inexpensive—the savings on parking alone could, over time, cover the cost of a new bike. A good bike, with a minimum of care, would last a lifetime. I rose and took my small box of tools from the pocket of my rear pannier, and I removed the chain ring, wiped it clean. Then I scraped the grease from the rear chain wheel. I pulled the chain from the derailleur and scrubbed it. I cleaned the rims, the spokes. I checked the brakes, adjusted the cable. Soon I would be headed back over mountains.

It was an easy ride south, and before I crossed the state line, I looked out over the milky surf of the coast. Oregon. Where grace outweighed theft and strangers were friends not yet made. Where golden hills looked out over blue waves and lighthouses still spread beacons of light through the fog.

Already I missed it and yearned to return.

# California

# To Eureka

NORTHERN CALIFORNIA HIGHWAY 101 was a beautiful night-
mare, with its fog-shrouded pines, thick redwood trunks, wildberry
scrubs, and ferns. Occasional light broke in visible rays through the
trees. And the road was suddenly narrow, with a shoulder that would
intermittently end, leaving me at the mercy of weekend warriors trying to test how close they could get. There were rental RV's and SUV's
and speeding sports cars. A camper, pulling a boat, moved back into
my lane before it had fully passed, the boat fishtailing beside me.

In Crescent City I stopped at the Redwoods National Park Visitor
Center, where I was informed that all of the campgrounds were full.
And the hiker/biker sites? That they couldn't say.

"Might be full. Might be not," said the ranger.

I tried to hurry, in case there were sites left. But the road outside
Crescent City was a steep five-mile climb, and then it was a series of
camelbacks, up hills and down. In the moist air my sunglasses fogged;
the world was an unsafe impressionistic blur.

And then I was descending, as fast as my vision would allow, and
I didn't see the pothole, only felt it, and the bike lurched, leaned,
and I swerved but managed to right it, didn't fall. The front pannier,
though, came unhooked and was dragging on the ground. I managed
to pull to a stop before rolling over it.

Once out of the forest, the road followed the coast, and I saw a sign
for the Redwoods Hostel. It was after five o'clock, and the next campground was twenty miles ahead, so I stopped and inquired about a
room. I expected that the hostel would be full, but it wasn't, and for
ten dollars I received a hot shower and a bed in a shared room.

The room I was assigned had two bunk beds, and when I walked
in, a frail elderly man with pale white skin and a white beard lay on
one of the bottom bunks, staring straight up. I set my gear down, and
then I introduced myself and stuck out my hand.

"I don't shake hands," he said.

I pulled back my hand. "Well, what's your name?" I asked.

He gave the question some thought. "Joseph," he said, finally.

Later, in the kitchen, a Chinese family sat around one of the tables. They didn't speak English, so we communicated with nods and smiles, and I listened to the percussive rhythm of their language. While I ate, a couple from Portland came in and set their baby in a high chair. The father fed the infant with a spoon, while the mom cooked their meal. They said that they were on a short vacation, on their way to San Francisco.

"I've never stayed at a hostel before," said the woman.

"I stayed at a lot of them in Europe," said the man. "They're very popular there. I don't know why they're not more popular here." He shrugged.

"Maybe it's because Americans snore," said the woman, and they both laughed.

I finished my meal and walked back into my room. Joseph was sitting in a chair against the wall, staring straight ahead. During the duration of my stay at the hostel I never once saw Joseph leave the room.

"Sounds like Mexico out there," he said. I listened and heard the baby babbling, the splashing of water, the clinking of plates.

"You've been to Mexico?" I asked.

"Yes," he said.

"Is it nice there?" I asked, wanting to keep the conversation going.

"Go see for yourself," he snapped.

Later, when I returned to the room to sleep, Joseph was still sitting in the chair, a book on his lap. His eyes were closed, his head down. He was very still. He looked like a statue in a wax museum. I watched, was relieved when I saw the rise and fall of his chest.

I was in bed reading when a French man came in. His name was Fabian. He looked at Joseph asleep in the chair.

"Should we wake him?" he asked. If we turned out the lights, Joseph might have woken, disoriented.

"Probably," I said.

Fabian went over, touched Joseph's shoulder, but he didn't wake. Then Fabian shook his shoulder lightly. Joseph opened his eyes, looked around.

"Do you want to get in bed?" asked Fabian.

Without saying a word, Joseph moved to his bed and lay on his back with his knees bent and his feet up against the top of the foot board.

The babbling coos of a one-year-old child and then the quiet murmurs of adults, the clink of spoon against bowl, all from the kitchen adjacent to our room. And I was awake, in a room full of men, Joseph and Fabian and a third man who had arrived in the night. The other men grumbled under their breath about the baby's attempts at language in the dawn.

I rose, walked into the kitchen, nodded at the couple, who apologized for their baby.

"Not at all," I said. "It was a pleasant sound to wake to." I wasn't just being polite. I meant it.

I walked outside and checked my bike, which was fine, locked to a rack beneath a tarp provided by the hostel. When I returned to my oatmeal, I could hear voices coming from the room where I'd slept, two voices, one with a soft, French accent.

Joseph was explaining, very articulately, and in precise detail, about the dossier that the government kept regarding him.

"They've been watching me for years, since the end of World War II," he said. "They know where I've been, who I've talked to. They keep a tap on my phone. They think I don't know."

"And why would they do that?" Fabian asked.

"Because," said Joseph, agitated, "of my connections to Germany, obviously."

I understood then why he wouldn't shake my hand, why he never left the room and kept his back to the wall. It struck me that a hostel was a peculiar place for a man who was certifiably paranoid.

Fabian, unabashedly, and gently, asked Joseph why he felt the way he did, what evidence he had. He engaged Joseph calmly in conversation, and Joseph was entirely willing to talk. Joseph had made me uncomfortable, and I had taken to avoiding him entirely. But Fabian was patient with him.

"Where are you going next?" Fabian asked.

"I never reveal my destination," said Joseph, "because I can't know who it is that might be seeking that information."

"That makes sense," said Fabian.

Before I left I shook Fabian's hand and told him I was glad to have met him. He seemed surprised by this—we had never actually had a conversation. But I meant it.

Fog again and water rolling onto a shore full of seagulls that, despite what I assume had been a life spent near the sea, rose squawking angrily at the ocean, as if surprised by its gall. I rode up a hill and then onto an alternate route, a road entirely devoid of traffic, which I found odd, given the redwood forest beauty and the fact it was still the weekend. But I relished it, taking advantage of the wide road and rolling hills. The fog drifted lazily through fanned branches, lifting, dissipating, until the sun broke through, creating a spotlight of beams, filtering through the trees. The road continued, winding through the redwoods, shady and cool, and even when the fog was gone and the sun shone bright in a late-morning sky, the forest floor remained in shadow, so thick and tall were the trees. I rode effortlessly, buoyed by the primeval beauty.

South to Trinidad, and an overcast sky hung over gray water, no light through the trees. I could feel my sweat, cold against my back. I had been avoiding a nagging feeling that had been building. It had been a flawless summer day of beautiful scenery, and I wanted it never to end. I wanted to ride and ride and ride. It was the thirty-first day of July, and like every July 31 of my life, I tried to block August from my mind, tried to will the summer not to end. To match what I'd done twenty years earlier, I'd need to ride 1,800 miles in two weeks. I did the math—nearly 130 miles per day. I heard the voice I'd been avoiding. I had to face facts—clearly, I was not going to make it.

*You are not twenty anymore.*

A decision had to be made. I could ride to San Francisco and then fly home. But I'd already been there, and I knew the coastal traffic would be heavy. My original plan on that first trip had been to ride all the way to the Mexican border and then across the southernmost

American desert. In August. Such was the foolishness of youth. Then, too, it was time that had forced me to alter my plans, had probably saved me from ending as buzzard feed in the Arizona heat.

I thought about all of those adventurers and explorers I'd long admired and wanted to emulate: Lewis and Clark, John Wesley Powell, the Peary Arctic expeditions; the American roadsters Kerouac, Steinbeck, Least Heat-Moon; and Odysseus, the hero of the greatest travel narrative of them all, a character whose very name was a synonym for journey.

But I was claiming kindred status to none of them. I was content now not to emulate but to admire them from the general safety of my reading chair. If this was an adventure, it was not heroic. I was simply a man on a bicycle, moving slowly again through the country he'd fallen in love with twenty years earlier. What I had in common with other sojourners was only that each of our journeys had to end. I was sad it would end, but even Odysseus had been returning to Penelope as fast as the day's technology would allow. And now there were planes, trains, rental cars. I didn't *have* to bike home.

Whatever romantic fantasy I'd held about the wiles of the solitary traveler was just that: fantasy. From the start I had relied on the kindness of others, the encouragement of family and friends. I hadn't been independent at all.

I rode into Eureka. In the night I gazed up from where I camped. Against the darkening sky, brightly lit for all to see, was the unmistakable yellow square and the red teepee design in front: KOA. The sound of highway traffic and the TV noise blaring from the small room above the campground office completed the experience.

It was time to get off the coast, add my two cents to the exhaust-filled air.

My bicycle journey wasn't over, but tomorrow, I decided, I would rent a car and drive to Modesto and from there continue east. Destination: Grand Canyon, north rim. I wanted to see Yosemite and Zion in Utah.

But mostly I wanted to do something the twenty-year-old had been unable to do: bike across Nevada, over the most solitudinal road in America, and then along the Extraterrestrial Highway.

# From Modesto to Yosemite and Mammoth Lakes

THE BICYCLE, SANS SEAT AND TIRES, fit neatly in the Dodge Neon, and I stashed the rest of the gear in the trunk. I pulled out of the rental car agency parking lot and drove back into Arcata and to a coffee shop, where alternative soul bounced from small speakers on shelves high in the corners and a teenage boy, with dirty-blond dreadlocks, talked to a man in an old green T-shirt that said THC; bright abstract paintings hung from walls painted orange and red. A woman sitting with her back turned at the table across from me leaned forward, revealing a macramé thong riding high above her jeans and a butterfly tattoo on the small of her back.

I finished my bagel and drove north to the Highway 299 exit. I adjusted the radio until I found an oldies station and turned it up loud. Sly and the Family Stone's "Everyday People" and Tom Petty's "Free Fallin'," and behind the wheel, I felt a surprising sense of freedom, a joy to be suddenly moving at sixty-five miles per hour. The drive east from the coast rose steadily into the Cascades on winding, curvy roads through pine forests and along the Trinity River, where kayaks and rafts moved with the rapids. In Redding I turned south onto Interstate 5, stopping only once for gas in Williams. And then it was over a bridge and into Sacramento. Elton John sang "Don't Let the Sun Go Down on Me," while the sun was indeed going down. And then through Stockton, intently watching the signs in the dark, not wanting to miss the turns, and I was in Modesto, where I checked into a cheap room. Outside, in the parking lot, men loitered in the ninety-degree-plus night heat, smoking cigarettes, and I hurriedly unpacked everything into the room, locking and latching the door behind me. I turned the air-conditioning on full blast, and amid the clanking noise I lay back on my bed. On the TV Lance Armstrong, who had just won his seventh Tour de France, was on David Letterman. I was inspired to ride again.

An August morning, and I walked back to the motel from the car rental return. I had heard Modesto could be a rough place, but the city struck me as a vibrant, friendly town. The lawns were all green, the gardens lush, the downtown streets lined with galleries and shops. It was hot. Until then I had scarcely seen a day over seventy-five, and suddenly I was faced with the prospect of 100.

I rode east on Highway 120, past long lines of strip mall shops, many with bars over their windows. The shoulder was wide but filled with debris, and I had to watch carefully for glass as I rode. But soon I was out of Modesto and riding on a road that was gun-barrel straight, through sweet-smelling orchards. It was hot, easily in the mid-nineties, and it felt good to sweat, to be moving under my own power again.

Out near the curb an old Hispanic couple stood by a mailbox. I stopped, greeted them. They smiled.

"What kinds of orchards are these?" I wanted to know, pointing to the long lines of trees in the yard.

They both shrugged, seemed confused by my question. When I asked again, the woman told me the name of the street I was on, and I realized they didn't speak English.

"Que tipo de frutas?" I tried, pointing to the trees.

The man nodded and replied in English. "Cherries."

"And almonds," said the woman, pointing to the trees planted across the street.

"Y los otros?" I asked, pointing back toward the way I had come.

"Peaches," said the man.

"Y walnuts," said the woman.

It made sense that the English words they knew named the crops that they grew. I continued east, stopping at a produce market. I bought an apple and a softball-sized peach. I stood outside in the shade of the store's porch and ate them both.

An old farmer in overalls and a green John Deere cap walked past me. He stopped and turned, looked me up and down, and chuckled. I wondered what his problem was.

"Good peaches, aren't they," he said.

And then I realized I'd been smiling like a child, the peach juice dripping down my chin.

La Grange arrived like a mirage, a town that stretched only the length of a single city block, with historic buildings. There was no sign of life, at least not out in the midday heat. At the edge of town there was an old jail cell, roughly the size of a garden shed. Behind the bars that lined the open doorway there was a small cot, and a pair of red long johns hung from a nail against the wall, next to a calendar from 1887. I walked up the hill to the old schoolhouse, where one could look out across hills of golden grass. The sky was a shade of light blue, with thin wisps of high cirrus clouds.

I struggled uphill, in the muscle-depleting heat, stopping often to drink water. My muscles felt tired, depleted. To my right the soft hills were a giant hand, its fingers stretching into Lake McClure.

In the early evening I rode into Coulterville, which, during the Gold Rush of 1849, had been a thriving mining town. Now it was a mix of abandoned buildings, with a handful of small businesses. A sign with an arrow pointing down a gravel road said, CAMPING. I rode past a swimming a pool and a small park to a park with run-down trailers. Along a fence, across from the trailers, there were a handful of grassy sites, with no picnic tables.

A woman sat on a chair beneath a tarp. She watched as I approached, a dull glint in her eyes.

"Is there tent camping here?" I asked.

"You'd have to talk to Frank," she said.

"Do you know where I can find him?"

"In his trailer," she said, gesturing toward a faded blue trailer at the front of the drive.

I knocked on the door, and there was a sudden fury of barking of dogs. And then the door opened, just wide enough for a skinny, shirt-less man to slip outside.

"What can I do you for?" he asked, and I asked him how much he'd charge me to pitch my tent.

He scratched his leg, thinking. "I don't know. There's no facilities, no running water."

I had just ridden over sixty miles in hundred-degree heat and was too tired to care. I told him that wasn't a problem—I just needed a place to sleep.

"Tell you what. You can pitch your tent anywhere along that fence. Five bucks. You can probably use the restrooms up at the pool."

I handed him the money. He slipped it in his pocket and stepped back inside.

In the dark I walked to the only pay phone in town, which stood on a steep sidewalk outside an abandoned motel. I dialed Joan. I was so tired from the heat, I had to lean against the phone. A teen on a skateboard came shooting down the sidewalk and crashed at the bottom of the hill, much to the delight of his friends walking behind him.

The next morning I rose before sunrise and quickly packed my bike. I wanted to avoid the midday heat. At a café I ordered a plate of fruit and asked the waitress about the road ahead. Was it hilly? She didn't know but asked three men sitting at a table behind me.

"Naw," said one of the men, "it ain't steep. Some up-and-down hills but not bad."

"The worst part," said one of the other men, "will be just getting out of town here."

I nodded and thanked them. I assumed he meant that the hill ended at the edge of the town, maybe a climb of a hundred yards or so. But instead I discovered six and a half curse-inspiring, steep, and winding miles. Already it was over ninety degrees. I had to stop often, and my leg muscles were uncharacteristically sore.

I struggled into Greeley Hill, where I rested in the air-conditioned library and studied maps. Then it was more uphill. The temperature rose to 103 degrees. Finally, I made the Highway 120 turnoff.

At a café in Buck Meadows a man sitting at the bar turned and gave me a smile of recognition. I had never seen the man before.

"You gonna make it to the park?" he asked. He meant Yosemite.

"I'm tryin'," I said.

When I showed no sign of recognition, he said, "We talked last night?" He stood up to walk outside, and as he did, he pulled a pack of cigarettes from his front shirt pocket. I was sitting by the door to an outside patio, which was the designated smoking area.

"You mean in Coulterville?" I asked as he passed.

"No. Not Coulterville," he said in disgust. He was a large man, with long mustard hair and a mustache.

"Where then?" I asked.

"I'll just let it be a mystery then, if you don't remember." He seemed rebuffed, and I felt guilty for not being who he thought I was. Or maybe the heat had left gaps in my recall.

I sat at my table and drank three large glasses of water.

"That your bike out there?" asked the waitress, a tall heavy-set woman, as she filled my glass yet again. I said that it was.

"Ain't you a fine line between bravery and stupid," she said. I didn't dare tell her to which side I was leaning, and she was kind enough not to speculate.

After a short time the man who recognized me from a place I'd never been returned.

"Are you sure it wasn't Coulterville?" I asked him.

"I've been to Coulterville once in my life," he said. "And it wasn't last night. It was at the hotel."

"I think you might have me mixed up with somebody else," I said.

He smirked and shook his head, as if I was being very naive. The exchange left me disoriented, and I felt guilty for not remembering an experience I'd never had in the first place.

I noticed a trailer park and campground adjacent to the restaurant. I stood stiffly, and as I paid my bill, I asked if there was a place nearby where I could shower. The waitress said she wasn't sure, but she agreed it was a good idea. Then she referred me to a man who I took to be the owner of both restaurant and camp.

"We're still redoing those showers over there. They're not officially open. But the water runs. You're welcome to use them," he said.

I asked him how much.

"You can use them for free. They're not actually open yet," he repeated.

I walked outside and across the lawn to the showers. There were no curtains on the shower stalls or the windows. I looked around. Nothing moved in the heat. I stood in front of a mirror. Who was I? I was riding a bicycle in 103-degree heat; my muscles were dead. I hadn't seen anyone I knew, with the exception of Joan and Winnefred in Washington, since I'd left in May. People who didn't know me claimed that they did, and who was I to argue? The face in the mirror was thin. White streaks of salt from my dried sweat ran down my face. For a brief and strange moment my identity fell away, and it wasn't me I saw in the mirror but a stranger.

I undressed and stepped into one of the shower stalls. But as I was reaching to turn on the water, I saw that the stall was occupied. A small, dark-green frog rested securely, at about eye level, on the wall.

"Whoops. Sorry," I said.

To a frog.

He didn't reply or budge or even blink.

So I moved to the next stall, checking this time to make sure that I was alone. And then I stood beneath water that was neither hot nor cold but lukewarm, no matter which knob I turned. Back outside it was still one hundred degrees, and it was just seconds before I was sweating again. The road outside Buck Meadows continued to rise, with no end to the incline in sight.

That evening as I rode, long reaches of forest shadows stretched across the highway, a cooling relief. I rode until just past dusk, and then, at a gravel pull-out, I stopped and carried the bike into the forest, where I set up my tent and hung my food from a high branch of a tree. Darkness fell quickly into a night that was still, not even a rustling in the tops of the trees. I was just miles from Yosemite.

It wasn't aesthetics that first drew white men to the Yosemite area. It was gold, which was discovered in the nearby foothills in 1848. The resulting encroachment of miners and traders led to conflicts with the Miwok and Paiute Indians who had long lived in the area. *Yosemite* is a word derived from *Uzumati*—which means "grizzly bear"—and refers specifically to an Indian tribe. The region was so named by Dr. Lafayette Bunnell, who was a member of a battalion that entered the park in pursuit of a small band of Ahwaneechee Indians, who had been accused of raiding local trading posts. *Taming* was the word they used. It was the first step in making Yosemite a refuge for tourists and nature lovers.

The history of Yosemite as a national park greatly complicates the notion of "pristine" wilderness. Man's influence is seen not only in the roads and buildings but also in the nature itself. Domestic plants and animals, introduced as early as the 1860s, altered the ecosystem. In

1878, under the guidance of preservationist Galen Clark, a moraine that had dammed the Merced River was dynamited. The result was a drier valley floor with fewer mosquitoes, more accessible to those who wanted to see nature in its "purity." The long-term effect of Clark's work was a forest growth that reduced the size of meadows. In 1860 there were over 750 acres of meadow in the valley. Today there are less than half that, and what remains is maintained only by clearing the forests. In 1923 the damming of Hetch Hetchy Valley destroyed an area of waterfalls and cliffs similar to those in Yosemite Valley.

Dynamite, dams, livestock, the removal of Indians who had long inhabited the land. In effect the wilderness had been "tamed" so that tourists could enjoy nature and cities could have water. "Indians walk softly and hurt the landscape hardly more than the birds and squirrels," wrote John Muir in *My First Summer in the Sierra*, "and their brush and bark huts last hardly longer than those of wood rats, while their more enduring monuments . . . vanish in a few centuries . . . How different are most of those of the white man, especially on the lower gold region—roads blasted in the solid rock, wild streams dammed and tamed and turned out of their channels and led along the sides of canyons and valleys to work in mines like slaves."

There was no longer such thing as "untouched by man," of course. Hadn't been for a long time. Yosemite was a peculiar and singular place. Not a wilderness but a study in human and nature relations that was unique among national parks, different even from Yellowstone or the Grand Canyon.

I entered the park, where I filled my water bottles and waited for the ranger station to open. Overnight my muscles had recovered, and the morning, while not cool, had been at least not unbearably hot, and I'd ridden uphill, on a winding road with little shoulder.

At the top of an eight-mile climb I stopped at Crane Flats. Already it was in the upper nineties. Lines at the gas pumps were backed all the way to the main road—RV's, SUV's, rental cars, vans. A woman, upon seeing me sitting on a bench beside my bicycle, said, "I'll bet you're glad to be on that bike when you see this chaos."

Maybe I was glad. Mostly, I was contemplating a sign that said, DO NOT MOVE THIS BENCH. The bench was the only seating, and it rested five feet from the shade. Three straight days of riding uphill in the heat was taking a toll. One of the symptoms of heat exhaustion was an increased heart rate, and I could feel my heart pounding. My legs felt heavy. It was a moral dilemma: should a man in my condition, sitting on a sun-drenched bench, ignore such a sign and move it into the shade? The conundrum was solved with patience. The shade shifted with the rising sun and eventually found me. Which is to say, I did not move from that bench for a very long time.

There was a new decision to be made. On the first trip I'd ridden to Tuolumne Meadows and over Tioga Pass. But I'd wanted to ride into Yosemite Valley. I'd arrived in Yosemite in late afternoon and was told that I wouldn't be allowed in the valley, as all of the campgrounds were full. So I'd missed much of what Yosemite was known for.

Now I wanted to see the valley, a decision made easier by the fact that it was sixteen downhill miles away. I'd been climbing, in the heat, for three straight days.

The ride was an exhilarating, treacherous descent, complicated by wind that alternated from side to tail, depending on the curves. There was no shoulder on the road, and I could see the traffic in my rear-view mirror. Posted speed limits were neither enforced nor adhered to; drivers pointed to scenery without watching where they were going. One car skidded into a pull-out just ahead of me, causing me to swerve and slam on my brakes. By the time I arrived on the valley floor I was a heat-frazzled bundle of nerves that the madness of the valley did little to alleviate.

The scenery, though, was magnificent.

And what was this place, this Yosemite Valley? Not really city, not really wilderness—the park on a Thursday afternoon in August was a Manhattan-style traffic jam. Inside the shops people nudged me out of their way or reached around and over me to pull items from shelves aggressively. A food court line stretched out the door. I bought a plate of spaghetti and waited for an empty seat. The tables were so close together, I had to hold my tray high and be careful to not bump anyone. When an elderly couple rose to leave, I hurried to their table, glad just for the chance to sit down amongst the crying children, snappy adults, and people with dazed looks in their eyes, all of whom had come to get away from it all but in so doing had brought it all with them.

"Excuse me?" asked a man at the table beside me. "Have you been here to Yosemite before?" The man was sitting with his wife and two boys, one sitting politely, playing with a toy Power Ranger, and the other, the youngest, asleep in his chair.

"Yes," I said. I didn't tell him it had been twenty years and that I'd never actually been to the valley.

"Could I ask your opinion, then?" he said.

"Of course."

"What should we see next? We arrived here this morning and have already driven the whole valley floor."

"How much time do you have?" I asked.

"We must leave for the coast tonight," he said.

They had driven all the way to Yosemite, having heard about the great valley scenery. Now, just past noon, they'd seen it all.

"You might try Tuolumne Meadows," I suggested. "Or Tioga Pass." I explained how to get there. He was grateful and kind. His wife smiled and thanked me. His sons were clean and well-behaved.

Outside I walked along a paved trail. People rode bicycles or skimmed past on roller blades. Many wore iPods, their heads bopping to the music. I looked up and saw for the first time the iconic Half Dome and Yosemite Falls, both of which seemed out of place, incongruous with the many famous photographs they had inspired.

I checked into a walk-in campground, which was surprisingly not full. The adjacent parking lot was crowded with cars. There were no trees in the campground. The sites were all shared group sites, square barren plots of land that held up to five tents. When I saw my site, my heart sank. There were four tents. A group of teenagers sat on the picnic table, drinking beer, their music playing loudly. Had I stayed, I might have made friends and learned to enjoy it, but it wasn't my idea of camping. In Idaho, where I'd slept in a town park, a woman had teased me. "Not exactly roughing it," she had said. But there I'd slept in solitude. Here in this famous national park there was scarcely room to breathe.

A bus was scheduled to leave for Mammoth Lakes at five o'clock. I planned to be on it.

I had two hours. I walked into a large gift shop and grocery store. People crowded the aisles, stood in lines. I could hear a man's voice frantically calling for his son. "Shawn. Shawn? Shawn!" Wherever I went in the store, I could hear him. Then I heard a female voice join in. "Shawn! Shawn!" The voices were frantic. I looked up and down the aisles, around the postcard racks, the glass shelves of shot glasses and wooden carved animals. I saw no child who seemed to be misplaced. Other tourists casually browsed the merchandise, unconcerned. The calls for the lost Shawn continued and then abruptly stopped.

I walked back outside. My head throbbed in the heat, which rose from the pavement and sidewalks. Outside, people hurriedly walked past, many talking on cell phones. Few were looking up at the famous falls or the granite cliffs.

When the bus arrived, I rolled my loaded bicycle and stood in the crowd that waited at the stop. I'd been told all of the buses had bicycle racks, but when the bus pulled up it didn't have.

"Bike racks?" said the driver. "No. None of the buses have bike racks. But if you want, you're welcome to cram it in, in one of the spaces underneath, if you can find the room."

The spaces were full of backpacks, but I managed to fit my bike and most of my gear, praying it wouldn't be damaged. And then I was seated comfortably in a big blue seat of the air-conditioned bus. I let out a deep sigh. After negotiating the valley traffic, we moved up the same road I had ridden down just a few hours before, and finally I relaxed. We stopped at Crane Flats and then headed up Tioga Road.

From the comfort of the bus seat I looked out at the narrow road. The bus hugged the corners tightly, and there was almost no shoulder. The road was steep and winding. But the main issue was traffic. I cringed each time we took a corner, imagining with horror any cyclist who might be riding there. Suddenly I had newfound respect for the twenty-year-old me, a parent-like pride. I hadn't considered how treacherous it was, had always ridden with a blind faith that all motorists would see me, wouldn't hit me from behind. Now I saw that to ride a bicycle on this road required a bravery and gumption that frankly I was glad I no longer had.

We drove on, rising through pine forests, past the sheer-faced rocks, smoothed from years of exfoliation. The road flattened out into meadows of wildflowers, ponds, and high mountain lakes. I could see Cathedral Rock and Half Dome in the distance. The sun shone against the mountain peaks, turning them light purple. Storm clouds brewed in the distance, and all that conservationists such as John Muir, Ansel Adams, and Galen Rowell had spent so many years of their lives working to preserve became clear to me, and I realized I was no different than any of those people I'd seen in the valley. What Yosemite required for full appreciation was time and exploration on *foot*. Glimpsing it aboard a bicycle—no less than in an RV—couldn't do it justice.

At Tuolumne Meadows there were five or six people waiting for the bus, including one dark-complected man. He was carrying a fully loaded backpack. His clothes were dirty, but he wore the glow of a man who had just been transformed. I watched him from my window as he loaded his pack in the bin under the bus. The bus was nearly empty now, most of the other passengers having been dropped off at various spots along the way. He boarded and sat across the aisle from me.

The bus rolled onto the highway, making a handful more stops along the way. The man's eyes were glued to the scenery outside his window. He shook his head, and in the reflection in the glass I could see he was beaming.

"Unbelievable," he exclaimed, looking out at the wilderness, in awe of the high peaks, the canyon, and the river below. Experience had gained him an appreciation that I envied. He had alert, brown eyes and crew-cropped hair.

We continued to the top of Tioga Pass and then started down the steep descent. Along a curve I looked out over the edge of the pass and felt a chill. It was here where two decades ago it had all nearly ended. But maybe I overdramatize it now; back then I believed I was invincible—believed that fate was on my side, that God would protect me from any harm.

It had been midafternoon, and I'd finally reached the nearly ten thousand–foot pass summit. Peering out over the granite cliffs, the mountains, the valleys, I was ecstatic. Since I'd left the coast, it had been a long four-day climb, but now I'd be riding downhill all the way into Nevada. I began my descent, pedaling hard. I did not need to be concerned, as I often am now, with failing eyesight. I was so attuned to the bike by then that it felt like an extension of my own body. Or perhaps I had not yet developed an appreciation for potential hazards. I didn't consider, for example, how you could hit a pothole or blow a tire or hit a rock and swerve and fall. I watched my cyclometer climb: twenty, twenty-five, thirty miles per hour. I rode, gliding, leaning into the curves, down the back side of that pass, my momentum gaining. Thirty-five miles per hour. I took in the increasingly blurred beauty of the scenery whizzing by, the blue lakes to my right below a steep drop-off and the cliffs on the other side of the highway. Forty miles per hour. The drier east side of the mountain, and I was flying, then, my reward for those days of uphill climbing, forty-five miles per hour. Then I came around a curve.

In my lean into the turn I was sucker-punched by a gust of wind, and suddenly I felt the slip. I'd leaned too far. I was falling—the adrenalin of panic, that split second when mistakes were made. I shifted my weight and, miraculously, didn't overcompensate but regained my balance and maintained it, braking slowly, gently, until I came to a euphoric stop.

I wore no helmet, having failed to replace the one that I'd lost.

I looked down at the drop, the trees, the rocks hundreds of feet below. I took a deep breath and wiped the sweat from my brow.

It was not until later—that night in my tent in a park in Lee Vining, as I replayed that scene in my mind—that I started to shake and my heart began to pound.

Slowly, now, the bus descended, and I looked out over that edge and tensed up. Even in the bus I was glad when we were all the way down the pass.

After a stop at Lee Vining the bus headed south, toward Mammoth Lakes. It was nearly dusk. I looked over at the backpacker across from me, and we started to talk. His name was Mark Phillips, and he had just spent sixteen days alone, hiking the John Muir Trail.

"It was incredible," he said. "Not easy. I had to ford several rivers. Some of them up to my knees. Once the water was so strong, I lost my sandals." He laughed, shook his head. "But it was beautiful."

"Did you have problems with bears?" I asked.

"No," he said. "The park service makes you rent a bear-proof container to store your food. I saw some deer. One night I heard something sniffing around my tent."

Mark lived in Houston, where he drove a dairy truck. He was headed back there the next day.

"I am already supposed to be back at work, technically," he said. "But my boss is pretty understanding. I never take sick days."

"Do you backpack a lot?" I asked.

"About every vacation," he said. "I've done trips in Alaska, Mount Rainier, and Machu Picchu.

"Were there a lot of people on the trail?" I asked.

"A few, not a lot. One night," he said, "I'd been out just about five days—I woke to voices. I looked out my tent with my flashlight, but there was still a little bit of light. There were two people, a couple. Lost. They were several yards from the trail, and they were headed toward a precipice—it could have been dangerous. I yelled at them. 'Hey. Stop.' And then I guided them back to the trail.

"Later I helped show them how to set up their tent. But they were doing it, hiking the trail."

We were silent then, and we each looked out the window into the darkness. I thought about how different his Yosemite experience had been from mine. I was impressed with him, for his demeanor and for his courage. I vowed to return to Yosemite someday, not by bike but with my backpack.

Mammoth Lakes was a mountain town, with an adventurer's charm enhanced by both its proximity to Yosemite and its local ski hill. Outside a bank a tall, lean man asked me about my bike trip. I told him how much I liked Mammoth, how it reminded me of Colorado ski towns. "Almost everywhere I've been in the West," I said, "people have complained about Californians moving in. It seems to me, though, that California has a lot of its own solitude and small-town life.

"It's always been that way," he said. "Back in the '70s, when I lived in Colorado, everything was 'Don't Californicate Colorado.' He laughed. "Where I live now" he said, "it's the Nevadans everyone says that about."

It was a sort of pretzel logic, particular to the West: if Californians were Californicating Colorado, it followed somehow that Nevadans were Californicating California.

"You know," he continued, "people everywhere associate California with Hollywood. Hey, Hollywood is a long way away for most of us. It's just such a small part of the whole state. I've lived all over the West. You know, it's odd," he continued, gesturing toward the mountains that rose and overlooked the town, "in all people's attempts to find the perfect life of peace and solitude, California just might be the best-kept secret."

The local bicycle shop was well stocked, and I purchased a spare tire, four extra tubes, eight $CO_2$'s, and a patch kit, all with Nevada in mind. It was paranoia that drove my purchase but a paranoia born from experience. Nevada's Highway 95 held for me a twenty-year-old memory that was full of both intrigue and fear. I felt a yearning to experience the vastness of it, to feel its disconcerting solitude. But I wanted no repeat of the complacency that twenty years earlier had left me standing alone in the desert, holding an irreparable tube and hollering into the wind.

# From Mammoth Lakes to Mono Lake

"WHY IN THE WORLD," asked the woman sitting in the bus seat in front of me, "is he stopping here?"

"Here" was a dry sandy pull-out at the side of a small break in the median of Highway 120. To the west, dry hills rose toward the sun, but to the east the land leveled out, and a single lane of highway converged into the horizon. We were on the bus from Mammoth, which was returning, ultimately, to Yosemite Valley. The answer to the woman's question was me.

Earlier I had asked the driver if he would drop me off at the intersection of 120 East.

He looked puzzled. "Yeah, well, 120," he said. That's where we're going. But you mean west."

"No," I said. "I mean east."

He had looked at me for a moment, cocked his head, thinking. "No one's ever asked me to do that before. But I don't see why not."

Now I stood up, and all eyes were on me as I walked off the bus. The driver followed and helped me to unload my bicycle and gear from the underneath bin.

"You wouldn't be here if you didn't know what you were doing, huh?" he asked.

"Every fool believes as much," I said.

He laughed and wished me luck. And then he stepped back onto the bus, and I heard the door close. I looked up. The woman was watching me through her window with a concerned look that didn't inspire confidence. And then the bus rolled back onto the pavement, and I watched it slowly disappear.

If the crowds of Yosemite Valley had made me agoraphobic, then surely the antidote lay before me. Once the bus was gone, there was nothing to do but ride through the sparse pine forests, where white prickly poppy flowers grew from the white sandy soil. The sky was a pale, metallic blue. Mono Lake spread out to the north, its eerie spires standing still, as if in mourning or in prayer.

The ride climbed a gradual incline, pleasantly cool in the shade, at an elevation over eight thousand feet.

I reached a summit, and then the forest turned to desert, and I moved through fields of sage and yarrow, the heat rising palpably with my descent, past striated rock formations and then into the furnace of Benton Hot Springs. The old store at the bottom of the pass, which I remembered for its antiques, was closed now, its paint fading. "ESTABLISHED 1852" was painted on the front. An old wagon wheel leaned against a post, and a rocking chair sat forlornly on the porch.

Two miles ahead I rode into Benton, a town with a single gas station and café at the intersection of highways 120 and 6. Across the street sat a truckload of squawking chickens. At the counter two men in cowboy hats and suspenders sipped cups of coffee.

I sat at one of the tables. I'd ridden nearly fifty miles already. My throat was parched from the dry dusty air. A couple came in and sat at the table next to mine.

The man nodded at my bicycle outside the window. "Where'd you leave from today?" he asked.

"Mammoth Lakes," I said. Mammoth Lakes was nearly a hundred miles away. I didn't tell him about the bus.

"I'm Michael," he said, handing me a business card. I read that he was a photographer from Kansas City. His wife was from Prague.

They had just driven from where I was headed. "How was the road?" I asked.

"Pretty desolate," said the man.

"Is there much traffic on that road?" I asked.

"That's the thing that got me," said the woman. "So little traffic."

My fear, I suppose, was not entirely irrational. Isolation, heat, long spaces with no towns, little to no traffic. What if I broke down, got sick, crashed, ran out of water? And yet already I had faced cold and snow, grizzly bears and bison, a crash, and drivers who inched too close at seventy-plus miles per hour. In the past I'd experienced hailstorms and heatstroke. I'd stood down a man who'd been stalking me, for what purpose, I never knew. Fear had never before deterred me.

Plus, I had a long-standing love for the desert landscapes of the American Southwest, which I'd hiked and camped and explored. Sure, there were rattlesnakes and scorpions and heat, and I'd have to be smart about water. But realistically, I reasoned to myself, there was really little about Nevada to fear. No, really nothing to fear at all.

But when I arrived at the state line and raised my camera to take a photo of the bullet-ridden WELCOME TO NEVADA sign, I realized I was shaking.

# Nevada

# Tonopah

NEVADA WAS A PECULIAR PLACE. *Strange* seemed a fair word to describe it, though it was a strangeness imbued with quirkiness and magic. Whatever fear I held was not driven by rational thought, but Nevada was a place where *rational* had limited bearing.

From Lee Vining to Tonopah it was 132 miles. This I knew because it stood as my single one-day record. But ultimately, that summer I hadn't been able to make it all the way across the state without the help of two men from Rachel and their pickup truck.

I hadn't originally planned to ride Nevada. Outside of Las Vegas and Reno, who does plan a journey there? When I did decide to ride east from the central California coast, I figured Nevada to be a simple two-to three-day ride, just a quick bridge to get me to Utah. For as everyone knows, the West is characterized by westerly winds. This confidence was buoyed by that long ride into Tonopah.

But then the winds had changed.

I'd ridden into a three-day flurry so strong that my speed was often reduced to six miles per hour. Then, when I had a flat tire, I discovered that my last tube had a slow leak. No problem. All I had to do was patch it. I took out my patch kit and discovered I had only one remaining. I carefully patched the tire.

But the slow leak continued. Roughly every five miles or so, I had to stop, refill my tire with a hand pump that required an exhausting level of effort. Twice, I'd tried to hitchhike. The first car passed without even slowing. The second, a trucker, slowed but then shrugged an apology and drove on. I watched as the truck grew ever smaller in the distance.

I had ridden on, stopping to pump the tire and then pedaling slowly against the wind, which grew in intensity. Wind inspires rage—studies have shown this. Among children playground fights increase on windy days, and in Italy a sirocco off the Adriatic Sea has been successfully used by lawyers as a defense for violent crimes.

Late in the afternoon fighter pilots from the Nellis Air Force Range had flown overhead. I rode, pushing onward against the wind, the sound of those engines above me, and I felt as if I weren't moving at all. It was like a bad dream in which you're being chased and can't move, can't get a foothold to scurry away from that which was ready to pounce. Except it was reality, albeit Nevada style.

I had attacked the wind, pedaled hard, grunting as I rode, angry. And then, when I felt the familiar wobble, I stopped, yanked my pump from the bike, and started pumping the tire in a rage. But the tire wouldn't fill, so I took the pump in both hands, like a bat, and slammed it against the pavement, with a fury that defied all reason. I slammed that pump until I felt it shatter, and plastic pieces were strewn across the pavement, the long tube of the pump now shaped in a V.

I stopped, realizing what I had done. Somehow the tire held enough air to get me over a pass and into Rachel, a town that wasn't really a town at all but a small smattering of trailers.

One of the trailers was a café. Two men worked inside, selling a small selection of grocery items and serving food and drinks at a counter. A single slot machine sat on one edge of the counter. I ordered lunch and explained my situation. The two men listened calmly, with compassion. That night they let me sleep in a small storage room in back, and the next morning they drove me to Caliente.

Now, in the middle of another August afternoon, I stood before the state line. If the twenty-year-old in the greatest physical condition of his life had struggled to cross this desert, what could I expect now?

There was nothing to do but find out.

I rode into a landscape I hadn't remembered, could scarcely imagine. Nevada by automobile may be monotonous, but by bicycle it was a place of stunning beauty, a landscape that was constantly changing. By early evening there was a skew to the light, a magnificent glow that seemed to be a cross between the blue of day and the golden hue of dusk. There was no accounting for that light. The sun was still high in a sky that was clear in a way that perhaps all skies once were, so clear that when I stopped to gaze at the landscape and drink water, I removed my prescription sunglasses and realized that even without them, I could see clearly. Large boulders, the size of tool sheds, lay haphazardly over the desert floor, as if they'd been dropped like marbles from the sky. Mountains rose in the distance, jagged incisors over the palate of alkaline desert.

My map showed a town called Coaldale, where I hoped to fill my CamelBak. But Coaldale was empty, save for a few dilapidated buildings that were falling quickly into disrepair. My water bottles were still almost full, so I thought I would probably be all right. Still, I tried not to drink, though I was thirsty. I rode into dusk, the night sky darkening slowly. The highway had no paved shoulder, and when truckers came up behind, I pulled off to the side of the road to let them pass.

Roughly thirty miles before Tonopah, I took a drink from my CamelBak and heard a gurgling noise, and suddenly I was sucking only air. My CamelBak was empty. I checked my water bottles. One was full and the other about half-full. I knew there was a rest area twelve miles this side of Tonopah. I hoped there would be water there.

I rode until the light of day was all but gone, wanting to take advantage of the cooler night. The light of dusk retreated slowly, but stars began to emerge. Brewing storm clouds covered the mountains, and I could feel the cooling winds. Long streaks of lightning flashed in the southern sky.

I pulled over at a rest area, which was just a gravel lot with two large metal trash barrels. And then I rolled my bike off the road, into the desert. There were no trees, just sparse scrub bushes of sage. My dinner consisted of a peach and a granola bar.

The wind rose up with an alarming intensity I was in no way prepared for. I looked up. The sky was completely overcast now, so fast had the clouds rolled in. Gusts blew with such intensity that I had a difficult time controlling my tent long enough to stake it down, a process complicated by ground that was very hard and packed such that the stakes wouldn't set. I struggled with the tarp, which was blowing like a parachute, and I thought it might lift me and carry me over the desert.

Finally, the tent was up, and I jumped inside, partly to use my body to hold it down. I feared the worst from a storm that had begun to spew rain. I read by the light of my headlamp until my batteries went dead. The wind howled, a deafening roar, like the devil's mocking laughter, welcoming me back to Nevada. The tarp came loose at one corner and whipped against the tent. Somehow I managed to fall asleep.

I don't know how long I slept, but when I awoke, it was silent. I unzipped the tent and peered into an entirely cloudless sky. There was no moon, but the stars stretched clear to the horizons and were so abundant that I could make out the silhouette of my bicycle. From the highway, when one of the few trucks would emerge from a distant rise in the east, which was over a mile away, the headlights would illuminate the inside of my tent, such was the clarity of the air. I stepped outside and gazed up at the sky. There were no city lights, nearly no traffic, not even light pollution from Las Vegas or Reno on the respective horizons. I was tired from the ride. My throat was parched, and my stomach growled. But I did not want to sleep, did not want the night to end.

Finally, I crawled back into my tent. But it was too hot, so I moved back outside, checking by starlight for scorpions and snakes. And then I lay flat against the desert floor and watched the sky until I fell asleep. When next I woke, a thin rim of red lined the eastern horizon.

I rode east. The sky grew lighter until the sun appeared, and I rode into a brilliant orange. The temperature was rising rapidly, so I tried to pace myself, not pushing too hard.

The downside to the clarity of the air was this: Tonopah appeared in the distance, a mirage-like Mecca standing at the edge of the Monitor Mountains. I pedaled for miles, yet it seemed no closer and in fact gave the illusion that it was drifting farther away.

I tried not to look straight ahead but focused instead on the desert. The temperature continued to rise. I afforded myself occasional swallows of water, still trying to conserve it, not wanting to pin my hopes too heavily on the rest area ahead. But as it grew closer, I licked my rough lips, already sensing the wetness inside my throat.

I'd ridden twenty-one miles by the time I reached Miller's Rest, and I leaned my bicycle against a picnic table, beneath a shade tree. I almost shouted in exultation at the sight of the drinking fountain on the side of the restroom building. I walked over and pushed the button and lowered my face to drink.

But no water flowed.

No problem. I could simply use the sink in the bathroom. But there was no water there either. Still, there were six water pumps spread throughout the grounds. I lifted the handle of one. Yes! I could hear the gurgle of water. I worked the pump up and down. There was a slow drip, and I got about an inch of water into my bottle. But that was all—no matter how hard I worked it. The pump was dry, as were each of the others.

Tonopah was only about ten miles. I'd be all right. I struggled up a gradual climb. At five miles I drank half the water and then, with three miles to go, half of what remained. A mile before town I finished it.

And then I arrived in Tonopah at last. Everything, it seemed, had shifted away from the west edge of town. Buildings were abandoned, many for sale, including the Sundowner Motel, where I'd stayed twenty years earlier. I remembered the motel for its large, comfortable room and for the first-floor casino. On that night, too, I'd crawled exhausted into town, though then it had been just after dusk, on a night with a full moon. For twenty years Tonopah had held a fascination for me, and always I'd envisioned it beneath that moon and a sky that had been a shade somewhere between pink and dull copper.

It saddened me now to see the Sundowner standing in the wilting heat, forlorn and empty. Ahead I saw a gas station, where I thought I could get water. But it, too, was closed and in disrepair.

Finally, I came to the Clown Motel, a building that was painted bright blue, with two floors of rooms, and on the porch in front of the office I could see a vending machine. I had exactly the right change. I bought a drink and downed it quickly. I wanted another.

All I had was a five-dollar bill, so I went inside to get change.

Against one wall there were shelves full of clowns: clown statues, cloth doll clowns, plastic clowns, small Barbie-sized clowns, large clown dolls with large clown doll feet. Clowns. Round red noses and big clown hair. But no clerk behind the counter.

I stood waiting. Finally, two people, a man and a woman, came inside. Talking to each other, they walked behind the counter and then into a back room. I waited. I could tell they worked there. They walked back into the office. Still, they didn't acknowledge me. I felt invisible. They seemed to be trying to solve some sort of maintenance issue, and I didn't want to interrupt them. Then they walked out from behind the desk and back outside. I stood alone in the lobby, just me and the clowns, their big clown smiles on their white clown faces. The room was air-conditioned—I was in no hurry. I sat down and waited. But no one else ever came in.

So, I rode farther into town and checked in to the Jim Butler Motel, where I completed both of the only tasks that needed to be done. Which is to say: I ate lunch and fell asleep.

Tonopah was not so much founded as stumbled upon, and the credit goes not to a man but to his mule. It was May 1900. Jim Butler was the miner's name, and his burro had wandered off without its owner's consent. Butler, so the story goes, chased the mule, and when it ignored his beckoning, the angry miner picked up a rock with the intent of disciplining it. But something to the feel of that rock was to his liking, and rather than throw it, Butler stopped to have a closer look.

The rock contained silver ore.

Tonopah quickly became "Queen of the Silver Camps," a thriving boomtown that rivaled San Francisco. In 1902 Wyatt Earp opened a saloon there. In 1915 Jack Dempsey fought Johnny Sudenberg in front of a spirited Tonopah crowd. The silver mine eventually produced over 150 million dollars.

The town may have been founded on silver, but the word *Tonopah* itself came from the Shoshone language: *little wood, little water*. The Shoshone and Paiutes had occupied this land long before Jim Butler had come along. The people, like desert dwellers everywhere, were once nomadic, moving with the seasons. You can drive through now and think how barren this land, how empty. Yet humans had once managed a life of subsistence here by gathering seeds and roots and making bread from piñon nuts. They'd found food, clothing, and shelter among the desert plants and animals—Joshua trees and cactus; rabbit, fox, and deer.

It made sense to me, that nomadic life—more sense, maybe, than settling down in a single town, more sense than scarring the earth for its mineral currency. Much was made of the idea of "searching for a home." But plenty of evidence suggested that humans were never meant to be a nesting species. One could easily spend a life roaming the Nevada deserts. The West was full of restless spirits. The landscape invited it.

In the evening I walked the quiet streets, which held little evidence of the town's one-time prosperity. At a restaurant/bar/casino my waitress seemed harried, overwhelmed. Worn-out. Everyone who came and went moved in slow, robotic motions. Words were hoarded, used only when necessary. Even when people paid their bills at the register, there was no banter beyond the exchange of thank-yous, which themselves were cut to the single word *thanks*. Was it the heat? Or did the open space and limited vegetation inspire tight lips? I noticed I wasn't feeling real social myself.

At the Central Nevada Museum I moved alone through the exhibits—photos of mining camps, army and fraternal displays, mineral collections, Indian artifacts. I saw no one the whole time I was there, and I thought the museum was untended until a phone rang in a back room and a voice answered it. I listened to the half of the conversation I could hear, a lot of "yeps" and "uh-huhs." Then the talking stopped. As I left, I could see a man sitting at a desk behind a plate glass window. But he never looked up.

Outside, a short boardwalk led past a restored miner's cabin, a shed, a store with brown bottles standing in the window.

I returned to the Butler, anxious for conversation. The woman who had checked me in had been very kind, had told me to let her know if she could answer any questions about the area. Now I was in a question-asking kind of mood.

But that woman was gone, replaced by a different one. I asked her about Highway 6, the road that I'd be riding on.

"I've never been on that road," she snapped. "All I ever have time to do is work."

I tried a different approach, told her I was on a bicycle, which had worked as an icebreaker before. I said I was concerned about possibly breaking down and wondered if she thought there might be much traffic that way, just in case a guy needed to, say, hitch a ride.

"You mean a bicycle bike, right?" She asked this with a tone of bewilderment.

I said that, yes, it was a bicycle bike. Suddenly I felt nauseous and hot.

"Well, can't pretty much everything on a bicycle be fixed pretty easily?"

Tonopah was 236 miles from Reno and 210 from Las Vegas. West to east, if you wanted a bike shop, you were looking at either Mammoth Lakes or St. George, Utah. In between there was a whole lot of isolation, where self-sufficiency was not some whimsical journey but a way of life. A guy rides out this way, he better be able to fix what brung him. Her point was well-taken. But the conversation came to a halt.

I walked upstairs to my room. It was August 7, summer was ending, and suddenly I yearned for home, a yearning so strong that I closed my eyes, imagined it: a Sunday morning in fall, and I wake, am lying in bed alone, the sound of dripping coffee, the opening of the sliding screen door. And birds! Blue jays, cardinals, yellow finches, robins, starlings, all of which I can recognize by their songs outside my window. And I hear Joan, on the patio outside, talking gently to Oscar, the neighbor's cat, who is no doubt rolling onto his back. And there's the smell of lavender and marigolds, of freshly mowed lawn. Home. For twenty years the West had beckoned, and finally I'd heeded its call. I was certain, this time, that when I returned, it would be for good, but I wouldn't be alone. And I would never stop traveling, would never end my forays into the desert, the mountains. I yearned for home and yet nurtured a restlessness I hoped never to tame.

The woman at the Tonopah Chamber of Commerce was talking on the phone when I walked in. I waited.

"Can I help you?" she asked, after she'd hung up.

I told her I was wondering about the road ahead, was looking for information. She pointed to some flyers lying on a table, told me to help myself. I asked her about mountain biking. It seemed to me that the whole area was a potential Mecca—mountains, rich history, endless camping. She showed me a book full of marked trails. She told me about other things the town had to offer—historic Victorian buildings, stargazing, mining history.

And then she said: "My son is going to jail."

She said this in a forthright manner, with no show of emotion, except for a sad tinge of resignation.

"He has a meth problem," she said. She shook her head. "There's so much pressure on the kids around here. Anyway, I'll send those copies of the trails," she said. "If I'm here. I may not stay much longer."

"Where will you go?" I asked.

"I'm from Buffalo," she answered. "I still have family there. Maybe I'll return there. I don't really know."

"It's hard, this town."

Earlier the morning motel clerk had said what a lot of small-town mothers say—that this was a great place to raise their kids. But trouble, it seemed to me, could find a person just about anywhere. Methamphetamine was just the latest in a long line of scourges, no more a city problem than it a small town one. In all the places I'd been and lived, from Alaska to Nebraska, meth was destroying lives. And central Nevada was apparently no exception.

I walked into the Tonopah hills, through residential neighborhoods. Lone Mountain stood as a backdrop to the mine below it and the town below that. I heard a soft cooing, coming from the end of a street, and as I approached the noise, there was a sudden flurry of pigeons, rising into the sky and away.

For lunch I stopped at a hotel casino. I walked through a room with new red carpet and lines of soft lighting and slot machines, where a handful of people were robotically pulling the levers to the occasional clinking of coins being dropped against tin.

I found the hotel restaurant in the back and took a seat at a booth. Shortly, a waitress stood looking down at me, her pencil at the ready.

"What's your soup today?" I asked.

"Lentil," she said. "You want a cup?"

"No," I said.

"Yesterday was chicken noodle," she said. "See, you're a day late."

"And a dollar short," I quipped.

"I know what you mean," she said.

"I *will* take a salad, though. With bleu cheese. When you get a chance."

"A chance is what I take," she said. "If I wait till I get one, you won't get a salad."

From the adjoining room I could hear the sound of taken chances, spun by levers.

Later I stood on the hotel balcony, which faced Main Street. I looked out at the old buildings. The evening storm clouds held a tint of green. Tonopah not only maintained its hold on my imagination, but its appeal had grown. It was a singular place, both haunting and real. Risks were being taken, families were being raised, hearts were being broken. It was rugged and idiosyncratic, the people conveying a reserved form of forthright, their language as sparse as the desert sage.

# The Extraterrestrial Highway

I HAD WORRIED ABOUT THE HEAT, but the central Nevada elevation ranged from 4,500 to 7,000 feet, and just before sunrise it was cool. After a day off the bike, I quickly fell into a hypnotic rhythm as I pedaled past the small airstrip, the scattered ranch houses east of town, white sage everywhere, mountains on the horizon, the desert hills with perfectly rounded tops.

I had always remembered this desert as a desolate, forlorn place, but now I saw beauty in its stability and solitude, believed that there was no such thing as the "middle of nowhere," that everywhere was a somewhere full of the life that suited it. Had I been in a car, shielded from the intricacies of its beauty, this stretch of road might have been boring. But by bicycle it felt alive.

Just after the sun rose, I saw three wild mustangs standing, watching. A few miles farther a black and white California king snake resting on the opposite shoulder slithered off of the road as I passed. In the late morning I passed another snake, a rattlesnake. It hadn't fared so well. It lay dead and flat on the road, its rattle gone, knife-cut and taken as a souvenir.

It was hot, upper nineties, but not unbearable, and a breeze pushed me gently, as if wanting to make amends for the trouble it had once caused. The sky was blue, and traffic was nearly nonexistent. By noon I'd ridden nearly fifty miles.

My map showed a place called Warm Springs, which wasn't a town but an old abandoned building. It looked about the same as it had twenty years earlier, except that now the pay phone that had hung from the wall was gone. On the hillside behind the building stood two old mining shacks, sagging, the wooden walls already beginning their decay from wall to mulch, a slow journey that—in the dryness of the air—would not soon be complete. I walked around the corner, scaring a lizard from its perch against the stucco. The lizard didn't move far and eyed me from its new site against a sagging shed at the rear of the building. I heard a trickle of water, walked over to it, and put my hand in a narrow stream. The water was hot, thus the name: Warm Springs.

The highway that ran southwest out of Warm Springs had not been named for aliens in 1985. It had simply been a desolate road, almost entirely devoid of traffic. It didn't become the Extraterrestrial Highway until 1996, and now a large blue sign just past the turn-off labeled it as such. A mileage sign showed Rachel to be fifty-nine miles away. Given its name, the road showed a disappointing lack of extraterrestrial evidence. It skirted the Reveille Range and then fell into a valley surrounded by mountains. No aliens. Just free-range cows, which turned and fled as soon as they saw me coming.

By two o'clock I'd ridden eighty miles, and I fell into that rarest of cycling rhythms, the kind that is accompanied with such ecstatic joy that exertion falls entirely away. I tried to suppress my enthusiasm, not wanting to jinx it, knowing that in Nevada good fortune could turn on a dime. But with each mile I felt a twenty-year anxiety slipping away.

In the distance, though, storm clouds darkened the sky. Lightning bolts flashed, and rain was visibly falling over the mountains to the southwest. The wind intensified, and I felt a few drops. Up ahead a Department of Transportation truck was stopped and two men were working by the side of the road.

"You get wet in that storm?" asked one of the men.

"It missed me," I said.

"Well, it isn't over yet," he said, pointing to the clouds in front of us.

But I managed to skirt the storm, its only effect on me the fresh scent it raised from the sage.

The road ascended sharply, leading through mountains. Just before I started the climb, I could see a pickup truck in my rearview mirror. The truck slowed, idling along beside me. It was a white truck, a Ford, the driver a middle-aged man with a cowboy hat. A younger version of him, a teenager I took to be his son, sat in the passenger seat.

"Where ya headed?" he asked.

"Rachel," I said.

The man nodded. I asked him where they were from, and he pointed. "Just up the road." He asked about my trip, where I'd come from. Twenty years earlier I'd seen only two cars on this route. Now I'd seen more—a car every twenty minutes or so. The population was growing, but a guy could still get lost in his own solitude out here.

"Well," said the man, "just thought we'd stop, make sure you're all right. You need anything?"

Just days before, had he asked, I might have taken a ride in the back of that truck. Now, though, I wanted nothing more than to pedal.

"I'm good," I said.

The man and his son smiled, wished me luck, and were gone.

Up over the Queen City Summit the pavement was still wet from an earlier rain, and then it was downhill until the road flattened out and I pulled into the Alien Capital of the Nation.

Rachel, Nevada, was a trailer town with a hotel/bar/café called the Little A'le'Inn. Inside one could drink a beer, order a steak, and peruse photographs of UFO's. A thick three-ring notebook held official reports of sightings. Corner shelves held alien coffee mugs, alien book marks, alien shot glasses, alien T-shirts, and UFO jigsaw puzzles.

I sat at the counter and ordered a Sprite from a woman appropriately named Joy.

"Where are the aliens?" I asked her. It was an annoying and unoriginal question, one she had every right to answer by rolling her eyes in disgust. But instead she pointed around the room at several men sitting at tables. The men all wore old T-shirts and had long hair and were deeply engaged in the reading of paperback novels.

"They're right there," she said.

I laughed. Earlier, as I rode, two military helicopters had flown so low overhead that I'd instinctively ducked. At the Little A'le'Inn I learned that this was part of what was called a "red flag." War games. The very unmilitary-looking men reading at the tables were not aliens but air techs, men whose job was to develop war strategies that could be simulated over the Nevada desert.

"I've been living here for five weeks," said Joy. "I had been working in Las Vegas. I'm a nurse. Been nursing for nearly thirty years. But I'd had enough of it, needed a break, so I quit, and I was headed back home to Texas when I stopped here for lunch. I started talking to the owner, and he offered me a job, said he had a trailer I could rent. I asked him how much. He said twenty-five dollars. I've been here ever since."

In addition to her job at the inn, she worked for a local farmer and was learning to drive a tractor. In her life so far she had worked in Alaska, Jamaica, and Korea. During her break she sat down next to me, smoked a cigarette, and talked about acupressure, acupuncture, and holistic health.

"In Korea," she said, "health care is different. It's all about balance, and the doctor's role is to keep the patient well before they get sick. To help them maintain a balance."

"And here?" I asked.

"Look, don't even get me started on the AMA, the insurance people, hospital administrations."

"You don't miss nursing, I take it," I said.

She flipped her hand as if to dismiss them all.

"Right now," she said, "I'm just enjoying life here."

Here in Rachel, in her trailer beneath the stars, working minimum wage, slowing down only for the occasional cigarette.

"You ever seen a UFO?" I asked the chef. She was seventeen. Earlier she'd told me she'd never before made a chicken fried steak, wanted to know if I was sure that's what I wanted. I told her whatever she did would be fine. Her cooking I trusted. The alien thing I was skeptical about.

"No," she said. "I never have, not yet. But my grandma has." She didn't smile or roll her eyes or give any indication that such a thing might be out of the ordinary. In Rachel it wasn't. In Rachel everyone knew someone who had seen a UFO.

In the evening the small bar was full with locals and alien aficionados. Two men had come all the way from Norway.

"What's the deal, really, with the UFO's here?" I asked Joy.

She shrugged. "Some people believe that the government does experiments at Area 51. There're rumors of alien bodies, spaceships."

"What do you think?" I asked.

She shrugged. "The world is full of things nobody knows for sure."

Kerry and Jamie had driven to Rachel from Los Angeles.

"It was either here or Yosemite," said Kerry.

They'd both been to Rachel before. Kerry, forty-five, was an actor in L.A. who'd once starred in a commercial. He had blond hair and was Hollywood handsome. Jamie had a round face and wore glasses and a sun hat. He was in sales. They seemed an unlikely pair. It was a fascination with the paranormal that they shared.

"I wasn't always into UFO's," said Kerry. "I used to think it was a lot of bunk. But one night I was camping with some friends, and we saw strange lights in the sky. The lights hovered, and then there was a bright metallic flash, and the lights were gone. It wasn't like they moved away. They just disappeared. Before that I never would have believed in UFO's. But that experience always stayed with me."

"Was it scary?" I asked.

"The thing is," he said, "it wasn't. I just wanted to see it again."

Kerry and Jamie were big fans of Art Bell, the radio talk show host best known for his intelligent on-air discussions about the paranormal. Bell lived in Pahrump, just north of Las Vegas.

"He's not on the radio anymore, sadly," said Kerry.

"But I still have a lot of his shows on tape," said Jamie.

"Have you been to Area 51?" asked Kerry, and I told him I hadn't.

"You have to go," said Jamie. "Actually, you can't go all the way there, just up to a line."

"There're two security guys in a jeep watching," said Kerry. "They're authorized to shoot you if you cross the line."

"They probably wouldn't, though," said Jamie. "They'd probably just arrest you."

"What do they do there?" I asked.

"If I told you," said Kerry, "I'd have to kill you. Actually, I don't know. A lot of people think they do experiments on aliens. But I think its mostly military experiments. Weapons. Chemicals. Who knows? It's all top-secret."

Outside the wind began to blow hard. I knew this not only because the trailer shook but also from the portable weather station sitting on a shelf behind the bar. We all watched the wind speed, which registered in red digital numbers. There were gusts over forty miles per hour.

"Aren't you glad you decided not to ride?" asked Joy. Earlier I'd told her that I might keep on riding into the night. Joy suggested I just stay in Rachel until morning. She was right. I watched those numbers and was glad to be staying.

"There was a guy rode through here about a month ago," she said. "He was only eighteen. From Georgia. He was really having a rough time. Winds up to fifty miles per hour. He stayed here for a couple days, just resting."

Through the window lightning strikes lit the sky.

Just then, two young women came in the bar. They hadn't come to Rachel seeking an extraterrestrial experience. They were from Norway. They'd driven a rental car to the Grand Canyon and were now on their way to California. They looked around the trailer. Though they tried to mask it, it was clear that a room full of actual aliens wouldn't have been more of a shock. Nothing in the guidebooks had prepared them for this or for the desert they'd just driven through.

Joy noticed their unease and immediately took to making them comfortable, inviting them in, giving them menus. The women were attractive and a long way from home, something not at all lost on Kerry, who'd been gawking since they walked in the door. Originally, said one of the women, they had planned to drive at least to Tonopah, maybe all the way to California. But then they saw the storm and decided they wanted no part of the desert at night.

"It was a good idea to stop," said Joy. "It's free range. A lot of cows on the roads at night."

The young women looked bewildered. "Is there not anywhere to stay between here and Tonopah?" they wanted to know.

"There's Warm Springs," said Joy. "Do you have a tent?"

They blinked a couple of times. No, they said. They had no tent.

"Do you have rooms here?" they asked.

"I think the inn is full tonight," said Joy.

"They could stay with us," said Kerry.

Joy and the two women all pretended not to hear.

"Don't worry," said Joy. "We'll figure out something. Wait here." She walked out of the trailer.

"That was a generous offer," I said to Kerry.

"I thought so," he said.

Jamie laughed. "All out of the goodness of his heart," he said.

Joy returned with an elderly man. He had a kind face.

"You girls need a room?" he said. "Here, follow me."

Rachel was a town that inspired such hospitality. Twenty years earlier I had staggered into town, wind-weary, thirsty, my tire flat, my hand pump broken. The two men who'd helped me had seen to it that I was taken in, made comfortable, and then had driven me the eighty miles to Caliente. I realized the trailer I was sitting in was in the exact same spot, might have been the same trailer. Rachel, despite its outward appearance, was a magical place, a place where all—extraterrestrial or non—were welcome.

That night my rain tarp whipped in the wind, making a harsh, slapping noise. Within an hour, though, the wind died suddenly, like a rock dropped from a cliff into mud. I looked out across the sky. No flying saucers or strange lights, just the Milky Way and stars so bright they illuminated the few remaining clouds. The sky revealed a universe so huge that the notion of us existing in isolation felt unlikely and life beyond this earth probable.

The road to Caliente led over two steep passes, the sun beating down. Near Oak Creek Summit I heard a sound like thunder, and when I looked up, I saw one fighter plane chasing another and then a cloud-like puff of smoke and a laser-sharp explosion, a single flare of light.

War games.

I rode out of the desert and into mountains of rocky cliffs and piñon forests. I made Caliente just before dusk.

The motel was small, two white buildings, each with three green doors. There was no office, but a driveway led back to a house, where a man was playing catch with a boy in the yard and two women sat in lawn chairs.

"Is this your motel?" I asked them.

"No," said one of the women. "You have to go back to the Chevron, check in there."

At the Chevron I was given a key. Room number 3.

But the motel rooms were numbered 1, 2, 4, 5, 6, and 7. I looked down at my key. Then I looked back at the numbers. I blinked.

It seemed my motel room was missing.

I walked back to the Chevron.

"Room 3 is missing," I said to the clerk.

"Not missing. Hiding," she said. "Check around back."

Sure enough, back through the driveway and around the corner, across from where the lawn chairs in front of the house now sat empty, there was room number 3. Why they chose to number it 3 instead of 7 was a mystery. But this was Nevada, and I liked it that way.

I walked up three wooden steps and onto a porch that leaned just a little askew. Inside, the room was small, the furniture old. But it was clean, and though there was no phone, it did have air-conditioning.

I was lying on the bed when there was a knock on my door. I answered, and a small boy, maybe six years old, looked up at me.

"Can I look for my sister's ball?" he asked me.

It seemed like a reasonable request. "Sure," I said.

He walked in, got down on the floor, and looked under the bed, peering in each corner.

"If you find it, can you bring it to us?" he asked.

"Of course," I said. And then he left, before I thought to ask him where he could be found. But I never found the ball.

Inside the Knotty Pine restaurant four men sat in a booth, drinking beer and flirting with a waitress who was too young to bring their drinks.

Outside it began to rain, slowly at first and then mercilessly, a driving passionate downpour, such that by the time I stepped outside, there were ankle-deep streams of water flowing down the street. I stood beneath a thin overhang and watched the rainwater that reflected the neon lights from the bar window bleeding streaks of red, blue, and yellow across the pavement. I walked back inside and tried to wait it out in the Knotty Pine bar, where four women played slot machines. Behind the bar a sign advertised KNOTTY BOYS T-shirts. The bar was filled with the sound of rain, jukebox country songs, and the clinking chimes and bells of the slots. But the mood was forlorn, subdued, the faces blankly staring—the women at their rotating icons, the bartender at the rain sliding down the window, and one other man into his beer.

When the song "I Love This Bar" began to play, the teenage employees from the adjacent and now closed restaurant sang along boisterously. They knew every word and sang them with a joy so pure that even the women stopped to smile. They loved this bar, they sang, even though they couldn't legally enter it.

It was my last night in Nevada, this land of solitude miscast as desolate and empty. It was a place of simulated games of war and alien aficionados swapping stories over beers in a trailer with photographs of UFO's on the wall, where motel rooms hid and people came from around the world to walk to the edge of a line they couldn't cross. Silver had been found here once, but always it had been a land where the most important commodities were shade and water.

The woman was eighty years old. She had bowl-cropped white hair, and she wore a white shirt and shorts. Her bony knees were covered with leathery skin, and I could not look at those legs without thinking of emus or flamingos or herons. I was sitting on a bench in the shade, outside a Laundromat. The Laundromat was closed.

She looked at my bike.

"I'll trade you," she said. And then she gestured toward an old single-speed parked across the street. It was a relic. Rusty orange now, it had once been bright red. A white basket hung from the handlebars.

"That bike is over forty years old," she said. "It doesn't run. The tires don't hold air. I'm looking for someone dumb enough to trade with me."

This was bad salesmanship, but I appreciated her forthrightness.

"And I look like just the guy, huh?" I asked. She chuckled but was gracious enough not to respond.

She walked across the street and placed a small bag of groceries into the basket. Then she slowly pedaled away.

I rode into Panaca, a Mormon town I remembered for its well-manicured lawns and a hamburger grill where a teenage girl with brown eyes had listened as I talked about the journey I'd been on. Panaca was different now, still clean but quieter. I wanted to see that young waitress again. But the grill was gone. And it hit me that the young waitress was also; she would be in her late thirties now.

Gone too was the boy who had told those stories, the stories he'd been telling for years ever since, to anyone who would listen. I walked inside a grocery store, where I bought a lunch, which I ate in the shade of the Latter-day Saints church lawn.

The climb to Panaca Summit began gradually, through the desert sage just outside of town. But then it was hot, and the road was so steep that even in my lowest gear, I struggled, sweat in my eyes, pulling the pedals slowly as I went. About halfway there the sun slipped behind clouds, a welcome reprieve, and then the clouds grew, gray and cumulous, and I could hear the clapping of thunder. Traffic was light, and I pedaled along, stopping finally at the summit.

My final six and a half miles of Nevada were all downhill, and I pedaled harder, a sprint, as if approaching a finish line, which in a way it was.

And then I saw the sign welcoming me to Utah—a skier gliding through the air in front of snow-capped peaks—incongruous where it stood in the summer desert heat.

I had finished what the twenty-year-old had been unable to do. At forty I had hitched rides in Colorado, Wyoming, and Montana. I had rented a car and taken a bus. I had stayed in more motels, and there was a nearly ten-mile difference in our average daily mileage. But in Nevada, and Nevada alone, the forty-year-old kicked the twenty-year-old's butt. I had long planned this moment, an exuberant raising of arms, a whooping yell. But deep down I knew that it had nothing to do with triumph and everything to do with circumstance. The forty-year-old had been mercifully blessed with a cooling cloud cover, a relatively calm wind that blew mostly from the west, and no mechanical issues. What I felt was an odd sadness.

I had feared Nevada, had considered hitchhiking, renting a car, taking another bus, all based on a twenty-year-old memory of wind and a bad tire. I had remembered it as a dusty, desolate, lonely place. But I had never forgotten it either, the intrigue of the desert, the history, the sound of the wind, the miles and miles of oh-so-little traffic.

I loved Nevada now, the sage, the Joshua trees, the endless sky and forever-changing horizon of stars and clouds, sun and mountains. I loved the quiet quirky friendliness of its people.

The journey was coming to an end. I would ride to the Grand Canyon, where my parents would be waiting. And then it was simply a matter of getting home. In less than a week I would meet Joan in Colorado Springs, and we would drive together back to Lincoln, our lives, and a new semester.

# Utah and Arizona

# Modena to Kanab

I RODE THE NINE MILES into the town of Modena, which was at the end of a gravel road. The town had originally been built along the railroad, and the tracks still ran past the long since abandoned station. A couple walking on the road said I could camp in town—they weren't really sure where, but they'd find a place. We walked past a neighbor's house. A woman came out, and they all talked. Then we walked on. But the neighbor woman came back outside and hollered for us to stop.

"Hey," she said. "The fugitive can camp here in our front lawn if he wants." The woman's name was Carol Rice, and it took me a second to realize that the "fugitive" was me. The couple seemed to agree this was a good idea, so I walked my bike back to the house.

"You know," said Carol. "We have a guest room. You might as well stay there if you want."

The room had a private bath and western-style oak furniture, air-conditioning, a television, and a phone. I lay down on top of a down comforter and a comfortable mattress. There was a knock on the door, and it was then I first met Vince, Carol's husband.

"Do you drink wine?" he asked. He had a full glass waiting. I walked out in the living room. The other neighbors were there, and I sat and listened to their conversation. I felt like I owed them, but nothing seemed expected of me.

I'd been invited into their home before I'd so much as told them my name. And I moved right in, so welcome did I feel. I was almost embarrassed by how easily I accepted their kindness. It wasn't that I had come to expect it. It just didn't surprise me. After three months on the road in America, whatever coarse grit of cynicism I'd left with had been nearly polished smooth.

That night we watched as the sun turned the storm clouds a bright shade of watercolor orange, and later I fell asleep to the sound of crickets.

In the morning Carol made cheese omelets with mushrooms and

hash browns and toast. Vince was thin with smooth gray hair and a natural tan. I had him pegged for being in his fifties, and I was surprised when he smiled and told me he was seventy-two. As we ate, he told me about the Burning Man Festival, which takes place, naturally, in Nevada.

"My daughter kept trying to get me to go with her," he said. "But when she described it, I thought it was just a bunch of weirdos. Then one summer she was seven months pregnant, and I didn't want her to be alone, so I went. There was this drumming group camped next to her. Well, I'm a drummer, and they let me join in. I've been going every year since."

Vince worked as a ranger at the event, helping to patrol the grounds and to keep them clean.

"Everything's no-impact camping. What people have to understand is that we have to abide by the rules of Nevada. That means no drugs. Unless you count marijuana as a drug—and I do—but we just tell people to keep it in their tents. We want people to have a good time but to behave themselves too.

"We do allow nudity, though. There's a lot of nudity at Burning Man. If nudity bothers you, don't go," he said.

"Nudity's not for everyone," said Carol. She got up to fill our coffee cups and then sat back down.

"That first year," continued Vince, "I heard this murmur, and I went to see what the fuss was about. There were women riding nude on their bicycles. I couldn't decide whether to run and get my camera or keep watching."

"What'd you do?" I asked.

"I kept watching," he said. "There were over three hundred women, all sizes, all colors."

I left Modena in midmorning, waving my gratitude to Vince and Carol before pedaling away. At Beryl Junction a sign pointed one way to Cedar City and another to St. George. I wasn't sure which way to take. I didn't yet have a Utah map.

There was a Goodyear tire shop not far from the intersection. It had a cooler full of cold drinks, so I took a Gatorade and waited at the counter. The door had been open, as was the larger garage door adjacent to the building. But there was no one around. A pickup pulled up, and a large bearded man with a dirty cap came in.

"They must all be at lunch," he said.

He walked behind the counter, and started writing a note.

"Can I pay you for a cold drink?" I asked him.

"'Fraid not. I don't work here," he said. "I just came in to shoot the breeze. Maybe they saw me comin'."

"You wouldn't happen to have a map I could look at, would you?" I asked as we both walked outside.

"Where do you want to go?" he asked.

"Zion," I said. "I'm not sure whether to go Highway 18 or up through Cedar City."

He patted his shirt pocket, which was empty. "Do you have a pen or pencil?" he asked.

"I do somewhere," I said, and started searching my handlebar bag.

"Wait. Hang on," he said. He walked back inside, and when he came back out, he had a pen. He pulled an old piece of cardboard from a nearby trash can and started sketching a map, describing each stop along both routes, the towns, and the distances each way. When he was done, he handed me the map. It was meticulously drawn, and I would later find his mileage estimates to be exact.

"Looks to me like I should take 18," I said.

"I would," he said.


At Snow Canyon the evening sun shone against red sandstone cliffs, and I cycled through a road surrounded by white rocks, red sand dunes, desert plants, volcanic rock. I took a site toward the back of the campground, which was protected on the back side by large rocks, well away from the main road.

In the evening the canyon walls were illuminated by brilliant lightning flashes, and outside the ranger station three wooden chairs rocked in the wind, as if inhabited by restless ghosts. I sat down in one and watched the storm.

That night I fell asleep to the sounds of a spirited desert—the wind,

rain against my tent, distant thunder. What I didn't hear was the nocturnal visitor that pulled the tortillas from my front pannier, which
was easily accessible through the hole that had been chewed by the
thief's Oregon cousin. And in the morning, preserved in the wet sand,
I found again the unmistakable tracks of a raccoon.

Foolish it was to store them there and no one but me to blame. Go
with God, my furry masked friend, I thought, I've made my peace
with you.

I rode out through the red dunes, their windswept ripples, texturing
the sand, and as I rode, I made the same vow I had made twenty years
earlier—to return, when I could spend more time. I'd made that vow
a hundred times, in a hundred places, since May.

I rode up the long hill from La Verkin, through Virgin, into Spring-
dale, and then into Zion, on a bike path that led to the Highway 9
turn-off. And then up, a not-at-all unpleasant climb, the monuments
of Zion rising high. The road was full of switchbacks, and with each
turn there was more to see, more to remember, more to make me want
to return. It felt good, that climb, and it climbed and climbed, but I
never stopped pedaling, never needed to stop and catch my breath.

Twenty years earlier a ranger, his car lights flashing, had escorted
me through the tunnel just before the top. Bicycles were no longer
allowed in that tunnel now, but a ranger helped me hail a ride with a
forestry student from the University of Tennessee. He'd spent his summer working in Idaho, and was now on his way back to Knoxville.
He dropped me off at Carmel Junction.

"It's too bad you're not going north," he said. "I could use the
company."

"I know what you mean," I said.

I watched him drive away and realized it was nearly over now.
I thought back to that twenty-year-old kid who rode out from his
parent's home one day in May and returned 103 days later. Unlike the
forty-year-old version, he never stopped to check a weather report,
didn't know such a thing as a cell phone, had simply ridden into the
world, come what may.

I rode into a town and checked into my last motel. Then I walked
farther into town, along a street that was lined with storefronts and

cafés. I browsed an upstairs gallery then ate dinner at a restaurant with outdoor seating on the sidewalk that faced the street. It was evening in Kanab, Utah, a cool eighty degrees.

It is midafternoon. Scorching hot. A sign on the bank says ninety-eight degrees. From where I sit at the sidewalk café I can see him sitting there on a picnic table in the sun. He is skinny, so skinny, a long narrow face, unshaven, his hair sun-bleached blond, his skin tan. He has just returned from the bank, where he used his credit card for a cash advance. He does not yet know about ATM machines. He is smiling, happy. He has money, health, faith. His bicycle is shiny, a new-model Trek, built for touring. He has no helmet. I walk over, sit down at the table beside him. He hands me his water bottle, and I drink from it.

"Where will you stay tonight?" I ask him.

He shrugs, smiles. "I don't know."

I could tell him. He will ride through Fredonia, will be in one of those grooves that feel so good that he will pass right through town without stopping, even though he knows he needs more food, a mistake that, given his youth and health, is really not much of a mistake at all. He will begin a ride up a steep climb, and it will start to grow dark, and he will slip quietly into the national forest and set up his tent behind a small group of trees, six miles south of Jacob Lake.

He is not thinking about the future now, though, is just enjoying the dry heat. I hand back his water, and he drinks from it and wipes his mouth with the back of his hand.

He is not thinking about the future.

He still doesn't know what he'll do with his life. But over the last three months he has learned to follow a path, to see what unfolds. He has learned that no wind, neither tail nor head, lasts forever.

I could tell him so many things, could offer wisdom, experience perhaps. But I would not dare to alter this journey he's on, so I remain quiet, don't tell him that his dropout days are over, that in fact not only would he one day finish a college degree, he'd go on to a career of university teaching and would eventually receive a Ph.D.

He already senses that the woman he's been calling his girlfriend is gone. He hasn't talked to her for weeks. In fact, by the time he returns home she'll be engaged to somebody else.

I restrain from revealing to him what I most want him to know—that one day he will find love and that she will be waiting for him when he returns from a journey very much like the one that he's on.

"Where do you want to be twenty years from now?" I ask him.

He gestures toward the red sandstone cliffs, which seem to be quivering, dreamlike, in the heat.

"Right here," he says. And we both laugh.

Night had fallen. I paid my bill, rose from my table, and walked slowly back toward my motel.

## At Jacob Lake

AUGUST 15, A MONDAY, and I rode out of Kanab into Arizona. And then it was back up the slow rising climb, through the trees, and into Jacob Lake. I pulled into the parking lot, and right away I saw a car with Colorado plates, a car that I immediately recognized.

Twenty years earlier I'd ridden to the Grand Canyon and then to Page, across the Navajo Reservation, where I'd camped twice by the side of the road. And then the Four Corners and into Cortez and Durango, where I'd spent two nights, before making my final push north, over Red Mountain and into Silverton, Montrose, Gunnison, over Monarch Pass into Poncha Springs, where I'd spent my last night in a sleeping bag on a picnic table behind a filling station. And then it was 111 miles, over Trout Creek, Wilkerson, and Ute passes. When I rode back down Crown Ridge Drive, I had been greeted with the cheers of neighbors, families, and friends.

But every journey was different. I stood, looking out at the scenery around me. It was good, I thought, to take a break from life halfway through and reacquaint oneself with the natural world, with physical and spiritual health, with one's own past. Now this journey, too, was a part of that past. There was nothing left but to go inside, greet my parents, and return home to Joan.

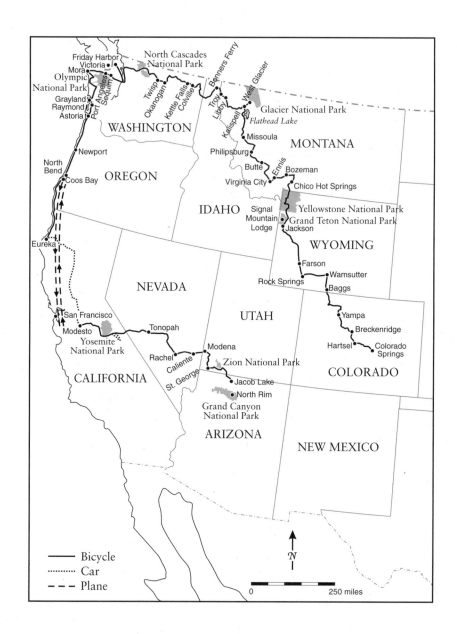

Bicycle

Car

Plane

0    250 miles

2005 Route

**In the Outdoor Lives series**

*Kayaking Alone
Nine Hundred Miles from Idaho's
Mountains to the Pacific Ocean*
by Mike Barenti

*Bicycling beyond the Divide
Two Journeys into the West*
by Daryl Farmer